THE ECONOMICS OF EUROPE

THE ECONOMICS OF EUROPE

What the Common Market Means for Britain

Edited by John Pinder

Published for the Federal Trust by

CHARLES KNIGHT & CO. LTD.
LONDON
1971

Charles Knight & Co. Ltd.
11/12 Bury Street, London EC3A 5AP

Copyright © 1971
Federal Trust for Education and Research

First published 1971

Printed in Great Britain by
Brown Knight & Truscott, London & Tonbridge

SBN 85314 123 1

CONTENTS

FOREWORD

THE idea of this book arose from a conference organised by the
Federal Trust at Wiston House on 7-9 May 1971, at which a
number of the authors presented papers that have been
developed into the chapters of the book. Because much of the
material they presented was quite new and extremely relevant to
the economic debate about British membership of the Community, it seemed desirable to publish it, together with other
contributions which should help the reader to make a full
assessment of the likely effects on the British economy. The
authors are to be thanked for producing their chapters very
quickly; and the Federal Trust for having made the project
possible by organising the conference initially and by subsequently providing facilities for getting the book together. It
might, indeed, be called the Federal Trust report on the
economics of Europe. The views expressed in it are, however,
entirely the responsibility of the authors, and do not necessarily
represent those of the Federal Trust or of any other institution.

Thanks are also due to Sir Alec Cairncross and Mr. Andrew
Shonfield for chairing the Wiston House conference; to the
Institute of Social and Economic Studies at the University of
York and to the Social Science Research Council for sponsoring
the study from which the chapter on taxation has been derived;
to the Committee on Invisible Exports for permission to
present the main findings of the study of invisible earnings which
was undertaken for them; to the Centre for European Industrial
Studies at Bath University and PEP for permission to draw on
the preliminary results of their study of the implications of
membership for British industry; to Michigan State University
for sponsoring the study on which much of the reappraisal of the
agricultural burden is based; and to the National Institute of
Economics and Social Research for permission to use the
comparison of the estimates of static balance-of-payments and
welfare costs, which appeared as an article in the August 1971
issue of their Economic Review and has been adapted to fit into
the context of this book.

J P

29 August 1971

CONTRIBUTORS

Ronald Cooper, Professor of Social and Economic Statistics, University of York.

Douglas Dosser, Professor of Economic Theory, University of York.

Tim Josling, London School of Economics.

Christopher Layton, Director of the Centre for European Industrial Studies, University of Bath

John Marsh, Reader, Department of Agricultural Economics and Management, University of Reading.

Marcus H. Miller, London School of Economics.

Alan Peacock, Professor of Economics, University of York.

John Pinder, Director of Political and Economic Planning.

Maurice Peston, Professor of Economics, Queen Mary College, University of London.

John Williamson, Professor of Economics, University of Warwick.

Stanislas M. Yassukovich, Managing Director, White, Weld & Co. Ltd.

Chapter 1

WHAT MEMBERSHIP MEANS FOR BRITAIN

by John Pinder

MUCH of the so-called debate on the case for British entry into the European Community has in fact been a dialogue of the deaf between practical people and academic economists. Industrialists have shown massive and prolonged support for entry because they believe it will increase our growth and prosperity, whereas exclusion would undermine our industrial strength. Those responsible for government have largely accepted this view, and have likewise held that Britain's political influence would grow inside the Community but decline outside it. Most academic economists, on the other hand, have discounted the benefit of growth on the grounds that they cannot quantify it. They have therefore concentrated on estimating the immediate 'costs' of entry: an expected loss to our balance of payments, commonly put at about £500 million; a rise in the cost of living due to higher food prices and the value-added tax; and a substantial net transfer into the Community budget.

The practical people have tended to accept that these short-term costs exist, although there have been doubts about the validity of the models on which the estimates are based and hence about the probable size of the costs. Most of them have, however, continued to support the case for entry because they consider that these costs are likely to be outweighed by the long-term gains. But many of the academic economists have opposed entry on the grounds that they dislike the costs, which are measurable, and are at best sceptical about the gains, which are not.

1

The argument between the two sides has been unsatisfactory because the academics have, on the whole, refused to fight on the ground where the practical people have based their economic case: the effect on industrial growth. The practicals have, for their part, despite their doubts about the economists' forecasting models, failed to produce much in the way of detailed alternative forecasts.

It is doubtless easy to agree that this has been a sorry state of affairs when the country is in the process of making its historic decision whether to join the Community. Until recently, it has not been so easy to see what to do about it. In the last few months, however, the results of several major new studies and of new thinking about the crucial economic issues have become available, which should enable both academic and practical people to form a more rational judgement of the economic prospects as a whole. It is the findings of these new studies and thinking that are presented in this book.

New studies provide new evidence

The most serious inadequacy in the argument so far has been the failure of the economists to produce any quantitative estimates of the effects of entry on growth. Professor John Williamson, taking as his starting point his own estimates of the effect on industrial trade, does much to fill this gap by his careful analysis of the growth effects, presented in Chapter 2 below. He stresses that his estimates are, in the present state of the art, inevitably rough and ready, but his work shows that there are sound reasons to expect a significant acceleration of the growth rate.

This conclusion is supported by the findings of a substantial empirical study that has been led by Mr. Christopher Layton, which complements Williamson's macroeconomic analysis by investigation at the level of the individual firm. Layton presents, in Chapter 3, some of the main considerations which do in fact underlie firms' decisions whether or not to expand capacity in the event of British entry into the Community.

These two contributions, taken together, offer material which should enable the reader to form a judgement on this central issue of economic growth, in a way that has not been possible hitherto. The following chapters are directed, rather, at questions relating to the balance of payments, the cost of living and the transfer costs, which have dominated the discussion among economists. The present authors have, however, been able to shed new light on these old subjects, partly because of new findings from major projects of detailed research, and partly as a result of the study of possible developments in policies in the Community, which most of the economic forecasting models assume will remain frozen in their present form, but which will in fact change over time and which are critical determinants of the economic consequences of membership.

Dr. Tim Josling's findings on agriculture (Chapter 4) depend in part on just such an assessment of likely price trends in Britain and the Community, and in part on a massive study of the effects on agriculture of enlargement of the Community, undertaken by Michigan State University with a team which included Josling together with another British and an Irish economist. Chiefly as a result of more detailed work on food consumption trends (by examining the effect of relative price changes as between, for example, the different types of meat), he shows effects on the balance of payments and on food expenditure that are markedly different from what has been usual in other forecasts. These estimates by Josling, which relate to the period up to 1980, are complemented by Mr. John Marsh in Chapter 5, where he considers the prospects for raising the incomes and reducing the numbers of people working on farms in the Community over the longer term, together with the feasibility of various policies to accelerate the process and their budgetary consequences for the Community and for Britain.

The estimates of the 'cost' of joining the Community which have been the common currency of economic discussion are based on forecasts of the balance-of-payments effects of industrial free trade and of the common agricultural policy, such as Williamson and Josling present in Chapters 2 and 4. In Chapter 6, Mr. Miller compares their results with the figures given in the 1970 and 1971 White Papers[1] and with two sets of unofficial estimates: those made by Professor Kaldor, and those derived from a model constructed by Miller and Spencer. This

---

[1] *Britain and the European Communities: An Economic Assessment*, Cmnd 4289, HMSO, February 1970; and *The United Kingdom and the European Communities*, Cmnd 4715, HMSO, July 1971.

enables the reader to see what the differences are between the estimates made in this book and the figures that have been put forward elsewhere, and analyses the causes of those differences. A complete assessment of the costs and benefits of joining depends, of course, not only on the industrial and agricultural forecasts but also on estimates of the effects on growth and on capital flows and trade in invisibles. These are left out of account in Miller's chapter—necessarily, because the sources with which the estimates of this book are compared do not present the findings of detailed research on these subjects. But as we have seen, Williamson has produced an estimate of the order of magnitude of the crucial growth effects; and in the chapters following Miller's the assessment is completed by an examination of the remaining aspects.

The agreement between Britain and the Community on the control of capital flows, and the provisions for limiting any adverse effects of such movements on the balance of payments, are analysed by Mr. Yassukovich in Chapter 7, where he also offers some judgements on the likely importance of different elements in the flows. In Chapter 8, Professors Cooper and Peacock summarise the findings of their major study of the short-term and the longer-term effects on the invisibles account. Then Professor Dosser, in Chapter 9, gives the principal findings of another new and important study, on the implications of tax harmonisation for the general level of indirect taxation in Britain, the cost of living, the distribution of incomes and the balance of payments.

Finally, Professor Peston offers a perspective for the economic debate by commenting on its relationship with radical and conservative elements in British life and thought.

Although some of their studies have been large and complicated, the authors have presented their findings in a way that is understandable to non-economists except in certain passages where it was necessary to deal in some depth with economic concepts that may be found difficult. Such passages are, however, a minority and the great bulk of the book is readily readable for the non-economist. Both specialists and laymen should therefore be able to decide for themselves whether they accept these two propositions: that the new evidence brought forward in the contributions to this book, taken together, provides a convincing foundation for the judgement that the economic gains from entry are likely by a wide margin to outweigh the costs; and that, given the terms which have been negotiated between Britain and the Community, this is likely to be true in the short as well as the long run.

Growth

The effects on growth are analysed by Williamson under the headings of the economies of scale, competition, and investment. His "central guess", based on a detailed examination of the quantitative indications that are available under these headings, is that the extra growth would add something in the region of $1\frac{1}{2}$ per cent to GNP by the end of the transitional period in 1978, or 0.3 per cent to the growth rate during the five years of transition. This would amount to £750 million on the basis of a GNP of some £50 billion in 1978. He also expects "at least some acceleration in growth" to be maintained beyond that period, partly because the same factors would continue to apply, and partly because a higher ratio of invesment to GNP, once it has been achieved, is not so difficult to maintain.

Crucial elements in Williamson's analysis are supported by the results of recent research which show that the existing members of the Community all enjoyed investment booms around the time of its inception, and that there has been a marked reduction in the export prices of their manufactures, and hence increase in the efficiency of those industries, during the subsequent decade.[2] The findings of Layton's survey of the prospects for industrial investment also confirm a number of the elements in Williamson's analysis and corroborate the order of magnitude of his central estimate.

The economies, and indeed the necessity, of large scale for important sectors of industry are demonstrated by Layton's work. He shows that expenditure of the order of £100 million is required to construct a modern petro-chemical complex or as the annual investment in expansion, modernisation and new models required to keep a motor manufacturer in the front rank, and that the American manufacturers of turbogenerators are also investing on the same scale. These are spectacular, though not

[2] These results were reported in *The Times* and *The Guardian* on 10 May, 1971.

untypical, examples. Smaller sums can create problems of
scale for other sectors of industry too in markets the size
of Britain's: the £10 million required to establish a complex
for the production of heavy trucks or to open up a major new
market for computers. Investments of these orders of magnitude
correspond, of course, to levels of market size required for
viability, put, for example, at two million vehicles a year for a
major motor manufacturer (not too far short of the whole of
UK production but less than one-fifth of that for an enlarged
Community), or at 8-10,000 mw of turbo-generator output a
year for a firm in Europe by the mid-1970s (compared with
5,000 mw produced by one of the two British manufacturers in
1970, and a total UK market of about that order of magnitude).
To avoid falling farther and farther behind, the manufacturers
of motors and of heavy electrical equipment clearly need secure
and free access to a market much larger than that of Britain.
For cars, the episode of the American import surcharge has
shown the need for greater security of access than the US
market offers; and the Community's fairly low tariff, even if it
remains immune from such shocks, would probably cause the
practice of exporting cars in knocked-down form from Britain
to the Community to become general. For commercial vehicles,
the Community's tariff of 22 per cent is a very serious barrier.
The situation of the motor manufacturers, though dramatic, is
not too dissimilar from that of many other branches of industry
selling into the private sector.

   The case of the turbo-generator is different, because they are
sold into the public sector, where 'buy national' policies are
widespread. A number of key high-technology products such
as aircraft, aeroengines and nuclear reactors, which like turbo-
generators also require investments on a growing scale and
hence an increasing size of market, depend to an important
extent on the public sector. European countries will have to
share their public sector markets, as they have begun to do, if
these industries are to survive. The background of close and
continuous political collaboration which is necessary if such
sharing is to be successfully sustained is not likely to be adequate,
as between Britain and the Community, unless Britain does in
fact join.

   The five major industries described in Layton's chapter

(chemicals, vehicles and suppliers, computers, aerospace and heavy electrical equipment) could in 1980 comprise two-fifths of manufacturing output, and economies of scale are important in each of them. He points out that economies of scale are also important in a number of other sectors, including key capital goods industries, so that over half of British manufacturing may benefit significantly from these economies. Increases in output per man through membership of 5 per cent by the end of this decade would, in the light of the evidence he has been accumulating in his survey, be minimal. This would imply an improvement of productivity for the economy as a whole of between 1 and 2 per cent—which accords with the conclusion of Williamson's macroeconomic work. Layton's survey thus helps to explain why British industry has been so keen on membership of the Community, particularly in view of the fact that the trend in technology will without any doubt increasingly emphasise the economies of scale in the years after the transitional period.

Some economists (for example, Kaldor), while accepting that growth will accelerate if the Government does not have to apply deflationary policies, have argued that entry will put such strain on the British balance of payments that governments will be forced to deflate any such acceleration away and, if anything, reduce the rate of growth. Williamson points out that any strain serious and prolonged enough to give rise to that danger could be dealt with by adjusting the exchange rate; and Yassukovich likewise shows that controls of capital movements will remain possible for as long as these may represent a threat to the balance of payments. In this they are certainly right. Economists who seized on the Werner plan and the Community's provisions regarding the control of capital movements, and brandished them as proof that the Community would put Britain in a straitjacket that would squeeze our economic growth, displayed little understanding of the political processes that operate in the Community. So much was clear from the start. But it was perhaps surprising how quickly and dramatically they were proved wrong, not only by the agreement reached between Britain and the Community on the control of capital flows (which the controls already operated by France plainly indicated as the likely solution), but above all by the several floatings of Community currencies that have since taken place.

However, even if it is foolish to fear a straitjacket, it would clearly be better for the Community, as well as for Britain, if the process of joining does not subject the balance of payments to a heavy strain. We look next, therefore, at the implications of the findings in this book for the British balance of payments.

Balance of payments

At the centre of all the estimates of the effect of British entry on the balance of payments is the common agricultural policy and its implications for imports of food and for Britain's net contribution to the Community budget.

The effect of the CAP on the value of food imports will be twofold: on the one hand higher prices, and on the other lower quantities due to the effect of the higher prices on production and consumption. The 1971 White Paper put the combined result of these influences at a deficit of £50 million at the end of the transitional period; and the centre of the range in the 1970 White Paper was £85 million. The estimate that Josling derives from the Michigan State University study is of a corresponding *gain* of approximately £150 million.

It is important to stress that, as has been indicated above, this difference is due mainly to the fact that the Michigan State University study has analysed food consumption at a more detailed level and has learnt, from the experience shown by the UK National Food Survey, that consumers respond to relative price changes by switching their purchases from beef towards pork and from butter towards margarine more readily than has been allowed for in previous estimates. The prospect of a substantial gain to the balance of payments is an unexpected consequence. The agreement on Britain's financial contribution that resulted from the membership negotiations provided for a net payment of some £200 million for 1977, and if this is deducted from the positive figure of £150 million, we are left with an estimate of approximately £50 million as the loss to the balance of payments due to the effect of the CAP.

There are of course consequences that arise for welfare as a result of dearer food imports and the payment into the Community budget, and these are considered in the following section. Since, however, one of the strongest criticisms that has been made of the proposal for British entry is that it will reduce welfare by forcing deflation because of the loss to the balance of payments, this finding that the loss attributable to the CAP will be small up to 1978—and, as we shall soon see, not much greater thereafter—is very significant. Because of the Michigan study's findings about the response of British production and consumption to higher prices, moreover, Josling shows that a devaluation would, by further raising the price level in terms of sterling, further reduce the value of imports (i.e. the import elasticity is greater than one). While nobody could want it to happen (and this book indicates that it will not), it is reassuring that devaluation in CAP conditions would be likely to reduce the deficit on agricultural trade, rather than increase it as some economists have claimed.

Williamson's estimate for industrial trade, on the other hand, is less favourable than those of the White Papers (as derived by Miller, for the purpose of comparison, in Chapter 6). He suggests a balance-of-payments loss of £100 million from the combined effect of tariff charges in the Community, the UK, and Britain's various preferential markets. He notes that this may be too pessimistic, in the light of a *Guardian* survey of British industrialists which showed their expectation that sales gains in the Community would exceed losses elsewhere; and Layton points out that the companies' answers to this survey carried the implication that their first reaction, in terms of investment, would be to invest more in marketing and service facilities on the Continent. This would cause a shift in the supply curve implying a greater growth of exports than would otherwise be expected—which would not be surprising as British firms would be presented with a trebling or quadrupling of their effective home market, while firms within the present Community countries would find theirs increasing by less than one-third.

Cooper and Peacock conclude, from their study of trade in invisibles, that "it seems unlikely that in the short term entry would have any sizeable effect one way or the other". In the long run, they are fairly optimistic about the prospects, pointing to "the expansion in the *total* volume of trade between EEC countries and not solely the volume of UK exports to the EEC" as a suitable indicator of the opportunities for expansion of net earnings of the City. They stress that Britain should use its influence within the Community institutions to secure liberal

treatment of invisible trade, while the other side of the coin is
their pessimism about the prospects if this British interest is not
taken into account—as it is hardly likely to be if Britain were
to remain outside.

Whereas these findings regarding invisibles are not unexpected, perhaps the most surprising result of all the studies
is Dosser's calculation of the effect on the balance of payments
of levying value-added tax at rates that would be likely to apply
within the Community. The rates assumed in the columns
headed '1969' in his Table 5 (page 207) may be taken as a
minimum, and at these rates a positive effect of around £100
million is indicated for the balance of payments, as a result of the
different incidence, product by product, of VAT as opposed to
that of our existing indirect taxation. Since a part of this is,
however, due to the effect of a VAT on food, which would
certainly not be levied before 1978, the effect by then is indicated
as an improvement of some £70 million.

The expected effects relating to agricultural trade, the
Community budget, industrial trade, invisibles and value-
added tax amount, then, to a loss of £80 million on the balance
of payments on current account at the end of the transitional
period. This figure is the result of either central or conservative
estimates for the respective items. The authors properly stress
the tentative nature of their estimates—which applies indeed to
any of the estimates which are put forward from any source.
The estimates are, however, derived from careful studies, and
while there is no magic in the particular figure arrived at, it seems
fair to suppose that the order of magnitude is a reasonable one.
It is also an insignificant one in relation to Britain's trade as a
whole and to the fluctuations which are bound to occur from
year to year owing to other causes.

Fears that have been expressed about the capital account of
the balance of payments turn out to be equally groundless.
Regarding direct investment, Yassukovich considers that "it is
certain that the UK lost a considerable amount of direct
investment from the United States" because of its failure to join
the EEC earlier, and that "further US investment in Europe will
be located to a large extent in the United Kingdom in preference
to Continental countries". He then examines the prospects for
direct investment across the Channel and concludes that "it is

difficult to visualise anything approaching a serious level of net capital outflow as a result of liberalisation of direct investment immediately upon British accession to the EEC". Finally, he reminds us of the prospect for continued controls over the out-flow of portfolio investment and of the safeguard that member countries can impose special controls if capital movements should endanger a country's balance-of-payments position.

We can conclude, then, that membership is not likely to cause any difficulty for the British balance of payments up to 1978. Difficulties may of course arise for other reasons, and if so it will be open to Britain, as a member, to take sufficient corrective measures, including, if need be, adjustment of the exchange rate.

For all but one of the elements in the foregoing analysis of the balance of payments, a similar trend can be expected for the years after 1977. The case of the budgetary contribution is, however, different. Here, the agreement with the Community provides for a further two years of transition, over which Britain is to move towards the same system of contribution as the other members: that is to say, the payment of 90 per cent of import levies and customs duties and a proportion of value-added tax not exceeding 1 per cent of total added value. The 1970 White Paper, Kaldor and Miller-Spencer all suggest that, on this fully-paying basis, the order of magnitude of Britain's net contribution, after deduction of receipts from the Community budget, would be around £400-500 million a year. Josling, on the other hand, puts the net contribution at about £320 million, and the 1971 White Paper implicitly (see Chapter 6 below) at £295 million.

The reasons for preferring Josling's estimates, based as they are on the new evidence of research into patterns of food consumption, have already been given. It can properly be argued that it is impossible to be sure whether his economic assumptions or those of the three former sources will be justified in the event. But it is essential to remember that the payment of large sums of money in tax involves not just economic forecasts, but political decisions. A net payment of the order of magnitude indicated by the earlier forecasts would imply British people would be contributing one-third or more of the total revenue for the Community budget. This would be manifestly unfair and, unless Britain had by then achieved the strength in its balance of payments and its economic growth that has hitherto been enjoyed by Germany, it would be unacceptable. The French representatives in the negotiations defended the tough line they took on the British contribution for the transitional period on the grounds that this would set, by implication, the ceiling on Britain's contribution in the definitive phase, because the British would not in fact be likely to pay excessive annual increments. The British, for their part, implicitly confirmed the realism of this French view, and the existing member Governments implicitly accepted it, when Britain secured the agreement of the Six to the proposition that, if unacceptable situations should arise, "the very survival of the Community would demand that the institutions find equitable solutions".[3] The British representatives did not feel able, in the context of the negotiations, to be more precise than that. But the net contribution of £295 million suggested by the 1971 White Paper offers an indication of the official view. With £100 million of receipts from the Community budget, it follows that a gross contribution of some £400 million is foreseen, or 25 per cent of the total estimated Community budget of £1,600 million. This would seem to be a reasonable percentage ceiling—well above the expected UK share of 18 per cent of the Community's GNP.

Unless Britain becomes so prosperous as to be unworried about such things, then, it can be taken that the net budgetary contribution will not be allowed in any year to exceed about £300 million. If Josling is right, the agricultural budgetary cost to Britain will not exceed this order of size in any case. There are, moreover, plans to develop Community spending under other headings such as technology, regional policy and the Social Fund, which could bring Britain a net gain and further reduce the budgetary cost; and reforms in the CAP or further reductions in the common tariff could reduce the bias against Britain on the revenue side. But if, despite these more favourable indications, the net cost tends under existing rules to exceed the level of some £300 million, then it is legitimate to assume that the rules will be modified.

It follows that the addition to the budgetary burden for the balance of payments between the end of the transitional period and 1980 or beyond will not exceed £100 million. With some

---

[3] *1971 White Paper, p.25.*

further gains to the agricultural trade balance expected by Josling, and none by Dosser if and when VAT is applied to food, together with the chance of substantial gains on invisibles by then, the balance-of-payments 'cost' in 1980 seems likely to be less than £175 million.

Welfare

The welfare gains or costs of membership — that is, the net gains or losses to the real value of British people's incomes — are not, for reasons explained by Miller in Chapter 6, the same as the positive or negative effects on the balance of payments. From the point of view of welfare, the net payment into the Community budget and, to a lesser extent, the cost of the rise in price of imported food are the most important. The implications for welfare of these together with the other elements in the different balance-of-payments forecasts are summarised in Table 1 on page 120.

The welfare effect of all the elements other than the Community budget is almost nil according to both Josling—Williamson and Miller-Spencer. The White Papers, without taking into account the findings of the new studies, imply welfare costs from those elements of about £200 million (1971 White Paper) and £200-300 million (1970 White Paper); and Kaldor puts it at about £300 million. Although there can be no certainty about it, it seems justifiable to prefer the estimate based on the findings presented in this book, because it takes into account new evidence based on detailed research which was not available before.

The welfare cost of the net budgetary contribution can be derived from the estimates of Miller-Spencer, the 1970 White Paper (central estimate) and Kaldor (central estimate) as some £650 million in 1980. The welfare costs derived from the work of Josling and Williamson and from the 1971 White Paper are, however, of the order of £350-400 million because they are based on a lower level of net budgetary contribution. The reasons why this latter view of the budget is more realistic have already been given. £375 million appears therefore to be the best central estimate of the welfare cost due to the budget. This is the total welfare cost if the remaining welfare costs are about nil, as suggested by Josling-Williamson and Miller-Spencer; or

£200-300 million if Kaldor and the White Papers are followed.

The figure against which these welfare costs have to be set is an estimate of the welfare gains from any acceleration of economic growth. Williamson puts this at some £750 million by the end of the transition period, and somewhat more by 1980. Thus this welfare gain exceeds what appears to be the best estimate of the welfare cost by a factor of two to one, or by an absolute figure of some £375 million by 1980.

If the more pessimistic estimates of £200-300 million of non-budgetary welfare costs were accepted, there is still a significant margin of gain. Even if one takes the mid-point of the total of Kaldor's very pessimistic forecasts of both elements of welfare costs, one finds a net loss for 1980 no greater than £200 million.

The most reasonable estimate for 1980 appears, then, to be a welfare gain around $\frac{3}{4}$ per cent of GNP.The gain may of course be greater or it may be smaller. There is also the chance of a loss of say 0.4 per cent of GNP. The balance of probability seems to be pronouncedly in favour of the gain. But it would, in any case, be rather absurd to lay great stress on estimates of the effect on welfare in 1980, while forgetting about the gains to be expected up to 1978 or the position in the 1980s and beyond. We saw that in 1977 the balance-of-payments loss is likely to be small because the net contribution to the budget is limited to about £200 million. With Williamson's estimate of a gain from extra growth of about $1\frac{1}{2}$ per cent of GNP by then, and after conversion to welfare costs and gains by the method used in Chapter 6, this gives a welfare gain of about 1 per cent of GNP at the end of the transitional period. Beyond 1980 too, it is only reasonable to expect that the extraordinary bias of the Community budget in favour of agriculture and against the consumer of imports—and hence against Britain on both counts—will subside. Both Marsh, in his assessment of the likely trend of the common agricultural policy and budget, and Dosser, in his final section on the Community budget, give reasons why this is to be expected. Thus it can be taken for granted that during the 1980s the net costs will begin to decline and the benefits increase.

In sum, the best estimate is a welfare gain of 1 per cent of GNP by 1978, declining to $\frac{3}{4}$ per cent of GNP by 1980 and rising again thereafter. The gain might be more or it might be less. There is even the possibility of gains up to 1978 being offset by a loss of up to 0.4 per cent of GNP in 1980, with a subsequent recovery to a position of net advantage. But it is hard to conceive that the possibility of a small but significant loss in the early 1980s could outweigh, in the judgement of the British people, the prospect of considerable welfare gains both before and after, and the strong probability of a substantial gain throughout.

The cost of living

The welfare gains or losses are measured for the nation as a whole. There is, however, also the distribution of these gains or losses among different groups to be considered. The effect on the cost-of-living index, which affects the real incomes of lower-income more than higher-income households, is a useful indicator of this.

The cost-of-living effect comes from the application of the Community's food-price supports and of its system of value-added tax, together with the prospect of further tax changes and the consequences of industrial free trade.

Josling argues convincingly that the influence of the food-importing countries in the Community will keep the agricultural prices rising more slowly than the general level of prices. This has in fact happened over the last eight years, to the extent of a decline of 2 per cent a year in real terms. Josling suggests, fairly conservatively, that the rate of decline in real terms may in the 1970s be 1 per cent instead of 2 per cent a year. He shows, at the same time, that if Britain were to remain outside the pressure in the UK would if anything be in the opposite direction, with the support of farmers continuing to move, as it has done in the last few years (under both Labour and Conservative governments), from the Exchequer to the consumer; and this trend he puts, again somewhat conservatively, at an increase in food prices of 1 per cent a year in relation to the general UK level of prices. These two trends combined give a rise in the price of food in Britain, if Britain were to remain outside the Community, of the same order of magnitude as that implied by the application of the common agricultural policy on British accession to the Community: some 15 per cent in either case, representing about 3 per cent on the cost of living.

This would, of course, preclude any special effect by way of a wages-price spiral, because the price trends would be similar whether Britain was in or out. Even if the whole of this additional rise in the cost of living were to be due to the CAP, however, it would still seem somewhat exaggerated to attribute any great spiralling effect to this kind of increase over a five-year period, after a single year in which the cost of living has risen by over three times as much.

As regards the Community value-added tax, this seems to be a dog that isn't going to bite. Dosser's finding is that on most counts it will make remarkably little difference when compared with the indirect taxes, purchase tax and SET, that were levied in 1969—let alone with the VAT which is now in any case being introduced. Thus the revenue raised by purchase tax and SET in 1969 was probably no less than would be raised by VAT at a rate which would fall within the band of rates at present contemplated for the purpose of harmonisation in the Community. Dosser finds that the rise in the cost of living, implied by the Community VAT, as compared with the 1969 system and rates of indirect tax, is likely to be of the order of 1 per cent, even after a reduced rate has replaced a zero rate for food— which would not happen in Britain until after 1978. When corresponding downward harmonisation of excise duties is taken into account—giving the British public cheaper beer, for example —even this small increase tends to melt away.

Associated with any such rise in the cost of living due to the introduction of VAT in the Community would be a regressive effect of a roughly similar order—which again would be barely perceptible before the introduction of the reduced rate on food, sometime after 1978; and this too should be largely offset by the downward harmonisation of excise. Changes of such orders of magnitude in the cost of living and the distribution of incomes can, in any case, readily be corrected, as Dosser points out, by greater payments to particular groups such as pensioners and by changes in the incidence of direct taxation; and, as Dosser makes clear, the VAT offers a broad enough tax base to make it relatively easy to raise the revenue required to improve the position of disadvantaged groups.

Finally, to set against any effects on the cost of living or the distribution of incomes due to food prices or VAT that are not offset by the reduction of excise, there will also be the downward pressure on the prices of manufactures that results from the removal of the UK tariff on imports from the Community.

The Commonwealth

This book is mainly about the economic effect of entry on Britain. But it also contains some implications for the Commonwealth and for other countries outside the enlarged Community.

It seems certain that the application of the CAP to Britain will have adverse effects on some producers of temperate agricultural products in the Western Hemisphere and the Antipodes. Thus Josling suggests that their exports of wheat may be 5.5 million tons, worth say £140 million, less than they would be if Britain stayed out.

To set against this, benefits are assured for the African and Caribbean countries and the other small islands of the Commonwealth (apart from Hong Kong, which will at least participate in the Community's scheme of generalised preferences) which accept the offer of association that is open to them. There are also the agreements relating to sugar and butter, which have satisfied the governments of the sugar-producing countries and of New Zealand. Josling's forecasts of production and consumption in an enlarged Community indicate, moreover, that there will be room in the Community market for imports of at least the agreed quantities.

Some particular problems remain, in addition to those for temperate agriculture. Thus no provision was made for the countries of the Indian sub-continent, apart from the application of generalised preferences, and the earlier suspension of the common tariff on tea and tropical hardwoods. Williamson's conclusion that there are sound quantitative grounds for expecting an acceleration of Britain's growth rate, confirmed qualitatively by Layton's work, does, however, appear to alter the balance of advantage for those countries. For their exports to Britain have up to now formed a diminishing percentage of their total exports, largely because of the relative stagnation of the UK market. With the British economy more dynamic, the prospects for the growth of their total exports to Britain would improve. The same consideration would, indeed, apply generally to Britain's suppliers, once transitional problems, arising largely from the application of the CAP, had been overcome.

Conclusions

The studies presented in this book show, then, that the
expectation of long-term net gains for Britain is probably
correct but that the fear of short-term net losses is probably not.
Any balance-of-payments effects are likely to be fairly small
and the gains to the growth rate and to welfare are likely to be
significant and could be very substantial. The effects on the cost
of living and the distribution of incomes are likely to be slight,
and any danger to less-privileged groups can be averted by
changes in direct tax and in social benefits.

This seems on balance to depict the most likely outcome. It
could, however, be better and it could be worse. But to accept the
latter possibility seems a small price to pay for the probability of
important economic benefits; for an insurance against exclusion from all markets in the event of protectionist forces
getting the upper hand in the world economy; and for the
expected gains in political influence.

Williamson writes in his chapter that he falls "in the category
of those who originally believed that the case for entering Europe
was entirely political and that the economic effects were unlikely
to be of much consequence in either direction". He now
considers that new findings which have become available
"seem . . . to change the balance of evidence". I too have
followed a similar line of development. I have been surprised by
the strength of the case that the new evidence seems to justify.
There is in my judgement now little room for doubt that
Britain should join on economic as well as political grounds.

For all that, one's final judgement is likely to stem from one's
philosophy. Peston, in the concluding chapter of this book,
points out that reluctance to enter is an essentially static and
conservative position: that readiness to join goes along with a
readiness to envisage change. For my part, the determining
factor, if all things were equal, would be my belief that the
methods of working together that have, despite difficulties and
setbacks, been evolving among the member states of the Community represent an important advance in political civilisation.
But it now seems clear that all other things are not equal: that
membership of the Community, being a major step in the
direction in which history is moving, accords with our economic
interest as well as our proper political development.

Chapter 2

TRADE AND ECONOMIC GROWTH

by John Williamson

BRITISH entry into the Common Market will result in tariff reductions, and as a result trade flows will change. That much is uncontroversial. One might also secure general consent to the proposition that these trade changes will influence real income, but there is profound disagreement as to the mechanisms through which this will occur. Some have even refused to commit themselves to any theory of the causal mechanisms involved and have resorted instead to such arithmetical banalities as telling one how much bigger national income would be after *n* years "if a rate of growth a $\frac{1}{2}$ per cent higher were to be achieved as a result of membership",[1] which prompted the TUC to retort that it also tells one how much lower national income would be if the growth rate fell by $\frac{1}{2}$ per cent as a result of membership. In my view there is an obligation on those who believe that the growth rate will benefit to show why. In seeking to do this I shall not draw rigid distinctions between 'static effects' and 'dynamic effects' or 'impact effects' and 'growth effects', since in my experience these classifications confuse rather than clarify analysis. If there are positive impact effects, then growth will be faster over the period during which they are being realised; conversely, faster growth must be explicable in terms of changes that could alternatively be described in terms of positive income effects.

My analysis will try to estimate the effects on real income

---

[1] *The United Kingdom and the European Communities*, Cmnd 4715, July 1971, p.16.

assuming that the Government maintains full employment by an appropriate demand-management policy irrespective of the balance of payments, and that the latter is maintained in equilibrium by any necessary change in the exchange rate. This may seem a startling contrast to the preoccupation with the effects on the balance of payments that has characterised much of the British debate. One is not denying that a balance-of-payments cost imposes a loss of real income, because any devaluation worsens the terms of trade and this certainly reduces real income; one is simply denying that it is proper to count any additional cost which would arise if the Government chose to counter a deficit through deflation unaided by depreciation. This assumption would be questionable if the EEC's ambitions towards monetary union meant that exchange rates were liable to be frozen during the transitional period, but the floating deutschemark and guilder have surely established that such fears are premature. (Indeed, this float may be taken as a reassurance that the Community is most unlikely to freeze exchange rates until there exist adequate alternative adjustment mechanisms that will enable exchange-rate changes to be safely dispensed with.) But the legitimacy of the assumption does *not* depend on a conviction (which I confess to lacking) that Mr. Heath and Mr. Barber can be relied upon to avoid irrational defence of an overvalued parity. The reason is that, if they prove to be obscurantist, an extra bit of deficit could just as easily be the final straw that persuaded them to overcome their reluctance to devalue (and thereby reduce the unemployment needed to preserve payments balance) as the cause of another round of stop-go.

A more fundamental objection to assuming away payments problems is that this also involves dismissing the theories of export-led growth which have been stressed by Professor Kaldor,[2] as well as by some of the Benelux economists.[3] Kaldor's version of this theory supposes that the growth of demand for an area's exports is the direct cause of its rate of

[2] N. Kaldor, The Dynamic Effects of the Common Market, in *Destiny or Delusion*, edited by D. Evans, Gollancz, 1971.

[3] For example, T. Peeters and J. P. Abraham, UK: the Benefit of Joining the Common Market, *Economische Statistische Berichten*, 1969 (in Dutch).

output growth, since the ability of the area to supply additional output is always assumed to be so elastic that the only constraint on higher output is the effect of a payments deficit in causing a limitation to be placed on demand. I find this theory intellectually untenable: there is overwhelming evidence, from British experience at the end of Mr. Maudling's period as Chancellor among other events, that the potential output an economy can produce at a particular point in time is quite rigidly limited by the resources it contains and the efficiency with which those resources are used. Foreign trade may well influence the efficiency of resource utilisation—indeed, discovering whether it does is what this chapter is all about. But to assume that output will always respond to an increase in export demand (and only in export demand?) is contrary to common sense, economic theory, and experience, as well as leading to such weird implications as advising the Germans never to revalue. The alternative version of the theory of export-led growth does not rely on any such unorthodox assumptions. It asserts that export expansion will encourage investment, largely by reassuring businessmen that they are not about to be assaulted by a debilitating deflationary package designed to shore up the balance of payments; that this investment will raise potential output and productivity and the latter will lower prices, thus improving international competitiveness and so setting the stage for further export expansion and the completion of a 'virtuous circle'. This seems to me a useful partial theory of the growth process, but it is not particularly relevant to assessing the consequences of Britain's entry to the EEC unless one can show that this will so improve the trade balance as to ensure an absence of future payments difficulties. If, on the other hand, the outlook is for continuing periodic crises resulting from excessive inflation, then a little bit more or less on the deficit will not be of critical significance: a favourable boost to exports will sometimes mitigate the deflation that would otherwise occur, but at other times it will delay a desirable devaluation and so retard expansion. In such circumstances an improved performance depends on better macro-economic policy and is not affected either way by membership of the EEC.

The two changes that can be expected to result from entry are an increase in trade and an increase in competition. An analysis of the effects of entry should therefore assess the consequences of these developments.

The effects on industrial trade

It is natural to start by asking how large an expansion of trade can be expected. In my view the best way of answering this question is to assume that British experience will be similar to that of other countries in parallel circumstances in the past. This of course requires a knowledge of the impact that customs unions have had on trade, and this is certainly not something that can be established by simply studying the historical statistics: it requires the elaboration of hypotheses as to what would have happened in the absence of integration. In fact, a paper of which I am joint author[4] is devoted to surveying the various attempts that have been made to analyse this question and adding a new analytical approach which has not previously been fully exploited, with a view to establishing the magnitude of the impact that the EEC and Efta had had on trade up to 1969. I propose to use the estimates developed in that paper to get an idea of the magnitude of the impact that Britain should expect.

The estimates presented in Table 1 relate to 1978. Since that is the year following the end of the transitional period, it is appropriate to draw on the EEC's experience up to 1969 (which was the first full year of a complete common market) in forming these estimates. Readers who have no interest in the tortuous ad hockery that is needed to brew a set of figures such as appear in Table 1 are advised to take note of the figures and pass on to the next section.

In order to construct estimates of trade changes one first needs an estimate of what trade would be if entry to the EEC did not occur. The provision of such figures is in itself quite a major forecasting exercise, which I am in no position to undertake satisfactorily. The figures for no-entry trade which I give in column 1 are no better than guesses which were arrived at by studying 1969 trade values and previous trends. They essentially assume that the price trends of the 1960s (rather than of 1970-71) will be re-established as the norm for the 1970s.

---

[4] J. H. Williamson and A. Bottrill, The Impact of Customs Unions on Trade in Manufactures, *Oxford Economic Papers*, November 1971.

Table 1: Estimated effects of EEC Entry on UK Trade in Manufactures in 1978

Column / Area	(1) No-entry trade (£ billion)	(2) Effects of entry on trade	(3) Percentage change	(4) Change (£ billion)
Exports				
EEC	3	$(40\% + 10\% + 10\%) \times \tfrac{2}{3}$	$+40\%$	$+1.2$
Efta	2	$80\% \times \tfrac{30}{160} \times \tfrac{2}{3}$	-10%	-0.2
Commonwealth	2		-10%	-0.2
EEC Associates	1		$+10\%$	$+0.1$
Rest of World	3		nil	—
Total	11		$+8\%$	$+0.9$
Imports				
EEC	3	$(40\% + 25\%) \times \tfrac{2}{3}$	$+45\%$	$+1.3$
Efta	2	$-\left\{\begin{array}{c}\text{Diversion}\\ \text{plus reversion}\\ \text{to EEC}\end{array}\right\} +(27\% \times \tfrac{1}{5})$		-0.5
Commonwealth	$1\tfrac{1}{2}$		-7%	
Rest of World	$3\tfrac{1}{2}$		$+5\%$	$+0.2$
Total	10		$+10\%$	$+1.0$

The next column displays the logic underlying the percentage change in trade shown in column 3 (and therefore the absolute change in trade, obtained by multiplying columns 1 and 3, shown in column 4). This logic is the core of the analysis and requires detailed explanation.

Exports to the EEC will rise for three reasons: trade creation, diversion, and reversion. Trade creation occurs when British exports increase at the expense of local production in the importing country. The Williamson-Bottrill estimate is that this factor led to an increase in intra-EEC trade of some 40 per cent. Trade diversion arises when the preference extended to Britain causes EEC countries to switch their supply source away from third countries towards us: this factor was estimated as increasing intra-EEC trade by 10 per cent up to 1969. Trade reversion occurs when the trade diversion from which we suffered as a result of being excluded from the Common Market is reversed, so that our exports replace supplies now bought in other EEC partner countries. This effect is also put at a potential 10 per cent because total estimated EEC diversion of \$1.9 billion was spread over extra-EEC imports of some \$17 billion. This gives a total potential export gain of 60 per cent. But the predicted gain is only two-thirds of this because the Kennedy round will reduce tariffs by about a third in any event.

Exports to Efta will be lower than they would be if Britain did not enter the Common Market. The trade creation that has occurred will not be reversed, because our Efta partners will either enter the EEC or conclude trading agreements that will preserve virtual free trade. But trade reversion will occur in so far as the diversion from which we have benefited was at the expense of the EEC—and this has been estimated as to the extent of 80 per cent.[5] Trade diversion would seem to have increased Efta intra-trade by something like 30 per cent; this means that elimination of the diversion would reduce intra-trade by $\frac{30}{160}$ (since intra-trade is an estimated 60 per cent higher than it would have been if Efta had not been formed). The total must again be reduced by a third to allow for the Kennedy round, giving an estimated export loss of 10 per cent.

---

[5] L. B. Krause, *European Economic Integration and the United States*, Brookings, Washington DC, 1968, p.56.

One probable consequence of joining the EEC is the loss of what remains of the preferential advantages favouring British exports in Commonwealth markets. It is difficult to know how much weight to place on this factor. At the moment our share of Overseas Sterling Area markets is still much higher than our share of third markets, but the difference has been narrowing very rapidly. In 1958 we supplied 51 per cent of the manufactured imports bought in the OSA, but this had dropped to 27 per cent in 1968—as against an almost constant 10 per cent in neutral markets. On this trend we shall not have any special position left to lose in Commonwealth markets by 1978. On the other hand, the erosion of our market share might level out before 1978, so it would seem prudent to allow for the possibility that tariff preferences would still be worth something if we did not enter the Common Market. A loss of 10 per cent of our Commonwealth market is a guess which seems to make a reasonably generous allowance for this possibility.

Membership of the EEC will also gain Britain preferential access to the markets of the countries associated with the EEC under the Yaoundé Convention and to those countries that have concluded trade agreements with the Community. (The first category covers most of ex-French Africa and the second most of the countries bordering the Mediterranean.) This should promote a useful though undramatic export expansion, which has again been guessed as 10 per cent.

The increase in imports from the EEC on account of trade creation has been assumed similar to the export increase of 40 per cent. It could be argued that the import increase is likely to be rather larger than that of exports because British tariffs are rather higher than those of the EEC, but as against this there is the consideration that the market enlargement will be proportionately far greater for British firms and hence one might expect a bigger response on the export side[6]. A rather greater allowance (25 per cent) has been made for the sum of diversion and reversion than on the export side, for two reasons: because

---

[6] A further reason for supposing that trade creation would cause imports to rise no more than exports is shown in Chapter 9 of this book, where Dosser indicates (in Table 5, p.207) that the introduction of VAT at the rates likely to be applicable within the Community would be likely to reduce imports significantly.

Commonwealth imports will see positive preferences in their favour replaced by positive discrimination against them, and because Efta seems to have been a more potent agent of trade diversion than the EEC. The total import increase is then reduced by one-third to allow for the Kennedy round.

Imports from Efta, the Commonwealth and the Rest of the World will fall as the direct counterpart of the diversion and reversion in the EEC's favour: no attempt has been made to allocate the overall fall of 7 per cent between the different areas. In addition, the Rest of the World will benefit from 'external trade creation' arising from the reduction of our tariff against them to the common external tariff. This effect has been put at a fifth of the 27 per cent rise in imports from the EEC attributed to trade creation, because the common external tariff is about 80 per cent of the British tariff. No allowance has been made for any increase in imports from the EEC Associates; any such change would be predominantly trade diversion and would therefore be offset by import decreases among the other non-EEC countries.

These figures add up to a net expansion in exports of £900 million, equivalent to 1.8 per cent of GNP if the latter is around £50 billion in 1978, and a net expansion in imports of £1,000 million. This would indicate a slight deterioration in the trade balance as a result of the complex of tariff changes involved. (This may be too pessimistic. For example, the *Guardian* survey of British industrialists published on 16 July 1971 showed that business expected that sales gains in the EEC would exceed losses elsewhere. But since this survey also showed expected gains slightly exceeding losses even *outside* the EEC I am not inclined to take it so seriously as to change my own estimates.)

I freely confess that I would not wish to stake my professional reputation on the accuracy of the figures in Table 1. That is why they are so heavily rounded: the common practice of quoting estimates like these to three significant figures is simply absurd. They are intended to provide a quantitative illustration of the two qualitative conclusions that seem to me both clear and important:

> (a) that entry will provoke a substantial increase in two-way trade with the existing members of the EEC;

(b) that the effects on the industrial trade balance will be
rather minor.

The theory of customs unions

There exists a well-established body of economic theory,
stemming from the original analysis of Jacob Viner,[7] concerning
the welfare effects of establishing a customs union. The purpose
of the theory is to enable one to appraise the effects that a
series of trade changes such as are shown in Table 1 will have
on real income. So far as an export increase is concerned, it
does not matter whether its cause is trade creation or diversion.
The distinction is, however, of fundamental importance on the
import side.

Trade creation is usually analysed with the aid of a diagram
like Figure 1. The domestic demand and supply curves are

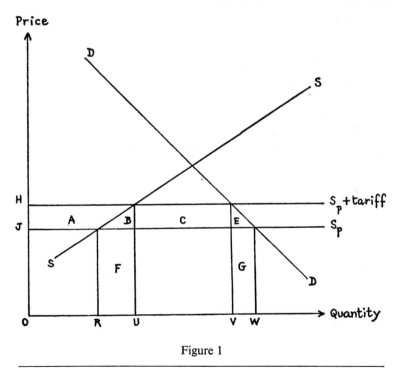

Figure 1

---

[7] J. Viner, *The Customs Union Issue*, Carnegie Endowment for International Peace, New York, 1950.

shown by DD and SS respectively, the partners' supply curve by J S_p, and the initial tariff by JH. Prior to the formation of the customs union domestic output is OU, imports are UV, consumption is OV, and price is OH. After the tariff is abolished the price falls to OJ and in consequence domestic output falls to OR, imports expand to RW, and consumption expands to OW. Consumers have a welfare gain of the areas A+B+C+E; of this area C represents a loss of tariff revenue to the government and area A represents a loss of quasi-rents to the domestic producers of the imported commodity, so that the net welfare gain is simply the areas B+E. This is (approximately, unless demand and supply curves are truly linear) half the initial tariff multiplied by the increase in imports.

The increase in imports of RU+VW will result in the displacement of the domestic factors of production that were previously engaged in producing RU of the imported commodity and VW of other products that are replaced by the cheaper imports. These imports have to be paid for by increased exports equal to the areas F+G. If the removal of foreign tariffs enables the exact amount of extra exports represented by the areas F+G to be sold at the previous supply price, then the welfare gain on the balanced trade expansion will be exactly equal to the areas B+E. In general there is no reason to suppose that this condition will be fulfilled. The demand for exports could grow by more than the areas F+G, in which case there would be excess demand and a tendency towards a payments surplus; the exchange rate would have to appreciate to re-establish equilibrium, and real income would benefit through the resulting improvement in the terms of trade. Or export demand might initially be augmented by less than F+G; in which case depreciation would be necessary and the welfare gains of B+E would be eroded by the resulting terms-of-trade loss.

Trade creation benefits welfare because it involves the replacement of relatively costly domestic production by cheaper foreign production. In contrast, trade diversion reduces welfare because it involves shifting the source of supply from a low-cost foreign source to a higher-cost partner source.[8] (The partner must be a higher-cost source because otherwise purchases would have been made there in the absence of tariff discrimination.) The loss caused by this diversion is measured by the difference in cost between the two sources of imports (which will on average be roughly half the common external tariff) multiplied by the amount of trade diverted. Trade reversion is of course the precise opposite of diversion, and gives rise to welfare gains that can be measured in a precisely analogous way.

The welfare effects of the trade changes shown in Table 1 are calculated in Table 2 using the methods that have just been described. Since the post-Kennedy round UK tariff is estimated as about 10 per cent, the gain from trade creation is 5 per cent of the increase in imports from the EEC attributable to creation. The welfare loss from trade diversion is half the post-Kennedy round common external tariff of about 8 per cent. Trade reversion from Efta should carry an average benefit of half the British tariff of 10 per cent, while reversion from the Commonwealth would be half the (lower) tariff faced by the Commonwealth: it is assumed that these two average to 4 per cent. External trade creation is credited with a benefit of 9 per cent, the average of the old 10 per cent tariff and the new 8 per cent rate, since the average extra unit of trade overcomes a barrier of that size.

The final element in the calculation is the terms-of-trade cost of correcting the worsening in the trade balance. I have presented elsewhere[9] a formula for calculating the terms-of-

---

[8] It has sometimes been claimed that trade diversion can raise welfare through beneficial consumption effects even though it reduces welfare through increasing the costs of imports. Whether this is true depends on the precise way in which one distinguishes between creation and diversion. It is correct if one makes the distinction in terms of commodities. The imports of a good for which trade is diverted to partners will increase because its price will be lowered, and this consumption effect will be favourable because previously a sub-optimal quantity of the good was being consumed. But in practice when one estimates trade creation and diversion one does not examine individual commodities in this way; one asks by how much imports increase in total and how much trade is switched from third countries to partners. This means that the increase in imports is already counted as a part of trade creation rather than diversion, and the latter is an unambiguous welfare loss.

[9] J. H. Williamson, *On Estimating the Income Effects of British Entry to the EEC*, University of Surrey, 1971, p.6.

trade loss resulting from devaluation. Unfortunately when I used this formula previously I substituted figures which appeared to be reasonable in the light of the experience of devaluation in 1967, without making a correction for the fact that when we are in the EEC one effect of the common agricultural policy will be to ensure that domestic food prices rise virtually in proportion to any devaluation. This, as Professor Kaldor has rightly emphasised, would raise the cost of any devaluation that was needed. In fact, according to my estimate it would raise the terms-of-trade cost from the 25 per cent that I previously estimated to about 33 per cent.

Table 2: The Estimated Welfare Effects of Trade Changes

	Estimated trade change £ million	Welfare gain or loss percentages	Change in welfare £ million
Trade creation	800	+ 5	+40
Trade diversion	350	− 4	−14
Trade reversion	150	+ 4	+ 6
External trade creation	200	+ 9	+18
Trade balance	−100	+33	−33
Total			+19

The end result of the calculations summarised in Table 2 is a net gain of £19 million, some 0.04 per cent of GNP. This is by any standards, and certainly in comparison to the sums involved in the agricultural arrangements, a trivial sum. One could argue that the appropriate tariff rate to use in evaluating the benefits of trade creation is the effective tariff of perhaps 16 per cent rather than the nominal tariff of 10 per cent, and by such amendments raise the estimated net benefit to perhaps £50 million without departing from the framework established by customs union theory. But, so long as one measures the benefits of economic integration by estimating the welfare triangles B and E, one is bound to get a small answer, because one is multiplying half of a small percentage tariff rate by the proportionate increase in trade, and multiplying that again by the proportion that trade is of GNP. Some economists have concluded that this establishes that entry to the EEC cannot be economically advantageous. But economic theory, though seldom departing so far from the available theory as to incorporate such curious concepts as import-led stagnation, is rarely complete. It is necessary to ask first whether customs union theory can really claim to be comprehensive.

The limitations of welfare triangles

In fact, customs union theory as presented in the previous section depends on three quite restrictive assumptions. First, it presumes upward-sloping supply curves like SS in Figure 1, and is not capable of handling correctly the case where scale economies exist. Second, it assumes that tariff elimination influences efficiency only through increasing trade, thus excluding the possibility that a more competitive climate could stimulate efficiency in the import-competing sector. Third, it assumes that the resources available remain the same and are simply redeployed between different uses, whereas it may be that investment is raised and so the available resources tend to increase through time. Before one could conclude that Table 2 is a useful guide to the expected effects of joining the Common Market, one would need to establish that relaxing these assumptions would not greatly change the picture that emerges.

There is to my knowledge only one study of the effects of integration that has adopted a method which would capture these additional effects if they exist, rather than using methods that exclude such benefits by assumption. This is a book by R. J. and P. Wonnacott[10] which attempted to estimate the gain to Canada through formation of a free trade area with the United States. The Wonnacotts estimated the cost of North American protection to Canada as a residual, by assuming that the small size of the Canadian market was the only factor which depresses Canadian wages below those in equally favourable locations in the United States. There may of course be factors other than protection and location that contribute to the wage differential (though it is not obvious what they are, since they do not include the capital intensity), in which case their estimate of the benefits of a free trade area would be exaggerated. But, since the Wonnacotts estimate the benefit

---

[10] R. J. and P. Wonnacott, *Free Trade Between the United States and Canada*, Harvard University Press, Cambridge, Mass., 1967. Actually their method would not capture any benefits that may come through the stimulation of investment.

to Canada as a gain of 10½ per cent of GNP, these other factors would have to be very substantial to undermine their conclusion that integration would produce much larger benefits than indicated by the welfare triangles. Unfortunately it is not possible to say exactly how much bigger their estimate is than would be produced by the conventional customs-union analysis, but it is at least 2.3 times as big and probably over five times the size. It follows that the best available evidence does not substantiate the legitimacy of the restrictive assumptions which are needed to conclude that the welfare triangles tell one all one needs to know.

This conclusion is corroborated by evidence which indicates that market size has a significant positive influence on industrial productivity. There is evidence that market size can usefully contribute to the explanation of international productivity differentials in cross-section regressions, and in addition bilateral productivity comparisons between a series of industries in a pair of countries have found that productivity differentials are greatest where the output differences are greatest.[11] After making all due allowance for such possibilities as that the observed association could to some extent be explained by high productivity causing large output rather than the reverse, these studies do provide evidence for believing that a large market is a significant factor making for high productivity. It is ridiculous to seek to dismiss this evidence by a casual remark about the prosperity of Sweden and Switzerland. Apart from the fact that both these countries have the same sized 'home market' as Britain (i.e., Efta), no-one is asserting that market size is of such dominant importance that investment, education and hard work cannot permit a country to prosper even on

[11] The cross-section regressions are found in UN Department of Economic and Social Affairs, *A Study of Industrial Growth* (63.II.B.2), 1963, p.7, and H. B. Chenery, Patterns of Industrial Growth, *American Economic Review*, September 1960, p.633; while the bilateral productivity comparisons are in J. H. Young, *Some Aspects of Canadian Economic Development*, unpublished doctoral dissertation submitted to Cambridge University, 1955; M. Frankel, *British and American Manufacturing Productivity*, University of Illinois Bureau of Economic and Business Research Bulletin 81, 1957; and D. Paige and G. Bombach, *A Comparison of National Output and Productivity of the UK and the US*, OEEC, Paris, 1959.

the basis of a small home market. One is at most saying that a doubling of the market might make them 5 per cent or 10 per cent better off.

It also seems relevant to note that businessmen, unlike economists with a good training in the theory of customs unions, do not believe that the Common Market is a trivial factor of no more than marginal significance. They are quite clear, as Layton shows in the following chapter, in stating that they expect the change in the environment resulting from entry to influence their decisions.

The evidence therefore points to the necessity of extending the analysis to cover scale economies, competitive effects, and investment. One cannot place any confidence in the results of studies which omit these factors.

Economies of scale

Perhaps the most interesting theoretical contribution of the Wonnacotts is their modification of Figure 1 to cover the case of increasing returns to scale. A slight adaptation of their diagram[12] is shown in Figure 2. One again postulates a domestic

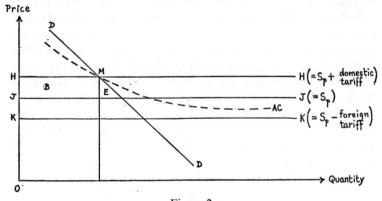

Figure 2

demand curve DD and a horizontal partners' supply curve JJ. The price at which partners can sell in the protected domestic market is shown by HH, and the price which exports would realise in the foreign market in the presence of tariffs is shown by KK.

[12] Wonnacott, *op.cit.*, p.288.

In the presence of increasing returns it is reasonable to postulate that firms will follow an average-cost pricing policy, since marginal-cost pricing would result in losses. (If, however, differential pricing in home and export markets were feasible, the firm might well find it profitable to move part way toward marginal-cost pricing in the presence of tariffs. This possibility is neglected on the grounds that anti-dumping policies limit the feasibility of differential pricing.) This means that whether or not domestic production occurs depends entirely on the position of the average cost (AC) curve relative to the demand curves introduced in the previous paragraph. Under protection, production will take place for the domestic market provided that the AC curve passes through M (as shown), or to the left of M, where M is the point defined by the intersection of the domestic demand curve DD and the foreign cum-tariff supply curve HH. Production for export would occur only if AC eventually fell below KK, enabling output to be profitably sold over the foreign tariff. If neither of these conditions were satisfied there would not be any domestic production.

Consider now the situation after abolition of both tariffs. Whether or not domestic production occurs will depend entirely on whether or not AC eventually dips below JJ. If it does not, then domestic production will not occur. If it was not occurring before, then the gain is simply the consumer surplus triangle E, and this is properly measured by the usual approach. If domestic production ceases, then the gain is the areas B+E (it should be noted that the quasi-rents of area A in Figure 1 do not exist under increasing returns, so that the whole of the gain to the consumer is also a gain to society at large); since area B is a rectangle and not a triangle, the conventional procedure halves the correct measure of the gain involved.

The major difference arises in the case where AC falls below JJ so that domestic production is maintained in the customs union. If exporting was occurring previously, it will now expand (and the value of receipts will expand still more because the foreign tariff revenue will accrue to the exporter). But if AC falls merely to between JJ and KK (as shown in the diagram), exporting will commence where previously production was confined to satisfying the home market. In either event the increase in output will reduce the cost of output for the home market and thereby yield benefits over and above those accruing directly from the trade expansion and measured by the customary welfare triangles.

In order to assess the size of these additional gains it is necessary to form a judgment of the importance of economies of scale. It is generally conceded that decreasing returns to scale such as are pictured in the rising supply curve of Figure 1 are virtually non-existent in manufacturing industry, but the evidence suggests that the normal condition is one of constant costs over the relevant range rather than of decreasing costs. There is, however, fairly compelling evidence that economies of scale are important in three circumstances[13]. The first arises in those industries which process liquids and are therefore subject to the so-called "0.6 Rule", according to which a doubling of capacity involves only a 60 per cent increase in capital costs because containers increase their volume with the cube of their dimensions while the surface area increases only with the square. The second occurs over a large part of the engineering industries where batch production is practised; a doubling of the product run often seems to lead to as much as a 20 per cent reduction in unit costs because of the learning process that accompanies repetition. The third case involves the possibility of spreading initial costs over a larger volume of output: this is, as evidence given in Chapter 3 below reminds us, of major significance in the high-technology industries.

Where scale economies exist they typically seem to be as high as 20 per cent. It is possible to get some idea of what this may imply for the welfare effects of trade expansion by taking an arithmetical example. Suppose that a firm with scale economies of 20 per cent has a 10 per cent increase in its total sales as a result of increased demand from the EEC following the elimination of tariffs. The 10 per cent increase in output will require only an 8 per cent increase in input and so, if the firm practises average-cost pricing, its domestic price will fall by about 2 per cent. If one normalises the firm's initial sales to 100, there is a social gain of 2 arising from the fall in the cost of previous output. In addition, of course, the additional

[13] J. R. Cable, *Scale and Economic Performance in Manufacturing*, unpublished, 1969.

exports of 10^{14} permit one to buy additional imports with a welfare value of 10.5 (without any terms-of-trade cost); that is the standard welfare-triangle gain. There is a further benefit in so far as the price fall stimulates domestic demand. Assuming that the resources needed to increase output are drawn from an industry with marginal-cost pricing or else from a decreasing-cost industry which closes down a production line entirely, this benefit can be evaluated by the difference between average cost and marginal cost, a factor of 20 per cent. With a domestic demand elasticity of —2 and zero initial exports one would have an additional benefit of $2 \times 2 \times \frac{20}{100}$, or 0.8, which is itself greater than the welfare triangle. The total benefit would be 3.3, some one-third of the increase in exports and over six times the sum suggested by the welfare triangle.

There is an alternative and somewhat more rigorous way to analyse the question. The increased output of 14 (10 for the EEC and four for the domestic market) requires an increased input of only 80 per cent of 14, or 11.2. Foreign exchange earnings would rise by 9.8, of which 7.6 (i.e., 95 per cent of 8) would be required to buy imports to replace the goods formerly produced by the factors that have now moved into export production. The payments gain of 2.2 could be used to realise a terms-of-trade improvement, thus yielding a benefit of 2.9. To this must be added the 0.8 difference between price and marginal cost on the additional domestic output, giving a total gain of 3.7 (or 38 per cent of the trade expansion).

In the above account scale economies are initiated by the rationalisation and longer production runs made possible by the wider market and realised through the medium of an increase in trade. It follows that it is still possible to relate the size of the benefits to the size of the increase in trade: it is just that the ratio is a much higher one, perhaps one-third. The next question is what proportion of the predicted trade creation of £800 million extra exports is likely to be realised in industries with increasing returns. One's casual impression is that the

---

[14] Less any terms-of-trade loss on exports that were being sold prior to entry. To the extent that such exports existed, a part of the gain of 2 will accrue to foreigners; but since any such price fall would tend to raise export volumes further, there would be an offsetting gain. It is assumed these factors cancel out.

increase in trade has tended to be concentrated quite heavily in this type of industry. By far the most impressive evidence for the importance of scale economies in traded goods is, however, the observed association between the increase in the volume of exports and the fall in the ratio of export prices to domestic wholesale prices. The obvious interpretation of this empirical association is that the export industries are characterised by increasing returns which can be realised through an increase in exports. Furthermore, it is generally hoped that the EEC will make rapid progress in eliminating non-tariff barriers in the next few years: since these are particularly important in the high-technology industries, future trade expansion is likely to be even more heavily concentrated in the areas where significant scale benefits are available.

On these grounds it would be reasonable to presume that scale benefits will be realised on the bulk of the £800 million trade creation. If, say, £600 million is credited with a welfare benefit of one-third and the remainder with the traditional derisory 5 per cent, the benefit of trade creation comes to £210 million or 0.4 per cent of GNP[15].

Competition

It is sometimes objected that, if scale economies were as significant as I have argued they appear to be, one would observe monopolies at the national level. This does not in fact follow, because oligopolists with decreasing costs could well find live-and-let-live a more advantageous strategy than the initiation of an oligopolistic war designed to bankrupt their competitors. But even if it were true that all scale economies could be realised by national monopolies, it certainly does not follow that such monopolies would be desirable or that that would dispose of the case for a market larger than can be provided by a single medium-rank country like Britain. It could be that the observed association between market size and productivity is explained by the opportunity a large market provides for reconciling adequate scale with sufficient diversity to satisfy consumers' tastes for variety on the one hand,

---

[15] This is still only about a half of the minimum figure suggested by some of the work that has been done on export prices, so there may remain a serious downward bias in the calculation.

and the maintenance of vigorous competition on the other.

It is perhaps easiest to illustrate the benefits of competition by examining the events that could be expected to follow the imposition of protection. Suppose therefore that a country had an industry manufacturing a product Z, consisting of a single firm which was operating at maximum efficiency and exactly satisfying the domestic demand for Z without making excess profits under free trade. Imposition of a tariff would not curtail the import of Z because none was being imported, but the monopolist would presumably take advantage of the protection he was afforded to raise his price, and this would curtail consumption causing a social loss that can be measured by the customary welfare triangle. The excess profits might attract new entrants to the industry, each of which would be of sub-optimal size and would therefore lead to waste. Even if new entry did not occur, so that production was not broken down into inefficiently-small units, it is quite likely that the protected monopolist might allow his costs to drift up over time.

Tariff elimination would presumably tend to reverse these changes. If it did, the resulting gains in real income would be realised without any increase in international trade. Moreover, the elimination of the sub-optimal-sized firms would involve once again reaping the scale economies potentially available, and this too would occur despite the absence of any increase in trade.[16] Thus it is mistaken to think that the benefits of joining a customs union are necessarily limited to a small (or even large) fraction of the increase in trade that it generates.

It is sometimes said that a multilateral freeing of trade such as occurs on joining a customs union would not lead to any net increase in the competitive pressure on industry: while import competition would indeed strengthen pressure on the import-competing industries, there would be a corresponding relaxation

---

[16] Scitovsky long ago claimed that the realisation of scale economies depends on an increase, not in intra-European trade, but only in competition. See T. Scitovsky, *Economic Theory and Western European Integration*, Allen and Unwin, 1958. Perhaps I am alone in ever having doubted the proposition. But I still suspect that in practice most scale economies are linked with trade expansion as described in the previous section.

in the pressure on the export industries. It is not as easy to visualise an export industry deciding it could relax because of favourable demand developments in its foreign markets as it is to believe the sequence following the imposition of protection that was described above, but presumably there could be an analogous effect. Nevertheless, there is a plausible argument for supposing that any such effect is likely to be considerably weaker. This stems from the presumption that production functions for the same industry are likely to be broadly similar in different countries. Suppose then that a country imposed a uniform tariff on all manufactured imports. Presumably some industries would react to this by allowing their prices and costs to drift up, while others would not. The former would cease to export, while the latter would continue exporting. What this suggests is that present export industries *are* export industries, at least to some extent, because in the past they let less fat develop. If this was because of some long-lived trait, then it seems reasonable to suppose that the process of improving their position relative to that of the import-competing industries would be likely to produce asymmetrical results, with the squeezing of the latter's position having a greater effect than any easing in the position of the former.

But there is another sense in which competition would be strengthened in the export industries as well. Suppose that one adopts the plausible postulate that businessmen have a trade-off between profits and lethargy that can be represented by a conventional-shaped indifference curve as shown by I I, in Figure 3. In the presence of tariffs there will be some attainable transformation curve between profits and lethargy that may for simplicity be represented by the straight line AB, and this will give rise to a utility-maximising point C. Tariff reduction will then have both an income effect and a substitution effect. The argument in the preceding paragraphs equated competition with the difficulty of making profits, and was therefore concerned solely with the income effect. It is certainly true that tariff reduction would push AB inwards for import-competing industries and outwards for export industries, and this would have an income effect that would decrease lethargy in the former but increase it in the latter, so that any net effect must be based on postulating some form of asymmetry.

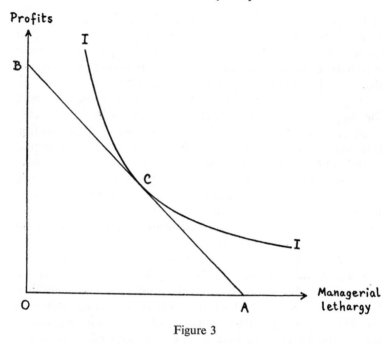

Figure 3

But tariff reduction would also produce a substitution effect. When the domestic and foreign markets are insulated by 10 per cent tariff walls on each side, it will be fairly unusual for domestic and foreign industries to be seriously in competition in both home and foreign markets (though no doubt this will happen to some extent where product differentiation is significant). Indeed, with similar costs there may not be much competition in either market; the home market may be available to home producers with very little effort, while the foreign market may not be accessible even if a great deal of effort is invested. In terms of Figure 3 this means that the level of profits will not vary much whatever the degree of effort or lethargy, so that AB will tend to be flat. Conversely, with one large market there will be the possibility of greater gains in export markets and also of greater losses in the domestic market, so that profits will respond more sensitively to effort and AB will be steeper. This will produce a substitution effect favourable to greater effort in both export and import-competing industries.

Even if there should be no asymmetry regarding the income effects, therefore, there is a compelling reason to expect the sharpening of competition resulting from the elimination of tariffs to lead to greater managerial effort. It is generally conceded that the major source of economic inefficiency is not the presence of market distortions, the cost of which is measured by the welfare triangles, but rather what Leibenstein has termed 'X-inefficiency': the technical inefficiency that stems from a failure to maximise.[17] The evidence suggests that the losses from X-inefficiency are substantial, and they are clearly the result of managerial inadequacy. There is therefore every reason to suppose that they would be reduced by a change which gave a greater incentive to managerial effort. It can be argued that the resulting increase in output would not represent a pure gain in welfare because it would be achieved at the cost of disrupting the leisurely working habits that constitute one of the attractive features of contemporary British life. There is an element of truth in this, but one can hope to rely on the trade unions to defend those elements that really do contribute to welfare (such as a civilised length of tea-break); casual observation suggests that there is also frequent under-utilisation of manpower which merely generates boredom, and it is this that one would hope to see reduced.

Competitiveness is not an easy concept to handle analytically, but it is hoped that the preceding analysis captures something of what is involved. There is one other aspect that may well be importantly influenced by entry to the Common Market: the ability of progressive firms to expand at the expense of the unenterprising. In a small economy the constraint on a firm's expansion set by the rate of growth of its market tends to be a serious one. A firm with the managerial capacity to expand more rapidly than demand for its products is growing can realise its potential only by increasing its market share, broadening its product range, or expanding the proportion of its output that is exported. Each of these strategies is, however, liable to encounter diminishing returns that will tend to drag the firm's growth rate back towards that which is consistent

---

[17] H. Leibenstein, Allocative Efficiency versus 'X-Efficiency', *American Economic Review*, June 1966.

with the growth of the economy. The first is increasingly likely to involve an oligopolistic war (and the smaller the economy the sooner this stage is likely to come), the second to take the firm outside the area where it possesses the expertise to succeed, and the third to involve an erosion of profitability as a result of the well-attested fact that selling over a tariff wall generally involves accepting lower profit margins than are customary on domestic sales. The fast growth of Britain's potential EEC partners should enable British firms with a high growth potential to realise this by sharing in the growth of Continental demand without eroding profitability. If the vigorous firms who wish to expand more rapidly than their home market are no longer subjected to the additional tax constituted by the foreign tariff, they will be better able to compete resources away from the stagnant industries that are content to follow the growth of the home market.

The benefits from relaxing the demand constraint need not be confined to the growth in international trade. This can be seen most clearly in the classic case of the benefits of being part of a rapidly-growing market—the case where the minimum optimal scale of new plants is large relative to the annual increment in domestic demand. In a closed economy this obliges an expanding firm to choose between constructing a fully-efficient plant that would be under-utilised in its early years and a sub-optimal plant that would have less excess capacity to begin with but higher costs in later years. The more accessible the foreign market is, the greater is the chance of the optimum-sized plant being chosen. The benefits of this choice would remain even in the case where exports were a purely transitory phenomenon and the plant's ultimate output was entirely devoted to the home market.

Unfortunately there is no basis on which one can quantify these competitive effects with any conviction. It seems clear that the potential benefits are large: indeed, if integration can produce really big effects (by which I mean anything over $\frac{1}{2}$ per cent on the growth rate) they almost certainly work through the types of mechanisms sketched in this section. But the size of the benefits really does depend on the managerial response: L-shaped managerial indifference curves in Figure 3 would imply zero benefits. I would personally guess that this factor is at least as important as the scale effects discussed in the previous section—but that remains a guess.

Investment

There is reason to expect that one effect of entry to the Community will be the stimulation of a minor investment boom (a boom, at least, in comparison to what would otherwise occur). It is certainly true that the founding of the Community was accompanied by an investment boom; it is also true that both British and foreign businessmen are reported to be planning to invest more to take advantage of the new opportunities; and theory suggests that one would expect a major shift in demand such as is represented by the predicted changes in trade flows to call forth additional investment. If one assumed that the additional exports of £800 million would generate a requirement for extra investment and one postulated a capital-output ratio of 3, that would involve additional investment of £2.4 billion over the five-year transition period.

It has become fashionable to denigrate the importance of investment in causing growth. The major reason for this is the supposed empirical finding that most growth is attributable to technical progress rather than capital formation, but this is not really an empirical conclusion at all; it is fed in at the beginning of the analysis in the form of an *assumption* that the social return on investment is no greater than the private return. Empirical estimates that have not pre-determined their conclusions in this way have yielded significantly higher estimates of the social marginal product of investment and therefore of the importance of investment in the growth process.[18] A central estimate of the rate of return would be about 20 per cent.

A 20 per cent return on investment of £2.4 billion would give additional income of almost £500 million. But it would be wrong to count all of this as a welfare gain, since the future income is achieved by a sacrifice of present consumption. A welfare gain of £250 million might be the right order of

---

[18] See R. M. Solow, *Capital Theory and the Rate of Return*, North-Holland, Amsterdam, 1964, and R. S. Eckhaus and L. Lefeber, Capital Formation: a Theoretical and Empirical Analysis, in P. N. Rosenstein-Rodan (ed.), *Capital Formation and Economic Development*, Allen and Unwin, London, 1964.

magnitude. (It is sometimes suggested that this should not be counted as a 'Common Market effect' because the Government could stimulate investment by other means in the absence of entry. Would that life were so simple! The fact is that the effectiveness of incentives to manufacturing investment is very much open to question, and anyway they involve an expensive transfer of income to shareholders. It therefore seems to me entirely proper to score the benefits of any increase in investment.) It can also be argued that any increase in the investment ratio which had once been achieved would be quite likely to be maintained beyond the transitional period. This is partly because the difficult process of pushing up the savings ratio would have been accomplished; partly because the capacity of the capital-goods industries would have expanded and this would make it more difficult for governments to pursue monetary policies that choked off investment; and partly because business would have acquired the habit of investing more freely. This would of course imply that the growth rate would receive a boost that could last far beyond 1978.

Conclusion

I fall in the category of those who originally believed that the case for entering Europe was entirely political and that the economic effects were unlikely to be of much consequence in either direction. The advent of the common agricultural policy prevented one from taking refuge in this cosy belief: in the absence of significant benefits from industrial free trade, entry would clearly impose an economic cost. The question of whether free trade with Europe would bring gains could no longer be brushed aside.

There seemed to be a real conflict between the results of customs union theory on the one hand and the reported impressions of those who had experienced integration on the other. In due course various bits of fragmentary evidence on the economic value of a large market size turned up, and the causal mechanisms that could explain an empirical association between market size and productivity became apparent: scale economies and competition seem quite able to explain what needs to be explained. But I remained hesitant about claiming more than that others should similarly refrain from dogmatism, because the connecting thread was a pretty tenuous one. The impressive study of the Wonnacotts, and the finding that the ratio of export to domestic prices is closely related to the rate of growth of exports, seem to me to change the balance of evidence. It remains true that any assessment of the magnitude of the overall benefits contains a strong element of guesswork. My central guess would be something in the region of $\frac{1}{2}$ per cent from each of the three extra sources distinguished (economies of scale, competition, investment), giving a total of $1\frac{1}{2}$ per cent on GNP by the end of the transition, or 0.3 per cent on the growth rate. I see no reason to think that these sources would be fully exhausted by the end of the transitional period, and would therefore expect to see at least some acceleration in growth being maintained into the future. While I would not rule out the possibility of the competitive benefits being more powerful than this analysis allows for, I think I would defend my guesstimate as indicating the order of magnitude a prudent man might gamble on.

Let me add finally that I am unconvinced by the argument that these benefits could be realised by unilateral free trade, multilateral free trade, or a North Atlantic Free Trade Area. Unilateral free trade would impose an immediate terms-of-trade cost of over 1 per cent of GNP, and would get only a half of the 'substitution effect' competitive gains. The Wonnacotts found that over 60 per cent of the benefits to Canada of a North American Free Trade Area would come from removal of the US tariff, and *at most* 40 per cent from unilateral free trade. Multilateral free trade would no doubt be economically splendid but is pie-in-the-sky for political reasons that I happen to find cogent, such as Europe's need for the political cement provided by even a low common external tariff. A North Atlantic Free Trade Area is equally politically pie-in-the-sky, but is less economically splendid. No; the best alternative to Europe that can realistically be expected is a perpetuation of the world much as we now know it, and—as the Dollar Crisis has emphasised—there is a not insignificant danger that the best might not materialise.

Chapter 3

THE BENEFITS OF SCALE FOR INDUSTRY

by Christopher Layton

FOR roughly a hundred years, or since the end of the American civil war, the long-term trend of growth in the US economy was faster than that of Western Europe as a whole. One major reason was economies of scale. For the first time in history modern industrialism developed within a continental economy. In the first half of this century the mass US market bred giant companies and new management techniques to control them. It generated mass-production technology for the first time. In the last 30 years there have been a whole new range of American economic developments that are a function of scale: a federal government market and federal government finance supporting advanced technology on a scale never known before in history. The result has been the creation of a new range of industries: computers and data processing, semi-conductors and integrated circuits, communications satellites. As a result, there is not merely a technological 'gap' between American companies and their competitors; in some areas they dominate the world.

The higher living standards and wage levels of the United States reflect in large part economies of scale, economies, not merely in the size of individual plants or factories, but in the total system. Within one enterprise the economies start with the purchase of components; they move into the production process where larger throughput makes profitable greater capital intensity using new technology and hence higher output per man; they can be found in handling, stocking and ware-housing, where the provision of standard products for a larger

46

market can cut costs; they are important in marketing and technical servicing where it can be a great deal cheaper and more efficient to market a homogeneous product over a market of two hundred million people than to launch eight versions in eight smaller markets. They are crucial in research and development, where the minimum threshold is rising rapidly in many industries, particularly those with advanced technology, and hence therefore a certain minimum sized market is essential; market size also determines the *speed* with which a new product can become profitable and therefore whether innovation is worthwhile. It is the current fashion to recall that big firms have extra costs in bureaucracy to carry; of course they do. But it is not only big firms that achieve economies of scale in a large-scale economy like America's. Small specialist firms—producing components, capital equipment, new-technology products— can also achieve economies in production and grow profitable faster by selling into a larger market. This is one reason why the small fast-growing high-technology firm is common in America and why risk capital is readier to back them than here.

At government level large scale in public purchasing of new technologies can carry products through the first difficult phase to profitability; a single programme of spending—on telecommunications or computer development—can bring far greater results and better value for money than the penny packets European governments separately dole out.

It is because British industrialists realise the cumulative impact of all this on productivity and profitability that they almost unanimously favour membership of a European economic union. As Samuel Brittan and others have pointed out *some* of the attributes of a larger market can be obtained by a combination of a national devaluation with unilateral tariff cuts. But there are many which cannot. There is no security or assurance of permanence of access to other markets; so if the climate for world trade should worsen the barriers could go up. There is little prospect of development of the common policies and common public market in the advanced-technology industries which are necessary if non-tariff barriers are to be removed and these industries are to obtain the benefits of a single open market. There is no prospect of achieving the rationalisation of government expenditure and effort in advanced technology which is one of the largest sources of waste in Europe. The international management of money and of companies will remain burdened by extra costs so long as taxes and laws are different and capital markets divided.

In what follows we look briefly at a few industries to suggest some of the processes by which they hope to benefit from economies of scale in an enlarged Community. These observations are preliminary findings derived from a research project being carried out jointly by PEP and the Centre for European Industrial Studies at Bath University: in this project we are seeking to explore the long-term industrial consequences of entry for a number of leading British companies.

The motor industry: scale in manufacturing

The motor industry is a classic case of such economies of scale in manufacturing. Mass production came first in the 1920s in the United States and brought with it a whole range of new types of capital equipment: the automatic transfer line, the well organised use of conveyor belts and integrated flow production. Many of these types of equipment and methods of organising them were introduced on a substantial scale in Europe only in the post-1945 years.

Today the volume of production per model, the capital per man, and the output per man of the British motor industry are far behind the American level. General Motors produces all the inside door panels for its regular models from one set of dies. It assembles different models in different places, but constantly seeks to maximise economies of scale in components, so that it achieves an optimal balance between the variety the market needs and scale. By contrast the British motor industry today still produces as many different models as the United States industry. That in turn feeds back diseconomies into the component industry.

In the safety glass industry, for instance, the basic processes are identical in America and Britain, but the variety of models in Britain over a much smaller output means a lower output per man, less automation of inspection and batch feeding of certain kinds of furnace which in America would take a continuous flow.

In the tyre industry too, the variety of British and European requirements means variations in some parts of the production process which add to cost.

A company such as British Leyland still has scope to achieve important advances in rationalisation (say in engine production) whether or not Britain is in the Common Market. All the same membership of the Common Market may be crucial. Why?

The blunt reason is that Europe is the only big market in the world whose consumers all buy the type of medium and small-sized car manufactured in Britain, and which offers the prospect of being completely open to British exports of volume cars in the next 20 years.

The motor industry has been shut out of Commonwealth markets in classic style. The fall in preferential margins for British exports to the Commonwealth has been widely documented. What is less widely understood is the nature of the tariffs and other regulations designed to foster local manufacture, which make what is left of the preferences of minimal value in countries such as Australia. Australia, for instance, has a 35 per cent tariff against British car exports (the most-favoured nation duty is 45 per cent) and a 27½ per cent preferential tariff on British components. But if manufacturers (from whatever country) assemble and then manufacture in Australia under a variety of arrangements, they obtain, for an initial period, the right to import components at a mere 7½ per cent duty until they build up local manufacture. Schemes with comparable effects exist in South Africa, India and now New Zealand. In Canada the 14 per cent preference, though more useful (the preference tariff is 0), does not apply against exports from the United States. The major Commonwealth markets (like other developing countries) may be good places to build car facilities with an eye to the future. But they do little to provide export markets which can help British factories at home to achieve economies of scale.

The United States does still provide an important potential market, especially for specialist cars. But the Japanese challenge to European exporters is rapidly growing as it is throughout the Pacific area. Transport costs begin to become important here. The US import surcharge imposed in August 1971 also underlined the fears manufacturers have about the insecurity of the US market in a time of protectionist pressures. If manufacturers are to invest in plant which achieves high-volume production they must have a political commitment that the market they depend on will stay open. This they cannot get in the United States.

A large enough base for large-scale production cannot be obtained by attempting to get a dominant position in a single national market such as Britain, and not merely because Britain is now the smallest and most stagnant home national market of any first-league car producer. Consumer taste and income levels are diverse and seek variety; in the words of T. N. Beckett,[1] Vice-President of Ford Europe "We live in an age of mass production but only to a smaller degree of mass consumption. There is a definite upper limit to the share of market which a manufacturer can expect to get—however attractive the car, however competitive its price, because of the desire some people at least have to be different". The rapid growth of imports of cars in every European country, which is expected to reach at least one-third of each domestic market by the mid-1970s (for Common Market members), therefore fulfils a crucial economic function. It is the only means by which the European motor industry can both supply consumers with the variety of products they want and achieve economies of scale.

In Mr. Beckett's words "with sales distributed over a wide range of markets, it will be possible for manufacturers to have the advantage of large production runs to a much greater extent than now. Europe will become one domestic market for vehicles. Dependence on a single national market within Europe will not be possible, and the international location of each manu-facturer's plants and the international coverage of the whole European market will be essential for survival".

Mr. Beckett suggested, in the same article, that "the special tooling, design and development by a major manufacturer of a new model to sell in Europe can cost, on average, including a share of power train expenditure, £50 million a time at current prices". To stay in the first league a company, in his view, had to attain investment of £50 million a year on new models and £50 million in expansion and modernisation. These kind of figures require a cheaper volume model to sell some 400,000 to 600,000 units per year to achieve viability and a company to

---

[1] T. N. Beckett, The European Motor Industry in the Seventies, *The Business Economist*, Spring 1971.

achieve an output of some 2 million vehicles (a figure also suggested by Signor Agnelli).

To a high degree the British motor industry is therefore already turning towards Europe, as it seeks these scale economies. It has no choice. Ford, since 1967, has been integrating its European operations—making the Escort and the Capri standard models for all Europe, manufacturing automatic transmissions for the entire company in Bordeaux. It took the view that sooner or later European countries would have to remove the barriers between them and that those who worked on this asssumption and developed a maximum division of labour between their manufacturing centres would be the first to benefit.

Nonetheless Ford's UK operations today are disadvantaged by Britain's exclusion from the Common Market in two ways. First tariffs do penalise the intra-company trading which it has developed as part of its European policy. As one Ford executive remarked, "we moved a bit ahead of history". Second, during the last 10 years there has been a massive shift in location of investment to Ford of Germany, partly to satisfy the growing German market, but partly to serve the Common Market as a whole. The shift happened long before Henry Ford got upset by British strikes and indeed at a time when Ford's management had, if anything, a predilection for Britain.

British Leyland now also has a five-year European strategy, designed to build up sales in Europe, outside Britain, from the present 200,000 to 500,000 cars by 1975-76. Under present plans some 270,000 of these units are expected to be from assembly plants on the Continent (in Italy, Belgium and Spain)—a big growth in Continental investment.

The major car companies that operate from Britain are thus all planning operations on the assumption that they must aim at a major share of the European market as a whole. The question is how Common Market membership or non-membership will affect the location, scale and efficiency of their investment in Britain within the framework of this strategy.

It should be noted first that the major direct effects on trade will not be felt by tariff cuts causing immediate price reductions and hence larger sales. On both sides of the channel motor manufacturers price their exports of cars to meet competitors' prices and absorb the tariff into their profit margins. This pricing policy reflects a long-term commercial strategy. Tariffs are already falling in the Kennedy round; Common Market membership for Britain has been expected for some time, and it takes 10 years to build up a strong marketing position in a European country; so the manufacturers fix the prices to meet the competition and aim to achieve a certain market share fitting their investment and production plans.

Nonetheless, removal of the tariff on both sides of the channel will have important effects, first by increasing the profitability of investment in marketing on the opposite bank. It will, for example, make it profitable for the first time for British Leyland to spend money on marketing in Europe's largest market—Germany; it may encourage American-owned companies to make Britain the source of a little more of their exports.

As the effects of this marketing investment build-up are seen in exports, effects will gradually be felt on investment in production and development.

One effect should at least be to slow down the massive switch in the location of investment by the US-owned companies from Britain to the Continent.

But there will also be an important change in the type and pattern of investment. If Britain remains outside the EEC a growing proportion of the Continental sales by a company such as British Leyland are likely to be exported in knocked-down form and assembled on the Continent.

This split in final assembly adds to costs and could make it difficult for some of the larger British manufacturers to stay in the volume car business at all by the end of the decade. Enlargement of the Community will make it more attractive to produce a complete model at each of a number of locations (including of course Britain) for the entire European market. This should bring economies of scale and a more efficient use of capital; it should also mean higher investment in Britain in the second half of the decade than will happen otherwise.

In commercial vehicles, removal of the Common Market's 22 per cent tariff is expected to bring substantial export gains for the British industry, though here too it will take time to build up service networks. The biggest potential gains will come if regulations on trucks are harmonised in a way which makes it possible for British-based manufacturers to use their expertise to enter the fast-growing heavy transcontinental truck market. At least two major manufacturers with British bases will have to decide in the next five years whether to build up centres for the development and manufacture of these heavy trucks and where to locate them. Outside the Common Market and with regulations that make it impossible for UK manufacturers to sell the largest trucks in their own home market, it is most unlikely that these investments will be based in Britain if they happen at all. If Britain is in the Common Market possibilities are brighter. At £10 million apiece, the investment required for such a heavy truck complex is no small sum even if it is less than the £50 million needed for a new car model.

Before 1975, the effects on domestic investment of all these changes should not be great but they will gather speed. Our estimate, derived from an assessment within the industry, is that by 1978 the net trade balance in vehicles between Britain and the existing EEC countries will have improved by £240 million over what it would be if Britain was outside (an increase in the value of exports of £360 million, and a growth of imports of £120 million). Losses in Efta should be offset by gains in EEC associates. Such an increase in output implies an investment of between £50 million and £100 million. A substantial part of this total should be financed by the improved efficiency of investment due to rationalisation and by higher profit margins on exports to EEC (less any reduction in profit margins at home).

Supplies of components in turn will be affected not merely by the better outlook for total investment in Britain, but by the rationalisation of models and assembly in the motor industry. 'One model in one place', for instance, could increase efficiency of the safety glass industry. More final assembly in Britain will probably bring a proportionate increase in this industry's British investment and output, for safety glass gets made where the assembly is done. In tyres, the great diversity of the European market and the nature of the production process mean that it will take a long time to achieve greater economies of scale in the tyre-building part of the production process. Nonetheless, as the market becomes more homogeneous, the tyre manufacturers will make small gains in efficiency.

Homogeneity could be much more important if the fully-automated tyre factory ever becomes feasible.

We have looked closely at the motor industry because it and its component suppliers are an important part of the economy and because it typifies potential developments in mass-production industries.

Inside the Community the Italian manufacturers of domestic durable consumer goods have already shown how access to a large market can permit price reductions through economies of scale. Between 1960 and 1969 three Italian manufacturers acquired domination of the European market for small refrigerators and washing machines. Italian output of refrigerators, for instance, grew from 500,000 out of an EEC total of 2,728,000 in 1958, to 2,800,000 out of 5,071,000 in 1966. Electric motors used in these machines, and manufactured in a single production plant by Fiat, perhaps achieved the biggest economies of scale. The products themselves were redesigned to get rid of slow, expensive hand-operations, like soldering in wires and components, and replacing them by quick installation of modular components. No one expects British manufacturers of those particular products to wrest the initiative from the Italians, who are already well-entrenched in the British market. But there are new durable consumer products, like colour-television sets, a boom product of the coming decade, where important economies of scale are possible. Let us take one small example, from the very early stages of the production process—manufacture of the glass for television screens and tubes. Here three chemical mixtures are needed: for black and white TV glass, for colour screens and for colour funnels. A complete glass production line costs some £5 million. Manufacturers are reluctant to invest on this scale without firm forecasts for the future. At present, therefore, lines are switched between products according to market needs. Each switch brings big extra costs, because of down time. A larger market might justify a third line with each operating continuously at much less cost.

So the manufacturers of TV tubes and glass for them will benefit and be able to produce more economically if, say, Mr. Jules Thorne's Radio Rental manages to apply his rental marketing techniques to Continental Europe and feed back orders to British producers.

Our example from the television business also illustrates a wider point, that some of the most important economies of scale are found in capital-goods industries, because they sell to rather few customers; it can make all the difference to the ability to cover development and tooling costs if you are selling to 30 customers instead of three. Philips, for instance, manufactures Plumbicon tubes for colour television cameras in one factory for the whole of Europe. If Britain is in the EEC there are areas in the same company, in Britain, where centres of excellence could develop faster to serve all Europe if Britain is in than if she remains out: night viewing systems and some areas of medical electronics are examples.

It should by now be a platitude to say that on both sides of the channel the successful specialist enterprise—notably in the engineering industry—will thrive, whether it is an independent company or part of a larger group. And of course the less successfull will go.

Capital goods

Economies of scale, in both manufacturing and development, are indeed to be found in the most diverse capital goods industries.

A good example is the industry that manufactures steel rolls for rolling mills. Despite its unromantic sound, technology is vital here for developing methods of heat treatment, alloys, the right balance of hardness and durability in the rolls; and for whole new technologies like spin casting. In the production process too there are important economies of scale to be obtained from repetitive machining of roll cylinders, and in the foundry. Such pressures, a few years back, brought about a concentration of the US steel roll industry into four major enterprises, serving an industry producing 130 million tons of steel per year. In Britain the Industrial Reorganisation Corporation intervened to help rationalise the industry into two major producers. One of these, by closing and selling off plant, and rationalising output between two others, has now achieved, within a space of four years, cost cuts of 10 per cent, in addition to absorbing increases in labour costs of at least 20 per cent. It now still has some spare margin of capacity, and EEC membership, with the removal of the 7 per cent tariff, could marginally help it to utilise this more fully, lowering costs further. The Continental industry has not yet gone through the process of concentration that has happened in Britain, so there are possibilities of, say, a merger with a Continental firm which could provide marketing outlets and bring a further process of specialisation (the partner might be a specialist in certain types of roll for both groups, e.g. iron rolls; the British firm for others). Such growth of the firm should permit a further strengthening of research and development (which amounts to five to six per cent of turnover today) to meet, in particular, the technological challenge of the big leading Japanese firm, whose spin-casting technology has come from a much larger conglomerate group.

Scratch a British company in capital goods with a number of divisions and you will almost invariably find a characteristic range of potential 'dynamic' effects. In one company of five divisions which we visited one small division had already become the world's largest exporter of a product thanks to economies of scale achieved by serving a large public sector customer at home. Membership will enable it to expand exports further, by applying its marketing skills, by expanding existing capacity, and then by investment where this becomes necessary.

A second division will grow faster through selling components to an expanding motor industry. A third has made a major investment in launching and developing a new product for which the UK market is growing more slowly than the market on the Continent. Membership comes at the right time to reduce the risk in that investment and make it more profitable sooner.

Companies with plants on both sides of the Channel—designed to provide a presence in each market—are already looking increasingly at the possibilities of rationalising output between them. For instance, a pump manufacturer with plants on both sides of the water, producing the bulk of his range in both cases, may concentrate output and development of large pumps, with their high technology, in Britain, while batch or flow production of smaller pumps is concentrated on the Continental side.

In yet other companies some of the 'dynamic effects' are, of course, to accelerate closure of uneconomic plant and release resources for new investment in successful products that are profitable. In yet other cases the initial competitive struggle may lead to mergers followed by rationalisation in the larger groups.

Chemicals: large plants; launching new products fast

A key industry whose production processes demonstrate economies of scale is chemicals, above all the vast new industry of petrochemicals and plastics that has emerged in the last 20 years. A modern petrochemical complex can cost over £100 million. An olefin plant, producing the basic building brick of the modern polymer-using industries, produced some 30,000 tons of ethylene in 1950; today's plants produce half a million tons and cost £25 million each.

Optimising the output of such a plant poses the following needs. First when the plant comes on stream the size of its output can depress prices dangerously (and they can rise before the capacity is put in); so these huge blocks of output need to be phased into as large a market as possible. Each plant, or series of related plants, produces a vast range of products and by-products at different phases in the production process. The optimisation of the design itself and of the use of the plant when built depends on a great deal of intra-trading in intermediate products. Partly for these reasons, the chemical industry in Europe has developed as a complex system, linked by pipe-lines (or tankers across the North Sea) and with a great deal of multilateral trade. And, as in vehicles, the last 10 years have witnessed a huge shift in the axis of investment to the Continent as the key firms such as ICI and Shell seek to share in European growth.

These trends have been reinforced by exclusion from other major markets. The failure of the United States Congress to repeal the American Selling Price legislation and thus implement the Kennedy round in full means that Europe is the only major market for chemicals relatively open to trade.

Quick benefits from entry are not expected by the chemical industry; at present it is too preoccupied with the problems of financing investment in a time of high inflation and with the loss of investment grants. But, for long-run, strategic reasons, this is one of the industries most committed to membership. Companies responsible for 98 per cent of the turnover of the industry supported the Chemical Industry Association's statement of support for membership of the EEC. Gradually, as the rather high EEC tariffs on some key organic chemicals and on plastics come down, further optimisation of the complex trade in intermediate products can be expected, perhaps accelerating the next major phase of investment in the mid-1970s. By the second half of the decade, the more potent secondary effects of being in or out may make themselves felt. The most important of these is that in a large market, new products and technologies can be launched and made profitable more rapidly. Again and again British companies (like ICI in polythene) have seen competing developments in America, which were not at first ahead technically, gain a market more rapidly there and thus acquire through feedback from the market place, and early monopoly profits, a world lead. In the economics of the product cycle, the company based in a large receptive market has an edge. But what is 'a market'? In many of the products that make use of chemicals, like synthetic clothing, European country markets still vary a great deal. Maximum rapidity in launching new products in the European market will come only as the market becomes more homogeneous. That homogenisation will grow as intra-trading grows and the chemical industry's customers in their turn launch and market products on a European scale.

This ability to launch products successfully into a rich and growing market will decide who is out in front in the chemical industry. In the next decade the development and marketing of non-weave textiles direct from the chemical, or of plastic paper, may change whole industries. By 1985, if Britain is still outside the EEC, a company such as ICI will have felt strong pressure to move its technological and managerial centre of gravity to the Continent where the growth is. If Britain is part of a more homogeneous, enlarged Community, the base for ICI's Europewide operations and its main technological centre is more likely to be Britain.

Advanced technology: expensive R & D, technical support and marketing

In many other advanced-technology industries the cost of research, development, engineering and technical support and marketing often raises the threshold of entry to a level which makes a large market essential.

The following projects have proved too expensive for even the largest single continent to support today:

Second-generation supersonic civil flight

Post-Apollo space exploration

The following developments and the marketing needed to make them pay are beyond the means of a national company operating mainly in a single national European market:

Semi-conductor and integrated circuit technology (the main growth of sector of electronics)

A family of computer central processors plus software

Nuclear reactors

Large modern aircraft

Large modern aeroengines

Communications satellite system

For good measure let us throw in heavy electrical turbo-generating sets. There are some strong companies in Britain and on the Continent, but they could not remain viable on the basis of small national markets.

Most of these products sell to and are helped financially by governments. In some cases (telecommunications equipment, electric power) there is total prohibition on trade in Europe; in others there are big obstacles. In some sectors, European-owned companies are barely in the business at all and it is already in the hands of US firms, who have applied in divided Europe the technology and skills developed in the wider American environment.

How much will membership of the Common Market provide the removal of non-tariff barriers, the development of common policies and procurement: in short the political action which can achieve the enormous potential gains in productivity and scale economies which are there? The public sector in Western Europe accounts for one-third to one-half of total investment. Far the largest gains in growth, productivity and wealth will be achieved if the advanced-technology industries, dominated by public markets, and in which Britain is still strong, can achieve the full benefits of integration.

Aircraft: faster rationalisation of joint ventures

Sceptics can be heard declaring both that integration of this kind (e.g. in aircraft) can be achieved anyway, in or or out of the

EEC, and that the barriers will never be broken down (e.g. in telecommunications). These contradictory thoughts misunderstand the change of climate which EEC membership should bring. The limitation on integration in the past in these advanced industries has been a lack of an overall political commitment and trust—the fact that governments and companies were not prepared to take the risk of a real opening of markets or cross-frontier mergers in industries vital to military and political power. If such common commitment cannot be achieved within the European Community it cannot be achieved anywhere else. Certainly the Community now gives these objectives of a common industrial policy high priority. Clearly the barriers will not be broken down overnight, but a realistic view might be that during the 1970s EEC membership will accelerate the pace of integration and the opening of public markets, though in one or two hard-core sectors like telecommunications and heavy electrical equipment, the full benefits will not come till the early 1980s.

In this short essay there is not space to analyse each of these major industries in detail. But some observations can be made.

In the aircraft industry, all the British industry's major development projects except the RB211 are joint projects with Europeans. But it is commonly alleged that the ad hoc character of these ventures—with their work-sharing and their committees—makes them more expensive than a development undertaken by a single company, perhaps by as much as 25 to 30 per cent.[2] Membership of the Community is expected to accelerate and facilitate the rationalisation of these ventures—through the establishment of a European company law, the harmonisation of taxation, and a climate of opinion which facilitates the formation of full-blooded European companies that can rationalise development and production as completely as a national company does. By 1980 a major transnational aeroengine company and two transnational airframe enterprises should exist in Europe in some form; but they will not yet have achieved a complete rationalisation of development and production.

National pressures and sensitivities will be too strong for works to be closed easily and a balance of effort between nations

---

[2]See, for instance, Henri Ziegler in a paper submitted to a symposium held by the Association Internationale de Constructeurs de Matériel Aeronautique, London, 13 September 1970.

will certainly have to be maintained. Nonetheless, within these limitations, considerable progress towards the ideal—in which, say, MK II of MRCA is being assembled in Munich, and a STOL aircraft at Weybridge, while common components for both are produced at a third location—seems likely. In the context of membership one might expect such rationalisation to have halved the extra costs of joint ventures, bringing an improvement in the efficiency of capital of the order of 10 to 15 per cent. Membership can also be expected to enhance the willingness of Community countries to invest in joint projects in which Britain is a member, bringing an increase in overall investment in the British aircraft industry. If Britain remains outside the Common Market, joint ventures will limp along. But the industry will not be able to achieve rationalisation so rapidly and in all countries mutually destructive nationalist pressures to acquire 'leadership' of projects will be strengthened. Britain, with smaller resources than its French and German partners, will not come off well from such in-fighting.

Computers: a climate for marriage

In the computer industry, membership has different implications for growth and productivity because, unlike aircraft where all the companies have national roots, there is a sharp contrast between the huge multinational sector dominated by IBM and the small national companies (ICL in Britain).

IBM already illustrates the economies of scale in production, software and servicing and research and development, which can be achieved by a multinational division of labour—even in a Europe divided between Efta and the EEC. Profiting by its experience of developing and manufacturing each one of its line of computers in a single manufacturing centre for the entire American market, IBM develops and manufactures each item of its computer range in one major European centre. Since its range of products is still narrower than ICL's, and its European turnover four times as large, production of each product is spread over a far wider turnover. The effect on manufacturing efficiency is illustrated by one statistic. Manufacturing cost accounts for somewhere in the range between 14 and 20 per cent of IBM's final price. For ICL the comparable figure is 35-45 per cent—with similar final prices. A far higher proportion of IBM's revenue is thus available to go into financing marketing, software, investment and profit. The gap between ICL and IBM (and a similar or larger gap exists between IBM and other European computer manufacturers) is a measure of the gains which the non-IBM sector of the computer industry could achieve if it too could attain IBM's present scale and methods of operation.[3]

The gains in efficiency and productivity for the computer industry through EEC membership will, therefore, mainly take two forms. For IBM there will be a modest improvement in profitability as the remaining costs of tariffs disappear and cease to be a burden on its already near-optimal intratrading. This process will be modestly helpful to IBM, UK, in its attempt to attract development centres within the IBM empire. For ICL the gains will come if membership accelerates and facilitates its advance towards the economies of scale and levels of productivity achieved by IBM. Moreover, the success and pace of that advance by IBM's main UK competitor may well decide, also, how large a proportion of IBM's own gains are distributed to consumers and the European economy and how much are remitted as profit to the United States.

The fall in tariffs will bring some small benefit to ICL, increasing profitability of exports to the Continent and thus contributing to financing European marketing—the main constraint on its growth, since opening up a new major market can cost some £10 million. But the important means by which membership accelerates ICL's increase in the scale and productivity of its operations will be the political support entry gives to ICL's attempt to combine with the French firm CII in a deliberate attempt to share and rationalise development, production and marketing costs.

If Britain joins the EEC, as expected, the computer union will materialise soon, and perhaps be followed by links with other partners. More important, this process should be supported by the gradual development, by the major European Governments, of common procurement policies and joint development

[3] For a further analysis of the structure and prospects of the European computer industry, see Ian Lloyd, *The European Computer Industry*, a report to the Science and Technology Committee of the Council of Europe (consultants C. Layton, Y. S. Hu).

contracts. In the second half of the 1970s, in short, one could imagine a European computer group producing a common range from two and perhaps three countries. The market penetration this tri-national presence would provide might have permitted the group to acquire 30 to 40 per cent of the European market instead of ICL's 18 per cent today, with important gains through scale for productivity and return on capital.

If Britain were to reject membership of the Community this autumn, it would be a sharp political shock to the budding ICL-CII partnership. ICL would almost certainly go on trying to develop European arrangements, but would be handicapped by political ill will and the possibility that any Community policy for joint development contracts and joint purchasing may develop without it. The possibility that Siemens may become the heart of a European computer industry in the second half of the decade will be enhanced and if ICL cannot find partners of this kind its long-term prospects look bleak.

The prospect for 1980 would, then, be for a smaller overall computer industry in the UK, mainly American-dominated, and probably with a substantial enduring balance-of-payments deficit for the import of larger computers in particular.

Heavy electrical equipment: when will public markets open up?

The heavy electrical industry (turbo-generators, transformers, switchgear) is one of the most dependent on Commonwealth markets, as its trade pattern shows. Moreover, in certain Commonwealth markets preferential margins are still useful (e.g. Canada—$12\frac{1}{2}$ per cent) and technical specifications give British products an important advantage. In Europe, by contrast, Buy National policies keep British products out almost entirely —just as the British exclude the Europeans. So it is not surprising that the industry first looked at the Common Market with scepticism.

A closer look, however, shows that here too scale is of growing importance; the full benefits of scale can be realised if the European Community succeeds in removing the barriers to buying heavy electrical equipment across the frontiers—in short succeeds in making the Common Market work.

The scale comes in both development and production, especially production of large turbo-generating sets. In an important recent study, Barbara Epstein[4] shows how, with the rising size of such sets (one 1,000 mw set can weigh 2,000 tons) and the constant improvement in their technology, the minimum sized output for a viable European firm in the mid-1970s will be some 8-10,000 mw of turbo-generating capacity. The British market bought on average 6,225 mw in the years 1965-68 (there has been a sharp drop since), and the largest annual turnover of any British firm has been the 5,000 mw achieved by Parsons-Reyrolle in 1970. For good measure, Barbara Epstein suggests that a minimum optimum scale for an American firm (with higher labour costs) in the mid-1970s will be some 15,000 mw of turbo-generator output per year. The logic of this argument is that if Europe hopes to raise its productivity and real wages to American levels, its firms will have to get up to this higher order of scale too. To put this in financial perspective, the Westinghouse company, one of the two great firms in the United States that does achieve this viable size, is currently investing £98 million over 3-4 years in the present step-jump in scale and technology of plant.

Commonwealth markets do not provide the kind of opportunities which are needed to jump the scale barrier in *production*. This is because in most cases high tariffs or government regulations require a large proportion of local production. Suboptimal plants are scattered throughout the developing countries —they usually employ derivative technology and build the smaller generating sets. Keeping competitive at world level requires a company to have a stake in the largest turbo-generating set business and technology.

How, then, has the British heavy electrical industry survived so far? One answer is that, despite tariffs and some restrictions, parts of the American market have been more open to exporters than markets in Europe. The pressures of scale, moreover, have already brought concentration in the industry (for instance in transformers) on a national basis; yet even this concentration has not brought complete viability, despite the prop of a protected home market. Nonetheless, in a world where the pressures of scale are great, the two British firms, GEC and Reyrolle

⁴ Barbara Epstein, *Politics of Trade in Power Plant*, Trade Policy Research Centre, 1971.

Parsons, are two of the four European enterprises (KWU and Brown Boveri are the others) which are in the first league of technology today and have the potential to form a nucleus of viable European firms on the scale Barbara Epstein describes.

What is the likely impact of Common Market membership on this scene? If Britain joins the Community, one can expect a gradual opening of public markets for heavy electrical equipment over the next 10 to 15 years. It will proceed in parallel with mergers and link-ups across frontiers which will permit rationalisation without complete extinction of certain producers. If Britain joins now, one, or hopefully both, of the two British firms will be important elements in the surviving, say, four European enterprises in 1985; certainly at least one major centre of large turbo-generator development will remain in Britain. Britain would be an important net exporter of heavy turbo-generating equipment to other parts of Europe (as Germany is) as well as the rest of the world, though this might be matched, in switchgear, by the development of France as an important centre, achieving economies of scale in this field. Investment resources will tend to be attracted to these points of strength.

Outside the Community, the British heavy electrical industry will be far more dependent on penetrating the American market, if it is to survive, and will have to do so from a narrower and more precarious home base. If it seeks American partners to help it penetrate the US market, as Reyrolle-Parsons has done in its link with Rockwell, the danger is of a gradual shift in balance towards the larger partner.

The pressures for scale, already apparent in large conventional electrical plant, become even more apparent in the nuclear industry—where the costs not only of turbines, but of reactors, and pumps and other equipment climb by a new order of magnitude. The way American water reactors swept Britain's first-generation gas reactors off the world market is well-known. Wisely, The Nuclear Power Group is now trying to build a systematic partnership with KWU in Germany for the worldwide marketing of reactors. The hope must be that this partership will ensure that the next generation—fast breeders—can be exploited successfully commercially on a world scale. If that new partnership is to be a successful one, a balance of equals, with a strong feedback of work into British industry, Common

Market membership is important. If KWU grows into one of the two major electrical groups in a continent where barriers to trade in electric plant are coming down, while TNPG continues to struggle as at present on the base of an erratic small national market, KWU will wear the trousers in the group.

Our discussion of the advanced technology industries so far has concentrated on the internal factors which dictate large scale in R & D, manufacturing and technical marketing. But scale is also important in the external relations of companies that use advanced technology. Much experience suggests that the acquisition of know-how through licensing tends to be unsuccessful if the purchasing company has no store of experience and skill enabling it to use bought knowledge well. When purchasing technological know-how the strong company tends to get the best price—not only in terms of cash, but in terms of minimum restrictions on the markets in which it operates and liberal access to further developments. All this affects the ability to apply bought knowledge profitably. Thus the search for scale in advanced technology spills over into industrial politics—the power factors which remain important in economic relations between companies and nations.

The impact of politics on growth

Because this book is about economics, this brief illustrative introduction to industry and scale has concerned itself with the economics of advanced technology. It is, however, the political significance of advanced technology which may well spur governments to act, and which has been the driving force behind the British application to join the Common Market. European governments do not want to be wholly dependent in terms of both defence and industrial strategy, on nuclear, computer, and aerospace industries controlled from outside. If Europe wants to have the ability to differ, on occasion, from its American partner and develop common foreign and other policies, it has to have the technological power base from which to act.

That argument is outside the scope of this book. It is clear, however, that the scale of the benefits Britain's advanced-technology industries can expect from the Common Market will depend largely on politics, on the speed with which the enlarged Community succeeds in opening up public markets, for instance for heavy electrical equipment or computers, on the degree to which Community solidarity accelerates the formation of European policies and companies in the aircraft industry. If the Community moves fast to open up public markets, much bigger and more rapid gains in productivity, through rationalisation and scale economies, can be expected. If it stays politically stuck, then even the modest progress we have suggested may not be achieved. The picture painted in the previous section represents a compromise between these extremes—the expectation that enlargement of the Community will indeed accelerate progress towards a European industrial policy but that the burden of national structures and habits will make the process slower than the ideal.

One major reason why industrialists, whose life is concerned with shaping the future, feel hopeful about all this is that membership of the Community will certainly give both the British Government and British industry a greater chance to share in shaping these developments. They therefore see membership as a valuable increase in the degree of control over the future and a reduction in its risks. British economists, by contrast, if they cannot put a figure on the impact on European technology of the politics of membership, may tend to discount this crucial factor altogether. They have usually been brought up to extrapolate figures, preferably figures decided by apparently invisible market forces. As the only figures about the EEC's future that have appeared to be readily available have been those concerned with certain aspects of the agricultural budget, extrapolation of this fragment of the picture has dominated the economists' debate in Britain.

The British industrial interest in joint policies in Europe, which provide a larger degree of control over the future, is not confined to advanced technology industries. In the chemical industry important economies could be achieved if the major European chemical companies could, by co-ordination, phase-in their big petrochemical investments smoothly so that huge simultaneous jumps in capacity are avoided and capacity grows in step with demand. The climate for such planning is likely to be better if Britain is in the Community than out. To take another example, the motor industry, which is becoming a Europe-based industry whether Britain joins the Common

Market or not, would feel greater confidence in its future if Britain shares in policies for the region.

If the gains of scale through common industrial policies depend on the political development of the Community, the gains of scale for the whole of industry of course depend on the will and skill of managements in seizing opportunities. It is not possible to predict definitely how British exporters and plant managers will respond to the Common Market any more than it is possible to be certain what the level of agricultural prices in the world and Europe will be in 1980. All one can do is suggest a potential. But the positive approach which British industry in fact has to the Common Market does provide hopeful evidence that opportunity may be seized. Following the many general indications of industrial support for Common Market membership (like the large majority of CBI members in favour, and the near-unanimous favourable vote of the Birmingham Chamber of Commerce, with its many small and medium-sized business members), the *Guardian's* survey of the top 200 companies provides further general evidence about *how* companies expect to respond. A majority of companies expect to increase their investment but—on the face of it surprisingly—this first reaction shows over twice as many planning initially to increase investment on the Continent as in Britain. This is because the first requirement for industry—as we have seen from some of our illustrations (vehicles, computers)—is to invest more in marketing and service facilities if it wants a larger share of Continental markets. Moreover, the effect of tariff reductions is to increase the relative profitability of investment in marketing on the Continent, compared with similar investment at home. Once the new marketing investment pays off, rationalisation of production or new investment in home capacity follow.

A further condition of maximising Common Market opportunities is wise government policies at home. One of the features of the Common Market's first 10 years which confounded prophets was that the fastest growth in productivity occurred not in Germany but in the more backward economies, such as Belgium, with its archaic industrial structure, and Italy, with its low level of overall development. It is an encouraging piece of indirect evidence for Britain, which has the lowest level of productivity growth and the third lowest absolute level of incomes per head in the enlarged Community. But the Common Market gains by Italy and Belgium were at least enhanced by domestic factors—in Belgium's case the remarkably favourable incentives given to investment, especially foreign investment in the country, in Italy's case a relatively favourable exchange rate and a reservoir of unskilled labour. Britain actually has a large reservoir of underutilised and far more highly skilled labour than Italy inside industry; it has underutilised resources of engineering and science graduates, which make it most attractive to foreign investors, particularly in advanced technology industries. But the speed with which these and the wider opportunities of the Common Market are taken up will depend, considerably, on the Government's will to adjust the exchange rate in good time, if it gets out of line, and to a lesser extent on the maintenance of investment incentives as attractive as those on the Continent.

Can potential be measured in quantitative terms?

Can we draw any quantitative conclusions from our analysis so far? The difficulties are clear. The Common Market is only one factor affecting the future prospects of British industry; isolating its effects is difficult. In particular, while the only realistic balance-of-payments assumption on which to try to forecast long-term effects must be that exchange-rate adjustments will at some stage correct any overall structural tendency to deficit or surplus, in the short term the competitive position of British industry depends on the timing of such adjustments— and both economists and industrialists tend to allow their long-term thinking about the effects of the Common Market to be coloured by short-term moods which reflect current rates of exchange (bullish in 1968 after devaluation, more bearish today after a period of inflation). The timing but not the nature of the long-term effects on investment can be affected by these moods.

Since economists, however, have not been reticent about forecasting the future impact of the common agricultural policy, when their forecasts have to be based, not on facts, but on guesstimates about such factors as the level of world farm prices, European farm prices, the response of British farmers to higher prices, the social behaviour of European farm workers and the future political climate of Europe, it should certainly be no more difficult to forecast potential long-term industrial effects of membership, including those in advanced technology which are as dependent as agriculture is on politics.

The examples given so far in this paper are illustrative, and clearly omit large areas of the British economy. Moreover, in some of the industries omitted (like textiles and shoes) economies of scale in production and technology are more rare than in the process industries (like chemicals), in the mass-production assembly industries (like cars), the capital goods industries, and the advanced-technology industries, whose R & D is so expensive.

However, the few examples we have given include key elements in the British economy. The chemical industry in 1968 was responsible for 10 per cent of the net output of British industry and for some 10 years has been growing at almost twice the output of the British economy as a whole. The vehicle industry, as far back as 1963, was responsible for $7\frac{1}{2}$ per cent of the output of British manufacturing industry while a further 3 per cent of industrial production (components, etc.) was dependent on the industry. These were the figures from the last census of production; the motor industry's share has risen farther since. The computer industry's output in 1971 was expected to be only some £200 million, but its growth rate of some 15-20 per cent per year means that by 1980 it and its major suppliers will also be a key component of the economy. By 1980 the five major industries we have described (chemicals, vehicles and suppliers, computers, aerospace and heavy electrical equipment—a slower grower) could represent over 40 per cent of manufacturing output. If one adds to the list of industries where economies of scale through the Common Market are important other key capital goods industries, including key growth elements of electronics, one finds that over half of British manufacturing may benefit significantly from these economies.

In the wider study being undertaken by the Centre for European Industrial Studies and PEP we hope to get further in quantifying some of the potential long-term gains of scale from membership. But even if the half of industry (in 1980) which we have described increases its output per man through membership by 5 per cent by 1980—a minimal gain in the light of the evidence we have been accumulating—and even if the rest of industry stands still in this respect, which it will not, this means an annual improvement in productivity for the economy as a whole of between 1 and 2 per cent.

An improvement of this order could mean that Britain's economy, by 1980, might have grown by some 42 per cent, compared with the 37 per cent predicted by OECD.[5] It would mean that output per head might still be level with Italy's, instead of being below that of all other Common Market members except Ireland. It is hardly an ambitious hope. But at least a beginning would have been made on halting the hitherto remorseless process of economic attrition by which the British economy is not merely growing slowly, but rapidly seeing the main centres of technology and the main locations of international investment in growth industries emigrate across the channel where the size and climate of a large market help them to thrive.

---

[5] *The Growth of Output 1960-1980*, OECD, 1970.

Chapter 4

THE AGRICULTURAL BURDEN: A REAPPRAISAL

by Tim Josling

AGRICULTURAL policy has rarely been so much in the news. The casual observer of the 'great debate' might be forgiven for forming the impression that the EEC had devised agricultural protectionism to appease the French peasantry, and that the UK was unwillingly being forced to follow suit. Farmers on the Continent would not share the view that the common agricultural policy (CAP) had provided them with a feather bed. The prices they receive for their goods have risen on average about 1 per cent per year since 1963[1] (and have accordingly declined by about 2 per cent per year in real terms), and the exodus from the land in the last decade is almost without parallel in recent history.[2] Our own support programmes involve payments per farmer much in excess of those in the EEC. The level of protection of agricultural production in the Six is not significantly higher than in the USA,[3] though con-

[1] The aggregate price index for the major CAP products rose by 8 per cent from 1963 to 1970; for cereals the total rise over this period was only 2 per cent: see Table 3, p.80, below.

[2] The EEC farm population fell from 15 million to below 10 million over the last ten years. This continuing exodus, and its implications for the common agricultural policy, are analysed by Marsh in the following chapter.

[3] The results of a study produced by Professor Vandervolle at Antwerp indicate the rate of protection for the 'value added' in US and EEC agriculture to be 80 per cent and 84 per cent respectively. The comparable figure for the UK is about 40 per cent. See: *Comparaison entre le soutien accordé à l'agriculture aux Etas-Unis et dans la Communauté*, Informations internes sur l'agriculture, 70, EEC, Brussels, 1971.

72

centrated on different products and with less felicitous implications for the trade of other countries. The methods used to support farm income do not differ materially from those we and other countries have used—and are equally ineffective at solving the serious social problems of rural development and agricultural adjustment.[4]

The CAP was devised as a way of allowing free trade in agricultural goods among countries which had, especially in the inter-war and post-war years, erected significant barriers to such trade. It involved the pooling of the control over third-country imports, thus in principle granting to all Community producers the same degree of protection against non-member countries. It also established a harmonised system of support buying so as to avoid the unwarranted movement of goods to take advantage of the support systems of other members. To date it has done little else. Each government maintains its own agricultural policy subject to these constraints. The spending on these national policies exceeds that on the common policy and shows no sign of diminishing.[5] This is as one would expect; countries have their own disparate objectives in their rural areas and their agricultural sectors face widely differing economic conditions. The monolithic aspect of the CAP vanishes when one examines the actual agricultural policy environment in the Six nations rather than the glossy brochures of Brussels. Moreover there is no evidence to suggest that the degree of agricultural protectionism has been increased by the devolution of the control of imports to the Commission and the Council of Ministers inherent in the CAP.

The CAP has been described in many places and its main features will be familiar to anyone who has followed the European debate.[6] For the major arable and livestock products the Council of Ministers, acting on proposals by the Commission, fix target prices which ideally the common policy would maintain. Derived from these target prices are minimum import or

---

[4] For a critique of the effects of price-support policies on farm incomes see T. Josling, *Agriculture: Britain's Trade Policy Dilemma*, Thames Essay No. 2, Trade Policy Research Centre, London, 1970.

[5] For an indication of the scale of national support policies, see J. Marsh and C. Ritson, *Agricultural Policy and the Common Market*, Chatham House/PEP, March 1971, p.179.

[6] See Marsh and Ritson, *op.cit.*

threshold prices below which any offers of imports attract a levy. The levy is thus variable depending on world prices. Our own minimum import prices for cereals, introduced in 1964, operate in a similar way, except that we until recently tried to persuade exporters not to ship to us below these minimum prices and so embarrass us with receipts from the levy. For export goods, the EEC allows for a variable export restitution to bridge the gap between high internal and lower world prices. This element of the policy has perhaps come in for the most criticism, especially from the USA who have now considerably curtailed their own export subsidy programmes and opted for supply control.[7] The EEC developed its policy at a time when it was a net importer of most agricultural goods; it has yet to adjust to a policy which is viable for an exporter—namely one which discourages output produced purely for dumping abroad at heavy exchequer cost. We have not used export subsidies extensively in this country.

Besides the import-levy system, the CAP also provides for intervention buying of agricultural produce when internal prices are depressed well below target levels. This gives a floor to the market for cereals, for beef and pigmeat and for some dairy products. The EEC finances any loss made by the intervention agencies in disposing of or storing these goods, though the agencies themselves operate on a national basis and retain some degree of autonomy. Though these are the two main pillars of the CAP, the details of its operation and of the application to various commodity markets are highly complex and invite abuse (both verbal and financial). In one sense it is a young policy; its main provisions date only from 1967 and its administration is only just beginning to be defined. In another sense it is old before its time; within a year of the operation of the single agriculture market its main author Dr. Sicco Mansholt was arguing that the CAP was not sufficient to perform the tasks for which it was designed.[8] The UK Government has

---

[7] For a recent expression of American concern, see the address by Senator Humphrey, *Agriculture's Place in International Trade*, copies of which are obtainable from the Trade Policy Research Centre, London.

[8] A European attack on the inefficiency of the CAP is to be found in P. Uri et al., *A Future for European Agriculture*, Atlantic Institute, Paris, 1970.

accepted the CAP as a reality; it is to be hoped that this does not imply a commitment to defend that policy against development along more constructive lines—the possibilities of which are discussed by Marsh in the next chapter. In such a development we have a paramount interest, as the remainder of this chapter will attempt to demonstrate.

Major changes required by UK adoption of the CAP

Although the philosophy and method of the CAP do not differ greatly from our own agricultural policy as it has developed over the last decade, the need to harmonise with the European system and price levels will involve some significant changes. At one stage, in the late 1950s, it was possible to characterise the British agricultural policy as one of allowing imports from the rest of the world—and in particular from the Commonwealth—to enter freely into this country. Farmers' incomes were supported by guaranteed prices set annually to take account of cost increases. But world prices fluctuated and at times fell to low levels as supplies from other countries were pushed onto world markets by export subsidies; it became convenient for the Government to control imports. Not only did this enable exchequer support to be limited but it allowed growth in the domestic market to be supplied from British farms. The change in approach to free importation of food predates the decision of the Six to use import levies as their main protective device. Rather than being an indication of our willingness to anticipate introduction of the EEC support system, the move to control imports and liberate the farmer from the reliance on Treasury handouts has developed in parallel with the CAP and in deference to the same world market pressures. After market-sharing quotas on butter and pigmeat came minimum import prices for cereals and 'voluntary' quotas on cheese. Imports of sugar, milk, and many fruits and vegetables were already controlled; of the major commodities only beef and lamb remained relatively free of import restrictions. In July 1971, these two commodities came under a variable levy system—thus completing a policy initiated under the previous Conservative administration in 1961 and developed during the period of the subsequent Labour administration. The adoption of the CAP would commit this country to the development of the new levy system to take the entire burden of support of grains and meats off the exchequer. It is of course possible that consumer reaction to higher food prices or pressure from overseas exporters might cause the Government to modify this policy if entry to the EEC was rejected. But in view of the Conservative commitment to a levy scheme, and of the budgetary problems of a complete reversion to the system of free imports by any subsequent government, it seems more realistic to assume the continuation of this policy even outside the Community.

The adaptation of our cereals policy will entail raising our minimum import prices to the levels of the EEC threshold prices. Imports from within the Community would enter without levy after the transition period, but would themselves be priced at the high internal EEC levels. In addition we would have to initiate a support buying scheme, run by an agency such as the Home Grown Cereals Authority, to remove grain from the market at times when domestic prices were depressed below the intervention levels. By contrast, the present levy scheme for cereals envisages fall-back guaranteed prices for farmers rather than intervention buying. There could well be considerable quantities of barley bought for intervention in this country at certain times of the season.

We would also have to introduce intervention buying for beef and for pigmeat if domestic market prices should fall to low levels. But intervention has not been extensive in Europe, and it would seem unlikely that this support mechanism would be more than occasionally used in this country. Intervention in livestock markets is in any case discretionary rather than automatic as in the grain market. For beef we would replace our new variable levy with a fixed tariff of 20 per cent and a supplementary tariff triggered by the relationship between domestic and guide prices. There would, however, be a revised import quota of beef for the enlarged Community, which would be exempt from this supplement. Virtually all our pigmeat imports will be from within the expanded EEC, if Denmark and Ireland join with us; the levy on third-country pigmeat imports will probably exclude competition from Eastern Europe. Our present prospective levy on lamb of about 11 per cent will have to be replaced by a fixed levy of 20 per cent on third-country (i.e. New Zealand) sales. No common support policy exists at present for lamb within the Six, and we would be free to continue our deficiency payments if we wished.

Of the EEC support policies for the major commodities, that relating to dairy products is perhaps the most difficult to translate to British conditions. At present our support system comprises three elements: a ban on imports of liquid milk, a statutory monopoly vested in the Milk Marketing Board which can dictate the uses to which domestic milk is put, and a government-controlled liquid milk price. Of these instruments the first and the third are likely to be revised with entry; the producer monopoly board is apparently unobjectionable to the EEC Commission. The Milk Board and the dairies will be able to direct milk into the relatively more profitable manu-facturing market and one would anticipate some imports of milk where transport costs were low—such as into Northern Ireland from the Republic. Dairy products entering from third countries would be subject to very high levies which would raise their price to the British consumer.

Policy changes for other commodities will be minor; no internal support system need be introduced for poultry or reintroduced for eggs. Potatoes at present are not covered by a common policy; for fruits and vegetables in general, our tariff system will need to be harmonised with the common external tariff rates and a system of supplementary levies based on reference prices adopted. Imports from the Community will of course be unrestricted after the transition period. A rudi-mentary market support scheme operates when prices are depressed to 'crisis' levels on the home market.

In general the CAP is not very effective at stabilising produce prices. Not only are there large price differences between areas of surplus and those where demand is high, and between places close to a port and those inland, but prices differ within and between seasons depending on the state of the market. The additional price uncertainty over and above that with which British farmers have had to contend could limit expansion plans somewhat. It should also lead to a considerable increase in market organisation as farmers get together to sell their produce. The Government would still retain the ability to introduce measures to control market fluctuations. The CAP provides the framework for market support; the implementation and administration of the policy is in the hands of the individual governments.

Effect on farm and consumer prices

Whereas the necessary modifications to our present support policy are known with reasonable certainty, the level of prices that such a policy will generate is still quite speculative. Two distinct exercises have been tried in the past; one is to assume that we instantaneously adopt the full CAP and to compare present producer and consumer prices with those that would obtain under this assumption: the other technique is to project prices into the future under alternative assumptions as to whether we enter or stay out of the EEC. The former exercise is easier but less useful. It is easier because we already know our prices and the present world and EEC prices—and it remains to translate the effect of the CAP to British conditions. If we could assume that UK, EEC and world prices would not change relative to each other over the next decade, this method of instantaneous price comparison would be legitimate. Such an assumption is implicit in the 1971 White Paper calculations of the agricultural costs. Tables 1 and 2 give estimates, for the major products affected, of the price increases which would be implied by an instantaneous translation of EEC rules and prices

Table 1: Comparison of Present UK Producer Prices with Equivalents under the CAP (products supported by internal price policy)

	Unit	UK farm price 1971/72	EEC equivalent 1971/72	Percentage difference
Wheat	£/ton	32.60	38.65	24
Barley	£/ton	29.00	35.10	22
Oats	£/ton	28.80	32.99	13
Fat cattle	£/ton LWT	247.00	310.30	24
(including subsidies)	£/ton LWT	298.50	310.30	12
Fat pigs	£/score DWT	2.93	2.93	—
Milk (pool price)	p/gall	19.0	23.5	24
(liquid)	p/gall	25.0	27.0	8
(manufactured)	p/gall	9.0	19.5	115
Sugar beet	£/ton	7.60	7.60	—

to British conditions. Farmers would therefore be receiving higher prices now if we had adopted the CAP several years ago. In particular the farm prices for wheat, cattle and milk would be considerably higher. But livestock farmers would face feed costs up to 30 per cent higher (depending on the cereal content of the feed rations they use); pig, poultry and egg producers would find their increased costs not recompensed by higher prices for their output. The average price difference, weighted by present farm output including those products not directly affected by the CAP, is 10 per cent. On the basis of such a price difference, the White Paper expected an extra 8 per cent of farm output by the end of the transition period.

The consumer faces price rises steeper than those enjoyed by the farmer. This is in part due to our present support system

Table 2: Comparison of Recent UK Average Consumer Prices, with Equivalents under CAP

	Unit	UK price (average, 1969)	EEC equivalent	Percentage difference
Beef and veal	p/lb	32.8	42.2	28
Pork	p/lb	27.1	27.1	—
Mutton and lamb	p/lb	24.1	27.7	15
Bacon and ham	p/lb	26.1	28.7	10
Liquid milk	p/pt	4.5	5.2	17
Butter	p/lb	17.0	47.5	179
Cheese	p/lb	19.1	30.9	62
Flour	p/lb	3.2	4.2	29
Bread	p/lb	4.5	4.9	10

Source: Average retail prices in 1969 from National Food Survey, MAFF. EEC equivalents assume full cost increases passed on to consumer.

which maintains farm prices above wholesale levels by means of deficiency payments; it is also the result of our different milk support policy which has enabled us to buy butter at the low and subsidised world price. Weighted by present food expenditure patterns these price rises average about 16 per cent: the cost-of-living index would rise by just under 3 per cent. These estimates are very close to those given in the 1971 White Paper.

This instantaneous price comparison would be acceptable if we had no evidence about future price trends in the UK and

the EEC. But this is not the case. We have, for example, the
recent history of both price policies and we have statements and
commitments about future price policies. Moreover we can
examine the underlying pressures acting on each policy. Table 3
demonstrates the remarkable stability of producer prices in the

Table 3: Recent Producer Price Changes, UK and EEC[1]

	Total change 1963/64 to 1970/71 (percentage)		Annual change 1966/7– 1970/1 (percentage per year)	
	EEC	UK	EEC	UK
Wheat	1	16	0.3	6.6
Barley	8	8	0.8	6.3
Cattle	29	38	3.0	5.7
Pigs	7	24	−0.3	4.5
Milk	15	15	1.0	2.3
Sugar beet	6	7	0.3	5.5

[1] Prices realised by producers inclusive of deficiency payments.
Sources: UK Annual Review White Papers and EEC *Statistiques Agricoles.*

countries of the EEC since 1964. This is to be compared with
a steady rise in farm prices in this country through the increase
in guaranteed prices at each annual price review. In the years
before 1964 there had been pressure to reduce UK farm prices
to control the exchequer cost of support at times of weakness
on the world market. With the gradual imposition of import
controls, it became possible to recompense farmers for the
major part of their cost increases and to encourage a 'selective
expansion' of home agriculture for the purpose of saving
imports. This process has been more marked since 1967 when
world prices themselves firmed. The decision to develop the
variable-levy scheme for most commodities completes this
release from Treasury control; indeed revenue from the levies
makes a welcome addition to tax receipts and helps to reduce
the level of direct taxation. Unless the present Government
were to alter radically its view of agricultural policy one might
expect price increases of 4 per cent per year at least for the
major farm commodities if we did not go into Europe.

A very different set of pressures operates in the EEC. On a
financial plane, all six governments are anxious to avoid a

recurrence of the surpluses which proved an embarrassment in 1969. Much of the burden of the surpluses was ephemeral—stocks which would normally have been held by private firms were transferred to the intervention agencies and exports which would have been commercial sales qualified for unnecessary restitution. But it is evident that those who set the unified price levels of the Six underestimated the technical advancement that has spread over much of European agriculture in the last few years. Price rises in the future are likely to be concentrated on those products which are not in surplus. Exporting countries within the Community fear the loss of their European markets if prices rise too fast and importing countries have no incentive to impose on themselves higher import costs. Presumably our own position within the Community would be a restraining influence on price rises, particularly rises in the threshold prices for butter, sugar and cheddar cheese. The EEC at present imports none of these three commodities in significant quantities; their tariff levels contain enough 'water' in them to allow flexibility in setting export restitutions. It would be unduly pessimistic to assume that we as major importers of these items would have no influence on their future threshold-price levels. With these pressures one would have to predict a more modest increase in farm prices in the EEC than in the UK as a non-member—perhaps 2 per cent per year over the decade.

The other set of price levels which affect the calculation of entry costs is that prevailing on the world market for agricultural goods. It is widely accepted that primary-product price levels do not keep up with general price rises for manufactured trade. Demand is relatively static, technical progress swift, and exporters' market power limited in agricultural markets. Moreover quality increases in industrial goods which tend to show up in economic statistics as price rises are largely absent in temperate food trade. But the depression in agricultural prices that persisted through the mid-1960s was nevertheless remarkable. Importing countries were isolating their domestic producers, and exporters were competing with help from their exchequers for shrinking markets. It is possible that these conditions could return. Certainly demand for cereals is unlikely to grow fast enough to keep grain prices on a rising trend if exporters abandoned supply control and developing countries in Asia speeded up their adoption of high-yielding varieties of wheat and rice. But there are reasons for thinking that world agricultural prices will remain firm. As inflation affects labour costs livestock producers are finding world price levels unremunerative. Although drought conditions certainly occasioned much of the cutback in Australasian butter production in the past year, cost inflation was an important additional cause. Inflation also affects transport and handling costs and raises import prices even when farmers in exporting countries receive stable prices. Treasuries in exporting countries are decreasingly willing to subsidise consumers abroad, and countries such as Australia and Canada are making an attempt to control supplies. The United States is becoming increasingly concerned about the loss of agricultural markets and is apparently prepared to mount a major trade initiative to curb price-depressing import policies in advanced countries. The EEC itself is taking more seriously the impact on other exporters of variable export subsidies—in particular it has agreed not to disrupt New Zealand's potential markets for dairy products in Asia. All these factors combine to suggest world prices rising by perhaps 2 per cent per year over the decade, with some livestock commodities—beef in particular— rising faster, while grain prices could remain somewhat below the exceptional 1970-71 levels.

Changes in world price levels put different pressures on different methods of agricultural support. When we in the UK ran a deficiency-payments system unsupported by levies, our guaranteed prices tended to follow world price trends so as to stabilise the level of exchequer expenditure. The levy system was designed in large part to break this link. From the consumer's point of view the variable-levy policy isolates the domestic market from trade conditions. The real level of support of home prices will fall as world prices rise. The recent rise in world prices has therefore moved our food prices up by more than those in the Community where the market isolation already exists.

A realistic assessment of the cost of entry would therefore require probable trends in policy and prices to be taken into account. Continuation of the present price differences in the UK, the EEC and the world market may be a convenient

assumption for the White Paper; the steady introduction of a
levy policy in this country irrespective of entry, a gradual rise
in world prices of livestock products, and a continuation of
relative price stability in the EEC would seem a more defensible
view of the future.

Implications of the CAP for producers and consumers

To estimate the implications of these policy and price
changes on farmers and on consumers it is necessary to look
at the probable effects on the markets for individual agricultural
products. Estimation would be much easier if one could treat
'agricultural production' and 'food' as aggregates, but most
of the important changes to be expected are production shifts
away from some goods in favour of others together with
corresponding changes in patterns of food consumption. A
disaggregated analysis is therefore imperative. There are two
well-known studies which attempt such an exercise, those by
Warley[9] and Jones[10]; similar analyses presumably lay behind
the agricultural and food-cost estimates of the CBI[11] report
and the White Papers,[12] but unfortunately these have not been
made public. Both Warley and Jones have been outpaced by
events, chiefly the devaluation of sterling in 1967. A more much
recent study coordinated by a team from Michigan State
University not only provides detailed estimates of production
and consumption of food in this country but also contains an
analysis of corresponding effects in Ireland, Denmark and
Norway, and discusses the impact of EEC enlargement on

---

[9] T. K. Warley, *Agriculture: The Cost of Joining the Common Market*,
Chatham House/PEP, April 1967.

[10] *United Kingdom: projected level of demand, supply and imports of
agricultural products 1970, 1975, and 1980*, Oxford Institute for Research
in Agricultural Economics and United States Department of Agriculture, 1969.

[11] *Britain and Europe: A Second Industrial Appraisal*, Confederation of
British Industry, 1970.

[12] *Britain and the European Communities: An Economic Assessment*,
Cmnd 4289, HMSO, February 1970; and *The United Kingdom and the
European Communities*, Cmnd 4715, HMSO, July 1971.

total Community agricultural trade.[13] The implications of this study for the United Kingdom are perhaps the more relevant in that they broadly confirm the overall food and agricultural cost estimates contained in the 1971 White Paper.

The study considered three alternative agricultural policy environments for the UK: a return to the deficiency-payment system of old, a continuation of the new variable-levy system, and adoption of the CAP. Production estimates were obtained by observing past farmer reactions to changes in the profitability of their enterprises. Consumer patterns were predicted on the basis of changes in food buying habits as recorded in the National Food Survey of household expenditure.[14] For each of 16 food items a relationship was found linking incomes, food prices, and inflationary trends to per caput consumption. The projections of production and consumption were extended to the year 1980. Although the transition to EEC prices should be complete by 1978, the production and consumption levels in 1980 are of interest in that they will determine to some extent our full contribution to the Community budget in that year.

The expected impact on farm output is shown in Table 4. Output of wheat, barley and milk is expected to be stimulated by adoption of the CAP, but the extent of this expansion is limited by the availability of arable land. Those livestock

Table 4: Estimated Change in Production in UK of Major Farm Products due to Introduction of CAP, 1980

	Index of 1980 production in EEC (1980, outside EEC = 100)
Wheat	106
Barley	113
Milk	114
Beef	90
Pigmeat	83
Mutton	100
Poultry	90
Eggs	84

Source: Study cited in text, modified by the present author to take account of negotiations on milk support scheme.

[13] *The Impact on US Agricultural Trade of the Accession of the United Kingdom, Ireland, Denmark and Norway to the European Economic Community*, Michigan State University (forthcoming). The study was sponsored by the US Department of Agriculture.

[14] *Household Food Consumption and Expenditure: 1968*, HMSO, 1971.

products which use grain as a feedstuff become relatively less profitable, though in all cases output in 1980 is higher than in 1968.

The expected changes in consumption patterns are of more general interest and warrant exploring in some detail. Table 5 gives the indices of per caput consumption in 1980 of the major food items considered in the study relative to the year 1968.

Table 5: Projected Indices of Per Caput Consumption in UK, 1980 (1968 = 100)

	Outside EEC	Inside EEC	Inside EEC, higher growth[1]
Beef and veal	107	82	101
Pork	148	156	180
Bacon and ham	113	113	119
Mutton and lamb	113	114	121
Poultry	127	127	135
Eggs	116	115	120
Liquid milk	100	100	100
Butter	120	85	92
Cheese	114	108	112
Margarine	83	119	115
Bread	82	83	76

Source: Study cited in text.

[1] 'Higher growth' assumption implies 3.4 per cent per annum real growth of GNP; other columns assume 2.9 per cent growth rates.

Column 1 shows consumption patterns if we continue the present variable-levy policy, phasing out deficiency payments over the decade. Column 2 gives the comparable figures assuming adoption of the CAP but with no change in the rate of growth of incomes. For those who predict an increase in our growth rate on entry into the EEC, column 3 shows the consumption pattern suggested by a rate of growth one half of 1 per cent higher (slightly above the increment to the rate of growth during the transitional period suggested by Williamson in Chapter 2). Total meat consumption is buoyant under each assumption, but beef becomes less attractive relative to other meats under EEC prices. Indeed in the case of entry beef consumption could fall 1½ per cent per year below present levels. The higher growth rate if achieved would just offset this decline. The only other significant change in consumption patterns is a switch from butter to margarine. Margarine consumption would normally fall as incomes increase; instead the study predicts a rise of 20 per cent over the decade under

EEC conditions. The reverse is true of butter where EEC prices would suggest a 15 per cent fall in the period up to 1980. The total quantity of margarine and butter together consumed by households is not markedly changed by EEC entry.[15]

The willingness of consumers, shown by the evidence available, to switch from beef to other meats and from butter to margarine implies that food expenditure rises by much less than that indicated by the food-price index. Both the food-price index and the cost-of-living index estimate the change in expenditure, and hence in the standard of living, on the assumption of no adjustment of consumption patterns.[16] But the more willing consumers are to substitute between food goods, the less will be the drop in living standards implied by price increases. Table 6 shows projected changes in per caput expenditure on some major food goods during the transition period to the higher EEC prices. Total per caput expenditure on food is higher by £2.59 per year with entry by 1978 relative to that implied by a continuation of present policies. Expenditure on butter alone accounts for £2.35 of this increase; expenditure on meat actually declines by £1.31 per head per year. The effect of the CAP on the standard of living will lie somewhere between the expenditure change (0.3 per cent) and the price-index change (1.4 per cent), depending on how much of the extra food costs are paid abroad as levies or higher prices for Danish and Irish products and how much remains in the pockets of our farmers and the domestic food industry. For that calculation one has to examine trade patterns.[17]

The projections of production and consumption can be used jointly to indicate our requirements of food from abroad. To

---

[15] The introduction of a 'cooking butter' as widely used on the Continent and sold at a lower price could arrest this switch somewhat.

[16] Taking each commodity and weighting by expenditure on that commodity in the base period will give a 'price-index' change that is an indication of expenditure change with no adjustment in quantities purchased. This will correspond to a loss in 'consumers surplus'—including internal transfers—which provides an upper bound to the true effect on living standards. Only in the extreme case where (a) all levy payments go automatically abroad, and (b) no adjustment in quantities purchased takes place, will this measure the real income loss to the country.

[17] See also the calculations by Miller in Chapter 6, below.

Table 6: Projected UK Expenditure on Major Food Items (£ per person), 1972–78

Year	Relation to EEC	Expenditure on major food items	Non-food expenditure	Beef	Pork	Poultry	Mutton and lamb	Bacon and ham	Butter	Margarine	Bread
1972		75.92	541.67	16.32	7.83	3.98	6.22	7.00	3.73	1.10	9.15
1974	out	81.29	612.29	17.42	8.91	4.28	6.81	7.63	3.90	1.11	9.88
	in	82.00	611.54	16.15	9.27	4.28	6.97	7.61	4.85	1.35	10.00
1976	out	86.71	692.21	18.78	10.07	4.59	7.37	8.19	4.11	1.13	10.35
	in	88.63	690.29	16.44	10.80	4.60	7.73	8.25	5.91	1.56	10.78
1978	out	92.08	782.71	20.57	11.17	4.86	7.88	8.65	4.36	1.16	10.53
	in	94.67	780.13	17.63	12.09	4.88	8.34	8.82	6.61	1.67	11.19

Source: Study cited in text.

determine the value of these imports it is necessary in addition to estimate future world and minimum import prices. Table 7 attempts such an estimation of food import costs for the years

Table 7: Food Import Costs, UK, 1972–80 £ million (current prices)

a) Outside EEC, present price policy				
	1972	1974	1976	1978	1980
Beef and veal	48.6	28.8	31.2	53.2	86.9
Pigmeat	68.7	42.0	53.6	49.2	23.6
Lamb	119.7	125.0	133.9	150.2	171.4
Cereals	168.3	141.6	99.6	90.4	89.3
Sugar	90.0	93.5	96.0	97.5	98.0
Butter	222.3	203.6	172.2	233.9	252.6
Cheese	50.7	52.5	53.1	52.1	54.4
Total, above	768.3	687.0	639.6	726.5	776.2

b) Inside EEC, transition period 1973–78					
					1980	
	1972	1974	1976	1978	total	of which, levy payment
Beef and veal	48.6	—	—	—	5.4	—
Pigmeat	68.7	57.6	87.0	134.8	147.8	—
Lamb	119.7	126.7	137.9	152.1	204.8	31.9
Cereals	168.3	143.3	84.4	—	—	—
Sugar	90.0	93.5	97.5	91.0	99.0	22.0
Butter	222.3	186.5	99.6	164.9	233.2	45.4
Cheese	50.7	44.7	38.1	34.7	53.9	24.2
Total, above	768.3	652.3	544.5	577.5	744.1	123.5

Source: Study cited in text, and assumptions of world prices. Imports are shown net of exports; export restitutions from the Fund are subtracted from levy payments in last column.

to 1980. The assumption is made that world cereal prices will remain steady but beef and lamb prices will increase by about 3 per cent per year. Butter prices are assumed to fall from this year's high levels but stabilise at about £400 per ton.[18] Imports are shown net of exports; a surplus of barley largely offsets the continued maize and hardwheat imports. The British market becomes self-sufficient in beef in the late 1970s following the contraction of demand occasioned by the higher EEC retail prices; pigmeat imports decline in the 'out' situation owing to expansion of UK production.

[18] Imports that come from other members of the enlarged Community (mostly from Ireland and Denmark) enter at a price in terms of foreign exchange which increases over the transition to be comparable with tariff-inclusive price levels for third-country imports.

During the transition period our payments to the Community budget are determined by a 'key' based on a percentage of Fund expenditure. From 1980 our contributions will include agricultural (and other) levy revenues. Since the table is expressed in terms of the foreign-exchange burden, the levy revenue during the transition period is excluded. Although these levies are imposed on third-country imports progressively during the transition, the yield accrues to the British exchequer and does not imply a foreign exchange burden. The 1980 import bill, however, includes such levies as are paid to Brussels on agricultural imports. There is, therefore, a jump in the foreign exchange cost of food in the period 1978-80. The amount of this agricultural levy is projected at about £150 million (see Table 7, b). Whether the net burden of payments into the Fund rises in 1980 depends on whether the agricultural levies and general import duties together with any required proportion of value-added tax receipt exceed the payments under the key at the end of the transition.

But in spite of—or rather because of—these price increases, our food import bill for the goods included in Table 7 is lower over the transition period than it would be if we did not adopt the CAP. This import-saving effect is shown in the diagram.

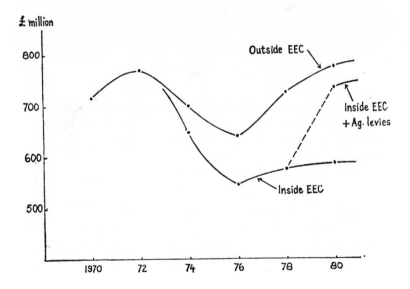

In technical terms, the response of producers and consumers to higher prices implies an import demand elasticity for food which is greater than unity.[19] The fall in import costs during the transition should provide a useful offset to the rising burden of the Fund payments and any unfavourable effect on industrial trade.[20] Those who have argued for years that domestic agriculture should be encouraged as an import-saving industry will not find such a conclusion difficult to swallow.[21]

Impact on agricultural trade

If these results indicate that the effect on consumers and on the balance of payments of the CAP have often been exaggerated, the reverse side of the coin is equally significant. A contraction of UK food imports has important repercussions on countries that have historically exported agricultural goods to us. The main third-country trade flows that are threatened are beef from South America and Australia, maize from South Africa and the USA, barley from Canada, and wheat from all these regions. In addition Australian sugar, butter and dried fruits, Canadian tobacco, cheese and fruit, and Polish bacon will be badly hit. New Zealand butter sales and Caribbean sugar exports appear to be relatively secure subject to a sympathetic interpretation by future British governments of the terms agreed during negotiations with the Six. The long-term implica-

[19] This property also suggests that if we were to devalue relative to the unit of account in which EEC import prices are fixed the further contraction of our food bill would help to restore payments balance.

[20] In fact the net payments into the Fund during the transition, rising from £100 million to £200 million, are almost entirely offset by the saving on food imports over this period. Williamson estimates, in Chapter 2, a negative effect of £100 million on the balance of industrial trade, though according to Dosser (Chapter 9), the application of value-added tax at Community rates might reduce this substantially.

[21] The present author retains his objections to the traditional arguments about using expansion of import-competing industries in place of exchange-rate adjustments and more general 'uniform-tariff' policies — as expressed in T. Josling, Agriculture and Import Saving: A Cautionary Note, in *Agriculture and Import Saving*, Hill Samuel Occasional Paper, London, 1969. In the present circumstance we would in fact be taxing the consumption of certain products, imports of which have a high social cost by reason of the transfers made across the exchanges to Brussels. Import saving under these conditions, in a second-best context, has some *a priori* attraction in narrow national-income terms.

tions for these economies will depend on the implementation of domestic policies by their own governments to promote development and aid adjustment.

More fundamental than the change in trade patterns is the potential shrinkage in the size of the world market for temperate agricultural goods. The Michigan State University study referred to above also provides an opportunity to estimate the possible effect of EEC enlargement on the net trading position of the 10 European countries concerned. Table 8 shows in the first column the potential damage to world markets that can be attributed to enlargement. In 1980 the European market for beef, grains and dairy products will be diminished if EEC enlargement takes place. Most of this change can be related to the shrinkage of the UK market for grain, butter and beef as

Table 8: Projected Impact of Enlargement of the Community on the Size of European Agricultural Trade

	Change due[1] to enlargement in imports of Ten	Change over[2] present Six imports
	'000 metric tons	
Beef	−593	−262
Pigmeat	700	−660
Poultry	175	−454
Eggs	204	−148
Grain	−5,732	−5,497
Milk (in butter fat equivalent)	−311	172

Source: Calculations based on study cited in text.

[1] Net exports of 10 countries in 1980 with no EEC enlargement minus the net exports of the enlarged Community in 1980. Positive figures show an increase in imports or reduction of exports from the Ten-country group arising from enlargement.
[2] Present net exports (1968) of Six-country EEC minus net exports in 1980 of enlarged EEC. Positive figures show a decrease in exports or increase in imports in the EEC following from enlargement, relative to the present.

consumers change food habits and farmers react to higher prices. Exporters excluded from the British market will face increased competition elsewhere in the world. For the cereal-using livestock products—pigmeat, eggs and poultry—the European market will expand relatively, though this may be

reflected in firmer European prices for these goods.[22] This
picture broadly confirms the fears by the major exporting
countries that EEC enlargement will further contract world
agricultural trade. Whether such a development will hasten a
multilateral pact on agricultural support limitation is a moot
point; certainly pressures for such a move will be intensified.

The second column of Table 8 is an attempt to estimate one
aspect of European trade which is of particular interest to the
UK. If European production outgrows demand over the next
decade then we would be faced with larger contributions to the
Community budget under present rules as surpluses are exported
with a subsidy. With the notable exception of dairy products,
the degree of self-sufficiency rises when the enlarged EEC
(in 1980) is compared with the present Six (1968). This implies
a reduction in import-levy receipts and an increase in export
restitutions. But the position should not be over-dramatised.
The largest item in column 2 of Table 8 is an increase in
grain exports (or decrease in imports) of 5.5 million tons. On
the basis of recent subsidy levels, this would involve an expenditure of £80 million. The implication for the Fund of all these
products together is an increase in expenditure on market
support over income from levies of about £100 million. This
suggests that predictions of a large increase in European
expenditure on market support are not borne out by the
evidence.

The implications for trade in agricultural goods may be the
most significant aspect of our adoption of the CAP. It would
appear that provided the Government takes steps to alleviate
the impact of higher food prices on low-income large families
and on pensioners, the cumulative effect on British households
is not likely to be severe. This does not exonerate the CAP—it
clearly is an inefficient and grossly expensive policy in relation
to its achievements. But the direct threat to the British economy
of adopting this policy even in terms of the balance of payments
is not serious. If it contributed to a collapse of the hard-won
liberal trade structure of the post-Kennedy round era then it
could greatly impair our living standards together with those

---

[22] As these needs are fulfilled by farmers in Europe or elsewhere, the
   demand for cereals will expand to offset the indicicated market shrinkage.

of many countries poorer than ourselves. In preventing this Britain has a responsibility. Clearly the decision on EEC entry will be taken on grounds much broader than agricultural trade relations. But if we join the Community an early priority will be the modification of the CAP to conform with accepted rules of international conduct. Obsession with the costs of entry should not blind us to the deeper implications for world prosperity and peace of further irresponsibility in the market for agricultural goods.

Chapter 5

THE CHANGING STRUCTURE OF AGRICULTURE IN THE EEC

by John Marsh

POLICY-MAKERS generally concentrate upon the implications of their decisions for the short, or at most the medium, term. Such an emphasis reflects the reality of political power where electoral processes demand presentable results every few years, if parties are to remain in office. It also accords with the limited capacity of the social sciences to predict far ahead with a high degree of certainty. In the present state of knowledge such fundamental elements of economic life as the size of the population or the level of national income can be foreseen with clarity for relatively few years.

Where the underlying framework of economic and social life is not expected to change, this disregard of longer-run issues may be tolerated. Where, as in the context of an enlarged European Community, this framework is itself being changed by the process of current decision-taking, neglect of the long-run issues is dangerous and likely to lead to mistaken policies. Nowhere is the need for a long-run view more evident than in agricultural policy. The acuteness of the current problems of the farming sector reflects the difficulty of reconciling rates of change in the size of its work force, the level of demand for its product and the disposition of its assets. Policy must seek not only to relieve the immediate discomfort of the agricultural population but also to afford such relief in a manner consistent with satisfactory rates of adjustment in these more fundamental variables. It is with these longer-run issues that this chapter, on the structure of the agricultural industry, is concerned. It seeks to show first, that there does exist a self-regulating process. Given the time-scale of a permanent Community this will eventually improve both the absolute and relative standard of living among farmers and reduce the costliness, to other sectors, of agricultural policy. Second, it argues that the current policy decisions can help this self-regulating process and so shorten the period during which income transfers from the economy as a whole to farming are needed.

For the United Kingdom the implications of such conclusions are vitally important. As the member of an enlarged Community with the smallest fraction of its population engaged in agriculture and the smallest fraction of its income derived from agriculture, any policy designed to transfer income on a Community scale from other sectors to farmers is bound to be relatively unfavourable. The disadvantages for Britain of a common agricultural policy are likely to remain as long as such transfers take place. On the same grounds, if there is a reasonable prospect that the size of the income transfer will diminish, this must make membership more attractive. Additionally, if by suitable current decisions the enlarged Community can both aid its farmers more effectively and shorten the period during which aid is required, Britain must have a vital interest in the development of the CAP in such a direction.

The nature of the issues

Agricultural policy deals with a variety of issues ranging from the health of people and animals to the strategic and diplomatic significance of farm production. At the heart of most policies for agriculture in developed countries there is, however, a common concern with the tendency for incomes in agriculture to be lower than those in other industries. This is far from the only issue with which agricultural policy-makers are involved but it so far dominates discussion, especially within the European Community, as to stamp its character upon the overall aspect of the policies which are finally adopted.

Incomes in agriculture tend to be low because there are too many people among whom the aggregate profits of the industry have to be divided. Improvement may come either from an increase in total output and profits or from a reduction of the number of people engaged in the sector, or both.

An increase in output must be related to the overall demand for agricultural goods at the farm gate. In recent years demand for food has risen, at the retail level, as per caput incomes in the Community as a whole have grown, but this growth in expenditure is associated more with the development of a more varied and better-quality diet than with a rise in the volume of food consumed. Hence the effect on the demand at the farm gate is less than in the shop and much of the increased expenditure has gone to the processing and distributive industries. In these circumstances the scope for EEC farmers to sell more is limited unless their products displace existing imports or find a market abroad. Such a process can take place only with the aid of subsidies, in one form or another, from the rest of the economy.

In so far as the aggregate market for farm output is relatively static, agricultural incomes can rise only if the number of farmers declines. The extent of the outward movement needed to raise farmers' incomes to equality with those in other sectors is further complicated by two factors. For many years most farm incomes have been below those of workers in other sectors. Quite apart from the need to adjust the size of the labour force to meet growing incomes in the economy, there is then a back-log of outward migration which must take place if agricultural incomes are to attain parity with existing incomes in other sectors. Again in recent years technical progress in agriculture has rapidly reduced the size of labour force needed to achieve a given level of output. If incomes are not to fall, or support costs to rise, a movement of manpower from agriculture must therefore continue to take place at a more rapid rate than would be possible in the absence of such technical development.

Within the EEC adjustment to these pressures has been remarkably rapid. In 10 years, during the 1960s, some five million people left farming. Despite constraints imposed by an inappropriate farm size distribution, new techniques have been adopted to such effect that output has, as Table 1 shows, risen very considerably.

Such spontaneous changes do not take place without difficulty. On the farm there is a need to adjust resource patterns, to enlarge farms and re-equip them with suitable capital equipment. In the market there is a growing requirement for

Table 1: Change in Production of Major Agricultural Products in the EEC 1954–58 to 1964–68

	1954–58	1964–68	% change
	'000 tons		
Cereals	48,400	63,500	30
Milk	57,000	71,900	25
Eggs	26,800	39,000	45
Poultry meat	500	1,400	180
Beef and veal	3,000	3,900	30
Pigmeat	3,600	4,900	35
Potatoes	49,400	40,200	−20
Sugar beet	33,700	46,100	35
Apples	3,500	5,700	65

Source: Selected Agricultural Figures of the EEC.
Ministry of Agriculture and Fisheries of the Netherlands, February 1970.

better product handling, improved processing and the presentation of goods in forms more convenient for the housewife. Among consumers there is sometimes resistance to new production methods, suspicion that food no longer tastes so good and a reluctance to abandon traditional patterns of purchase for the standardised, refrigerated and pre-packed offering of the supermarket. For the rural community, the diminution in the size of its population leads to the breakdown of established social patterns and a threat to the prevailing environmental and ecological balance. In a world context the whole idea of restricting food production, whilst many people in poorer countries remain under-nourished, poses an acute moral dilemma.

If the agricultural labour force were not allowed to decline, however, the prospect would be one of increasing poverty both in relation to other parts of the economy and in relation to earlier years. The implication must be, not that policy should impede the outward flow of manpower, in the long term, but that it should seek to relate the flow to a creative programme which will generate lasting solutions for these important consequential problems.

Some indication of the scope for policy decisions intended to raise farm incomes and establish parity with incomes in other sectors can be derived from Table 2. This table, although not dissimilar in some respects from the situation of the Community,

Table 2: A Simplified Illustration of the Relationship between Key Variables relating to the Income Level of Farmers and other Workers

	Active agricultural labour force	Aggregate net output of agriculture	Agriculture output per caput	Total non-agricultural labour force	Gross domestic product	Product per caput	Average output of agriculture as percentage of average non-agricultural sectors	Percentage of GNP that would need to be transferred to raise agriculture per caput income to same level as average income per caput
1	10	35	3,500	70	450	6,400	54	6.4
2	5	35	7,000	75	480	6,400	109	...
3a	5	47	9,300	75	600	8,000	116	...
b	5	47	9,300	75	720	9,600	97	0.4
4	4.89	47	9,600	75	720	9,600	100	...

...nil or negative.

is essentially a numeric illustration of the effects upon relative income of different rates of growth in output and in the size of the labour force. The first row (1) sets out an initial set of assumptions concerning the value added (net output) of agriculture, the total output of the economy and the number of people involved. These assumptions are broadly in line with the experience of the Six around 1970. Row 2 explores the significance of holding output constant but transferring 5 million of the labour force from agriculture to other sectors, where their per caput addition to output is assumed to be equivalent to that of workers currently engaged in non-agricultural activities. The effect is to raise farm incomes per caput somewhat above those of the rest of the economy. Although such an assumption of constant output with a 50 per cent cut in the labour force is clearly arbitrary, it implicitly reflects the observable tendency for technical progress to permit other factors to replace the men who have gone. Row 3 examines the situation where an equivalent movement takes place in the labour force but output grows both in agriculture and in industry. In row 3a farm output rises by one-third and non-farm by one-quarter. This induces a situation in which farm incomes are higher than non-farm. Row 3b allows non-farm output to rise by 50 per cent and farm output by $33\frac{1}{3}$ per cent. In this situation, although the gap between per caput incomes in agriculture and other sectors has narrowed greatly compared with row 1, farm incomes are still below those of workers in other sectors. Finally row 4 examines the implications of a situation in which output increases by 50 per cent in non-farm output and $33\frac{1}{3}$ per cent in farm output and output per head is assumed to be equal, in terms of the sustainable size of the agricultural labour force. This proves to be 4.89 million. In other words, if under the output conditions of 3b, parity is to be achieved, a further 110,000 jobs have to be found outside agriculture.

Parity of incomes may be achieved by transfers, through subsidies or similar devices, from the rest of the economy to agriculture. The final column of Table 2 indicates that, in the situation postulated, the proportion of the income of the rest of the economy which it would be necessary to transfer to attain such equality decreases sharply as the labour force declines and as the rate of increase in farm output exceeds the increase in output of the economy as a whole.

These arbitrarily chosen figures illustrate a number of rela-
tionships important to the policy-maker. First, the nearer it is
intended to approach parity of income from the mechanism
of the market, the larger must be the exodus from agriculture.
Second, the more gross domestic product rises, the larger must
be the corresponding reduction in agricultural employment or
rise in agricultural output. Third, the smaller the increase in
agricultural output, the smaller the size of the labour force
which can be retained in agriculture.

Table 3 sets out basic statistics of the type employed in
Table 2 for the EEC of Six in 1958 and 1968. During this
11-year period some improvement took place in the relative
position of agricultural output per head compared with output
per head in the economy as a whole. If, for the moment, we
assumed that the rates of change recorded in Table 3 were to
continue unchanged into the future, then, in something like
35 to 40 years, output per head in agriculture would be equal
to output per head in the economy as a whole. At this point
there would be some 2.5 million employed in agriculture and
83 million in the rest of the economy—i.e. about 3 per cent of
the total labour force would work as farmers. Perhaps of more
interest is to examine the effects of continuing such arbitrary
assumptions to 1985. Row 4 indicates that on such a basis,
farm incomes would have reached two-thirds the level of
non-farm incomes and the farm labour force be something less
than 6 million people.

Such an assumption of constant rates of change over a period
of 30-40 years is clearly absurd, even if for the period to 1985
it may not be too far wide of the mark. However, with the aid
of Table 2 we can interpret the effects of making different
assumptions concerning the relevant variables.

Table 4 indicates the Commission's expectations concerning
the development of the agricultural labour force to 1976. The
rate of decline foreseen is rather lower than that which prevailed
during 1958-68. Other things being equal this must mean that
incomes will take longer to reach parity than implied by Table 3.
However, the rate of outflow is considerable and by 1976 a
rather higher proportion of the total farm labour force (71 per
cent) will be in the two older age groups than in 1971 (67 per

Table 3: Changes in Net Output per head in Agriculture and the Rest of the Economy in the EEC, 1958–68

	Active agricultural labour force (million)	Total contribution of agriculture to GNP (billion units of account) (current market prices and exchange rates)	Agricultural output per person engaged in agriculture (units of account)	GNP (billion units of account) (current market prices and exchange rates)	Total labour force (million)	Average output per worker (units of account)	Average output of agriculture as % of average non-agriculture	% GNP required to raise agriculture income per head to 65% of average	% GNP required to raise agriculture income per head to 100% of average
1	1958	16	15.94[1]	983	158	72	2,205	47	4.5[3]	12.3[3]
2	1968	11	29.30	2,764	381	74	5,150	54	1.7	6.8
3	Annual % change 1958–68	−3.8	5.7	9.8	8.3	0.3	8.3	—	—	—
4	1985[2]	5.7	71.0	12,500	1,470	77.6	19,000	65	0	2.5

Notes: [1] Agriculture's contribution to GNP is based on statistics giving the % GNP derived from the industry. The figure used is that for 1967 and probably overstates the value of agricultural output.

[2] The figures for 1985 are based on the assumption that the rates of change recorded in row 3 continued unchanged from 1968–85.

[3] No allowance is made for the effect on GNP of income transfers. Such transfers would lower GNP so that the figures recorded probably understate the proportion of GNP which would need to be transferred to retain the 65%–100% levels of parity.

Sources: For 1958, *The Common Market Ten Years On—Selected Figures*, EEC Statistical Office, 1968.
For 1968, *Basic Statistics of the Community*, EEC Statistical Office, 1970.

Table 4: Development of Active Agricultural Population in EEC, 1961–76

	1961	Forecasts 1971	Forecasts 1976
West Germany	3,518,143	2,163,700	1,863,217
France	3,853,831	2,885,102	2,543,688
Italy	5,664,127	4,002,198	3,480,037
Belgium	253,922	169,707	136,667
Netherlands	442,385	378,693	303,824
Luxembourg	19,325	16,000	14,000
EEC	13,751,733	9,615,400	8,343,433

Agricultural Population as Percentage of Total Active Population

	Germany	Italy	France	Belgium	Netherlands	EEC
1961	13.67	28.22	19.45	7.22	10.22	18.9
1971	9.03	18.3	13.1	4.52	7.83	12.09
1976	6.76	16.9	10.56	3.62	6.52	10.49

Forecast Age Distribution of the Active Agricultural Population in EEC

Age groups	1971	%	1976	%
Up to 19 years	335,245	3.5	306,071	3.7
20–29 years	1,105,612	11.5	808,054	9.6
30–39 years	1,713,330	17.8	1,333,366	16
40–59 years	3,460,284	36	2,912,230	34.9
60 years and over	3,000,529	31.2	2,983,712	35.8
Total	9,615,400	100	8,343,433	100

Source: Agra-Europe report, March 1971.

cent). We may, then, expect some acceleration in the rate of departures in the 20 years following 1976. It is clearly important for policy-makers seeking income parity that retirements should not be offset by a parallel growth in recruitment. Hence stress must be placed not only on schemes, such as the Mansholt plan, which help existing workers to leave, but also upon providing suitable education and job opportunities to permit rural school leavers to find employment in other sectors.

During the years recorded in Table 3 agricultural output rose substantially. In part this was due to the larger volume of production (see Table 1) and in part to increases in prices paid to farmers. By 1968 the Community was approaching self-sufficiency for a wide range of agricultural products (Table 5).

Table 5: Degree of Self-sufficiency in the EEC, 1967/68

	%		%
Wheat	112	Citrus fruit	51
Rye	100	Wine	96
Barley	106	Full cream milk	100
Oats	95	Skimmed milk	100
Maize	46	Cheese	103
Total grain	91	Butter	117
Rice	80	Beef ⎫	89
Potatoes	102	Veal ⎭	
Sugar	95	Pork	100
Vegetables	103	Poultry	98
Fresh fruit	90	Total meat	94

Source: Basic Statistics of the Community, EEC Statistical Office, 1970

Further expansion in the volume of output is likely to encounter difficulties in finding a market within the Community. Some relief may be afforded by the accession of the UK to the Community, but changes in British consumption and production levels may tend to diminish this, as Josling has shown in Chapter 4. In the long run continuous increases in output must reach a point beyond the absorptive power of the Community. At this stage goods which have to be removed from the Community's market, for storage or sale abroad, will represent a substantial and growing cost to the Community's budget. Thus pressures are likely to emerge to reduce, or at least not increase in step with inflation, the prices paid to farmers. The Community has in recent years kept the rate of growth of agricultural prices about 1 per cent per annum less than the rate of growth of its general price level, and a continuation of this trend would maintain a downward pressure on the growth in the value of farm output. It is apparent from the figuring of Table 2 that if the rate of growth of farm output is curtailed the difficulties involved in seeking income parity with other sectors are intensified. Greater emphasis would then be needed on the reduction of the size of the farm labour force, or means found of supplementing income which do not require higher prices or a larger volume of production.

Between 1958 and 1968 Gross Domestic Product in the EEC grew rapidly. Table 3 exaggerates the real change, in so far as it does not allow for the falling value of money. Since the argument of this chapter deals with parity of output between workers in agriculture and other sectors, and since agricultural output, too, is measured at current market prices, the comparison made is not invalidated. It seems improbable, however, that similar rates of increase in GNP can be sustained over a very long period. A downward adjustment in the rate of growth of GNP would, as Table 2 emphasises, make it easier to attain parity in relation to a fixed rate of increase in agricultural output. Incomes in farming and non-farming should then reach equality more quickly but at a lower level than is implicit in Table 3. In fact, as we have already seen, there are strong reasons to believe that growth in farm output may slacken. The effect of taking together these two factors—slower growth in GDP and in farm output—is to restore the period required to attain income equality and to imply that incomes, when equal, will be lower than a constant rate of increase based on Table 3 would suggest.

Apart from the effects of a slower rate of growth in output upon the date and level of income at which parity is attained, it is clear that slower rates of increase in GDP will have a substantial influence upon the prospects of moving manpower from farming to other sectors. A strongly expanding economy will tend to attract resources away from agriculture and so help its labour force to contract. For the policy-maker this situation presents a dilemma. Rapidly expanding GNP will aid the transfer of resources and ensure higher per caput levels of income. It will, however, make income parity more elusive. The commonly expressed view that agricultural income problems are best resolved by maintaining an expanding economy is true where the primary concern is the low absolute level of farm incomes. Where parity is a principal goal of agricultural policy it is not necessarily true. In this context assistance to the outward movement of manpower becomes more important, and also more likely to be fruitful.

The other variable which affects the prospect of parity is the size of the non-agricultural labour force. If GDP is assumed to be fixed, then the larger the non-agricultural labour force the nearer will the system approach income parity, although at a lower level of income than if there were fewer people. In reality this is taking note of a formal variable over which policy seems likely to have little influence. The rate of growth in population in Western Europe averaged about 1.0 per cent between 1958 and 1968. There seems little reason to expect this to accelerate in the remaining years of this century. Improved methods of birth control and changing social attitudes might lead to some reduction in the growth of population, whilst the labour force may be affected by longer periods of formal education and a decline in the number of women at work. However, it seems improbable that changes in the labour force will significantly alter the per caput level of income of the economy as a whole.

Before leaving the admittedly schematic data of Table 3 it is important to note its implications for the cost of agricultural policy. The figures for 1985 suggest, on the basis of the simplified assumptions employed, that parity of incomes might be attained by transferring an ever-decreasing fraction of the total income of the non-agricultural sector to agriculture. Thus the burden which agricultural support policies represent for the rest of the economy is likely to decline. This is true although the figures employed in Table 3 indicate that the total size of the transfer would rise from some 26 billion units of account in 1968 to 37 billion ua in 1985. More realistically, it should be noted that absolute parity of incomes is unlikely to be sought. Political pressures for additional aids to agriculture are likely to diminish considerably once farm incomes reach 70-80 per cent of incomes in other sectors. Table 3 shows that, if its assumptions were correct, no transfer at all would be required to attain 65 per cent of parity. A 75 per cent level of parity could be attained by the transfer of approximately 0.6 per cent of GNP, equivalent to some 10 billion ua. If the element of inflation built into the rate of growth specified in Table 3, some 3 per cent a year, was to be deducted, this would give a transfer of some 6 billion ua in 1968 prices, to be financed from a substantially larger GNP. The assumption, implicit in Table 3, that agricultural prices will maintain the same relationship to other prices as existed in 1968 is however unlikely to be true. In real terms the prices paid under the CAP have, as already mentioned, declined since they were first fixed, and it may be expected that this tendency will continue during the next 15 years. As a result the receipts of the farming sector, from the market, will compare less favourably with receipts by other sectors. Thus in the simplified circumstances postulated in Table 3, should the decline in real prices amount to 1 per cent a year up to 1985, then the transfer payments needed to restore farmers' incomes to a given level of parity with non-farm incomes would have to increase by a further 0.6 per cent of GNP, or 10 billion ua in current prices (again some 6 billion in 1968 prices) on the assumptions of Table 3. This would, then, be the whole transfer needed to provide 65 per cent of parity, in the face of prices declining by 1 per cent a year in real terms, while double the sum would be needed if 75 per cent of parity were to be achieved. As will be argued later in this chapter, the bulk of any such payments will be financed by national governments transferring money from their own taxpayers to their own farmers, and the level of such payments will clearly reflect the governments' political decisions. The purpose of this section has been to give some idea of the progress that is likely to be feasible in agricultural incomes at rates of transfer from other sectors of the economy which are not too far out of line with what member governments of the Community are transferring from their taxpayers to their farm people now.

The contribution of the common agricultural policy to income parity

The somewhat formal argument developed in the previous paragraphs confirms the view that there exists a self-correcting mechanism within the economy which will, given time, lead to a situation in which further income transfers to agriculture will not be needed. For those who visualise the significance of a united European economy in terms of the twenty-first century rather than the next few decades this is an important and reassuring conclusion. For many, however, such comfort will seem too distant and the problems of the intervening years more significant. For both groups it is evident that during the next 40 or 50 years incomes in agriculture, although approaching other incomes, will remain relatively low.

As a result, for the remainder of this century, at least, agricultural policy will continue to play an important part in the economic thinking of the European Community. It is therefore appropriate to review the adequacy of present arrangements for agriculture against the background of this longer-run consideration.

From the outset the primary goal of agricultural policy was to reach a settlement which would permit the Community to proceed to a full Common Market by the end of the transitional period. This in itself was difficult as the history of protracted discussion and delicately balanced compromise makes plain. In the process the attainment of a good agricultural policy, which would ease the inevitable process of adjustment facing the sector, was an important but secondary goal. Although the agreements which were finally negotiated represent a considerable political success it is hardly surprising that they do not correspond to the economic requirements of the agricultural industry.

Of the CAP's two parts, that which seeks to maintain prices has attracted most attention, commanded most expenditure and resulted in most difficulties. The element which is intended to promote structural adjustment, to assist farmers and the ancillary industries of agriculture to respond to the economic and technical opportunities of the mid-twentieth century, has been relatively neglected. The Commission is well aware of this deficiency and since the publication of the Mansholt Plan in 1968 has stressed the need for a more effective structural policy. Some successes have been scored by Dr. Mansholt. The price increases negotiated in 1971, as on previous occasions since the Community's prices were first fixed, do not fully compensate for the effect of inflation, but in the same package, the Council of Ministers approved arrangements which would permit member countries to carry out many of the proposals of the Reform Programme of 1968 and 1969 with an element of aid from the common fund of the EEC. There remain many obstacles before the Community can be said to have a truly common or adequate structural policy for its agricultural industry. Two of the more important difficulties require more explanation.

First, structural reform proposals must be designed to enable the rationalised farm to earn a satisfactory income for its occupier and to generate an adequate return on the capital employed. To do so existing capital assets must be reorganised and new capital invested. Such processes once undertaken are not easily reversed or amended. The basis of reorganisation must be the expected pattern of returns on the capital involved. To calculate such a return estimates are required both of the physical productivity of the farm as reorganised and of the prices which will be received for its products. At the moment the CAP seeks to maintain prices in order to protect the incomes of existing, badly placed, farmers. Whilst this may be defended on grounds of social policy it establishes a price level which is indefensible as a basis for investment. Capital deployed on the assumption that current prices will be maintained can generate a satisfactory return to its owner and user only if this price level is sustained. Since the present prices involve an income transfer to agriculture and since a reformed agriculture should be able to produce a given output at lower cost, the implication of investment based on existing prices being maintained in real terms is a continuing and ever-growing income transfer. The separation of price policy and structural policy is thus a fundamental weakness of the CAP. What is needed is a device which will enable agriculture to carry out investment based on an expected level of price which will not demand continuing support from the economy as a whole.

Second, the proposals for structural reform impinge much more clearly on the social, legal and institutional arrangements of each member country than do the price arrangements. This makes the challenge to established legal and administrative frameworks more apparent. Further, since within the Six, and even more in a Community of Ten, the present structure of agriculture varies greatly, the same proposal may have very different effects in different parts of the Community. For example, the offer of an annual payment of $1,000 to farmers who retire early would be well below the average earnings of most British farmers but well above incomes received by many farmers in Italy. Such considerations have led the Community to adopt permissive rather than mandatory arrangements for structural reform, allowing each government to apply its proposals within local conditions. There are real dangers in such devolution. A country which drags its feet on structural reform may calculate that, as a result, it will secure a larger fraction of the EEC market for farm goods and, if in doing so it generates Community surpluses, it will have to bear only part of the cost of their disposal. In the absence of some limitation to Community liability for surpluses, progress towards a more uniform approach to structural reform must await a closer degree of harmonisation in legal and social security provisions applied by member states. It will probably require, too, a considerable reduction in the differences in farming patterns among the member countries. Both requirements are likely to be satisfied as the Community matures but in each case progress is likely to be measured in decades rather than years.

The immediate possibilities for the policy-maker are thus somewhat limited. The development of a common structural policy for the Community as a whole is likely to be approached by stages rather than at one bold step. As a result greater reliance must be placed on the ability of the Community to manipulate the prices farmers receive. Even here the options are narrowly defined. Substantial price increases would generate output which could not be sold within the Community and which would therefore lead to an unacceptable rise in the costs of the CAP. On the other hand, an attempt to cut prices suddenly would encounter fierce political resistance both among the farming community and within the Council of Ministers. In recent years the most that has been attainable has been a gradual squeeze on the real price level as a result of the failure to increase farm prices in step with inflation.

The fact that prices cannot be raised, nor a prolonged increase in the volume of production be viewed with equanimity, means that within the CAP arrangements significant constraints are placed on the level of agricultural output. As we have seen, such constraints require a continued rapid outflow of agricultural manpower if the level of farm incomes is to be raised and parity with other sectors approached. However, the rate at which men can be moved from farming is not easily accelerated without unacceptable social cost. To a large extent out-migration will hinge on such independently determined variables as the age distribution of the agricultural population, the location of new industries and the overall growth of the economy.

Agricultural policy alone can affect these matters to only a marginal extent.

If neither price policy nor structural policy can, over the next decade, secure a satisfactory level of income for many of those who work in farming some new initiative in agricultural policy will be demanded of an enlarged EEC. At this point it is possible to trace a coincidence of interest between the Community of Six as a whole and that of the largest new member, the United Kingdom.

A policy for the coming decades

The central difficulty with the common agricultural policy, for the United Kingdom, is that any system of inter-sectoral transfers in favour of agriculture in the Community as a whole will involve a disproportionate contribution from Britain. This arises because of the relatively small share of agriculture in her overall economic activity. Critics of membership in Britain have a point when they complain that we would, under Community rules, be required to finance adjustments in other countries which we have already made for ourselves.

The British Government, in its 1971 White Paper,[1] refuses to speculate upon the size of the Community's budget, or of UK contributions to it, beyond the end of the transitional period. This reluctance to name a figure is understandable. It must be understood in the light of the Community's assurance that, if unacceptable situations should arise, "the very survival of the Community would demand that the institutions find equitable solutions" (1971 White Paper, p. 25). Any long-term assessment of the possible size of the UK contribution to the common agricultural policy must then seek to probe the boundaries of acceptability to the various countries involved.

The cost to Britain of transferring the proceeds of import levies to the common fund may, as Dr. Josling suggests in Chapter 4, prove to be lower than earlier, gloomier forecasts had predicted. The proceeds of customs duties on trade with third countries could fall as a result of further trade liberalisation moves within the framework of Gatt. On both these scores it seems possible that the receipts of the Community from 'its

---

[1] *The United Kingdom and the European Communities*, Cmnd 4715, HMSO, 1971.

own' sources of revenue might be less than expected. If the Community's budget were not to be reduced a greater burden would fall on revenues raised through taxation, equivalent to a value-added tax of up to 1 per cent.

Moves in this direction would reduce the discriminatory and adverse effect of the way in which Community finance is raised so far as the UK is concerned. They would not, however, diminish the importance of the fact that Community expenditure on agricultural policy in Britain would be proportionately less than in other countries. Hence the British Government would have an incentive both to restrict further increases in agricultural price levels, which would tend to raise levies, and to contain any increase in the aggregate size of Community expenditure in support of agriculture. In short it does not seem implausible to suggest that increases in the net cost to Britain of the CAP beyond £300 million are likely to prove unacceptable.

At this point a British government might effectively exercise a veto on further development within the Community. It is clearly in the common interest that such an extreme situation should be avoided. Within the Community there exist other political pressures which are likely to restrain any uncontrolled rise in either prices paid to farmers or the overall cost of the CAP. It seems certain that some compromise would have to be sought between the contending interests.

The position is most difficult for those governments that have a large proportion of their population engaged in agriculture. In France, Italy and Ireland, pressures to improve the incomes of farmers are likely to be especially strong. In the Netherlands too, the CAP system, which enables exports to be sold, within or outside the Community, at higher prices than would otherwise prevail is likely to be strongly defended. For these countries gains seem probable from further price increases and an accompanying growth in the EEC budget.

Such a view is, however, essentially short-run and short-sighted. In a longer-run context the wealth of each of these countries is most likely to be enhanced by an increase in the overall prosperity of the Community. This would require for exporting as well as importing countries a shift of resources, especially manpower, from farming but it would permit a more rapid rise in living standards for all sections of their population

than would otherwise take place. If agricultural policy were
allowed to become so costly as to substantially impede economic
growth then these countries, with others, would suffer. Again
it is clear that each of these countries might reasonably expect,
on the basis of comparative cost, to become permanent suppliers
of agricultural products to the rest of the Community. Maintenance of high prices through the CAP means that producers
in importing countries are encouraged to remain in business
and even expand their output. As a result surplus production,
which can be sold only with the aid of subsidies for export or
denaturing, is likely to grow and the cost of the CAP to rise.
In such a situation political pressures from countries which
make major net transfer payments in support of the CAP—
West Germany and the UK—would become very important.
Such pressures might lead to a system of quotas to restrain
production, with the accompanying probability that they would
frustrate the attempts of agricultural exporting members to
secure a larger, permanent share in the market of importing
members. Alternatively, the pressures might lead to attempts
to reduce the 'common' element in the financing of agricultural
policy. As a result the burden of maintaining the livelihood of
the farming population might fall increasingly on the countries
with relatively large farming populations.

The failure of the Community to increase prices, in step with
inflation, since their initial fixing, and the intention that by far
the larger share of the cost of Community structural reform
programmes should be borne by the member countries, under-
line the strength of the resistance to a growth in the cost of the
CAP among existing members. British attitudes are likely to
reinforce this resistance. It seems unlikely, therefore, that
expenditure on agriculture at a Community level will rise as
rapidly over the next decade as during the past 10 years.
Although the evidence presented in Table 3 suggests that
agricultural income parity might be approached with the
transfer to agriculture of a diminishing fraction of the income
of other sectors, it makes it plain, too, that even in so favourable
a situation the total size of the transfer, measured in units of
account, would rise substantially. Complete parity of income,
attained by transfers between sectors, is unlikely to be attained.
If it were it would remove healthy pressures which tend to

redistribute resources into a more productive pattern. However, the persistence of marked inequalities of the order experienced in recent years—farm incomes some 55-60 per cent of non-farm incomes—would lead to discontent among farmers and embarrassment for politicians.

Table 3 suggests that by the mid-1980s, if prices are squeezed downwards at a rate of some 1 per cent a year in real terms, the total transfer needed to raise farm income levels to 75 per cent of the level in other sectors could be of the order of $12 billion at 1968 money values, and that a ratio of 65 per cent would be reached with transfers at about half that level. The resources for such transfer payments would be derived, as at present, in part from the national governments and in part from the Community budget. Since strong resistance must be expected to any sharp increase in expenditure from common funds upon agriculture, the Community's contribution to these transfers would certainly be limited. If the funds available for the execution of the common agricultural policy were to be 4.5 billion units of account, and some 2.5 billion ua were required to maintain the common price level, Community support for other types of agricultural policy would be limited to some 2 billion ua. A British gross contribution to a budget of this size would, if it was proportionate to Britain's share in the Community GNP, be some £300 million; and if it were as high as 25 per cent it would be some £400 million. A larger contribution than this would certainly seem inequitable and would, as suggested above, probably be regarded as unacceptable by a British government, which could rest its case on the Community's assurance that was cited on page 110.

Continuing Community support for agriculture, limited to this order of magnitude, would imply that the major share of farm support costs would continue to be met from the resources of national governments. To ensure that national policies were consistent with the interests of the Community as a whole, the available common funds seem likely to be used as a lever. Thus something like one-fifth of the costs of approved structural or income policies might be met from Brussels—and this would be consistent with the orders of magnitude indicated by the illustrative figures given in the preceding paragraph. Such payments would be greatest in those countries where incomes are lowest and the structural problems more severe. Britain would therefore gain relatively little in the short run, but her longer-run position would be improved.

The British interest can, in the light of the above, be quite shortly stated. It is first that the rate of adjustment should be as rapid as possible so that the period during which inter-sectoral transfers are needed is shortened. Second, the cost of adjustment must, as far as possible, fall upon the countries concerned and the remaining cost be distributed in terms of ability to pay, rather than in relation to net imports of food.

The Community, too, would benefit from measures which increased the effectiveness of the common agricultural policy in raising farm incomes and which contained its cost. Greater effectiveness requires further adjustment in the labour force and in agricultural structures. If it is to promote such adjustment, in a situation in which significant restraints exist on the extent to which prices can be manipulated or structural reform financed from Community resources, some separate device for aiding the incomes of farmers who remain poor is required. On a small scale the Community has already recognised this for Italy in its arrangements of May 1971. In West Germany, measures taken following the revaluation of the deutschemark show a similar concern to protect farm incomes whilst maintaining the common Community price level specified in units of account. Should such a system of support become more generalised throughout the Community, prices might more easily be used to indicate to modernising farmers the probable value of their output. In this way a more easily sustained pattern of agricultural activity could be created.

A variety of ways in which this might be attained have already been proposed.[2] The essential feature is that the farming community shall not find its longer-term welfare impaired by measures which fail to encourage it to modernise and adjust to a stable long-run price level as rapidly as possible.

In a policy such as has been outlined, the UK would find that its contribution as a result of the price provisions gradually

---

[2] See, for example, J. Marsh and C. Ritson, *Agricultural Policy and the Common Market*, Chatham House/PEP, March 1971; *A New Policy for Agriculture*, Federal Trust, 1970; and P. Uri *et al.*, *A Future for European Agriculture*, The Atlantic Institute, Paris, 1970.

declined, as Community and world prices became closer. If, as seems possible, world prices of the products Britain imports rose, then the disadvantage of the CAP for the UK would be further diminished. Contributions to structural reform might tend to rise, but here the difficulties of creating a truly common policy are so substantial as to place limits on the extent to which common financing would be appropriate. Income support would represent a new form of expenditure. For this the most acceptable basis for finance seems to be a combination of social payments from member governments and a common element related to the overall income level in each country rather than to net imports. This would diminish the proportion of cost borne by the UK although, since her receipts would be relatively low, there would still be a net income outflow to the rest of the Community. Such an outflow seems inescapable so long as there is a policy transferring income to agriculture without adequate compensation as a result of other policies. However, in this case the payments made in respect of income support would decline as the existing farming community retired. In terms of the long-run structural adjustments considered in this chapter, this might significantly shorten the period during which the UK was at a disadvantage as a result of the operation of a common policy for agriculture.

Apart from its capacity to meet more adequately the overall goal of raising incomes in agriculture such a policy would have several important long-run benefits. First, it would allow for differing regional emphasis in income support, designed to meet the very heterogeneous conditions to be found within the Community. Second, it would permit available resources to help most those members of the farming population who are, under existing arrangements, poorest. Third, it would open up the possibility of a more constructive dialogue concerning world trade in agricultural products. On each of these scores the Community as a whole would benefit and the interests of the UK be safeguarded.

Conclusions

This chapter has attempted to place the agricultural problems of the EEC in a longer time context. In doing so it has demonstrated that there does exist a process of change within agriculture and the economy at large which, if it is not impeded, will ultimately raise farm income levels and close the gap between them and incomes from other types of employment. This process is, however, even on the most favourable assumptions likely to be protracted and does not afford relief to the immediate pressures on the farming community. As a result agricultural policy has a positive role to play for many years. The arguments developed here indicate that a more positive policy is politically feasible and that such a policy should not demand a large increase in the EEC budget or in the level of UK contributions after the end of the transitional period. This policy would indeed represent a lower cost to the Community in real and eventually in money terms, and a corresponding reduction in the UK contribution could therefore ultimately be expected.

Chapter 6

ESTIMATES OF THE STATIC BALANCE-OF-PAYMENTS AND WELFARE COSTS COMPARED*

by Marcus H. Miller

THE purpose of this chapter is to bring together in comparable form some published and unpublished estimates of the effects on the United Kingdom balance of payments[1] of entry into the EEC, and the resource costs associated with them. The effects referred to are the 'static' effects measured at the end of the transition period,[2] no account being taken of any 'dynamic' effects,[3] nor of the transitional arrangements.

---

*This chapter is an article that appeared in the *National Institute Economic Review*, August 1971, adapted to take account of the work presented by Williamson and Josling in Chapters 2 and 4 of this book.

[1] Excluding invisibles and private capital flows, other than payments to, and receipts from, the Community budget.

[2] For the 1970 White Paper this would be for 1978. It has now been agreed that, while most of the transitional arrangements will be complete by then, there will be two years (1978, 1979) when some limit is placed on the rate of increase of the UK contribution, see 1971 White Paper, paragraphs 94 and 95 (the principal proposals for the transitional arrangements governing the budgetary contribution, and some of these estimates for the liability at the end of the transition period, are shown later in this chapter). The estimates of this chapter should thus be considered as applying in 1980, in that they do not assume UK contributions to the Community budget to be limited by any such short-run correctives, and no account is taken of the timing of the incidence of the resource costs listed, important though this may be.

[3] These dynamic effects are taken to include economies of scale and the effects of increased competition and investment.

Altogether, seven separate estimates are involved in the comparisons. One is based on combining the results of the work by Josling[4] on food and by Williamson[5] on trade in manufactures. Another estimate is built up round the figures given in the 1971 White Paper.[6] Two further estimates are drawn directly from the 1970 White Paper,[7] and correspond roughly to the 'high' and 'low' elasticity calculations given there. Two are drawn from Kaldor's work.[8] These are the 'high' and 'low' estimates he gives, based on balance-of-payments variants drawn from the 1970 White Paper, for each of which he has calculated the resource costs. Finally, there is an estimate based on a general equilibrium trade model constructed by John Spencer and the author of the present chapter.[9]

For present purposes the raw data given in these various estimates are deficient in several respects. In most cases, for example, the sources described do not provide a resource cost calculation while some others do not give explicit figures for the amounts expected to be transferred to the Community budget, or do not indicate clearly the breakdown of costs arising from adherence to the common agricultural policy (CAP). As a result it was necessary to work through a number of additional computations in order to provide the missing information, and of course to do so on the basis of assumptions compatible with those made in the original estimate concerned. This inevitably

---

[4]See Chapter 4, above.

[5]See Chapter 2, above, but note that the effects included there due to economies of scale, increased competition and investment are *not* included with the Josling-Williamson figures reported here as they fall under the heading of 'dynamic' effects. Williamson's work is a development of his earlier study. *On Estimating the Income Effects of British Entry to the EEC*, Surrey Papers in Economics, No. 5, University of Surrey, June 1971.

[6] *The United Kingdom and the European Communities*, Cmnd 4715, HMSO, July 1971.

[7] *Britain and the European Communities: An Economic Assessment*, Cmnd 4289, HMSO, February 1970.

[8] N. Kaldor, The Dynamic Effects of the Common Market, Chapter 4 of *Destiny or Delusion*, edited by Douglas Evans, Victor Gollancz, 1971.

[9] M. H. Miller and J. Spencer, *The Static Economic Effects of the UK Joining the EEC and their Welfare Significance*, London School of Economics, 1971 (mimeograph).

involved a certain amount of 'guesstimation' and it should in fairness be pointed out that the final sets of estimates compared include many elements of attribution and reconstructions, some of which may in detail be wrong. But it is not felt that there is any major inconsistency or implausibility involved in the procedures used, which are explained in some detail.

The need to explain and justify the steps taken to place all the estimates on a comparable basis does, however, somewhat complicate the task of presentation, and the reader is asked, in the first instance, to take some of the figures 'on trust'. The precise basis for the additional computations is subsequently made clear.

The plan of this chapter is therefore to proceed immediately to the comparison of the basic figures, i.e. the balance-of-payments and resource-cost (or welfare) effects which are given in Table 1. This table identifies the main categories of cost or gain involved, and after explaining the nature of these the next section draws out the main features of the alternative estimates. The following two sections then explain the basis for the food costs attributed to the 1970 and 1971 White Papers as a result of application of the CAP, and deal in detail with the methods used to derive resource-cost figures from the balance-of-payments estimates. A further section deals briefly with various aspects of the scale and timing of the UK contribution to the Community budget. A final section draws up some broad conclusions.

There are two appendices to the chapter. The first of these gives some details of the Miller-Spencer model, the results of which are included in the basic comparison. It should be emphasised that the Miller-Spencer model was designed to investigate the relative importance of different aspects of entry and not to provide detailed value estimates. The results are reported here largely because the methods used to estimate the resource costs in this chapter, when applied to the output of the model, gave reasonably good estimates of the actual welfare changes, thus providing some warrant for the use of the crude 'welfare multipliers' described below. The resource costs of correcting a balance-of-payments loss are estimated in this paper on the basis that the price adjustment to equilibrium is effected by devaluation. Appendix II provides a formal analysis and an illustrative figuring of the additional resource costs arising where

Table 1: A Comparison of Some (Static) Balance-of-Payments and Welfare Costs of Entry[a]

£ million, 1969 prices

	Josling-Williamson	Miller-Spencer	1971 White Paper	1970 White Paper		Kaldor	
				elastic	inelastic	'low'	'high'
1. Gains from trade creation	— / *58*	— / *56*	— / *...*	— / *...*	— / *...*	— / *...*	— / *...*
2. Balance-of-payment deficit on manufactures	100 / *33*	151 / *54*	... / *...*	35 / *12*	58 / *70*	(125) / *20*	(275) / *50*
3. Import saving on food	—225 / *—74*	—480 / *—172*	—140 / *—47*	—320 / *—107*	—200 / *—240*	— / *—*	— / *—*
4. Cost of the rise in price of imported food	70 / *87*	167 / *206*	190 / *238*	235 / *294*	255 / *485*	200 / *267*	200 / *267*
5. *Sub-total*: Cost of entry before official transfers	—55 / *—12*	—162 / *32*	50 / *191*	—50 / *199*	113 / *315*	(325) / *287*	(475) / *317*
Official transfers							
6. Levies on food	81 / *101*	282 / *350*	80 / *100*	167 / *209*	176 / *334*	200 / *267*	200 / *267*
7. Customs duties	240 / *300*	222 / *275*	240 / *300*	240 / *300*	240 / *456*	240 / *319*	240 / *320*
8. Value-added tax	—b / *—b*	—b / *—b*	75 / *94*	—b / *—b*	—b / *—b*	— / *—*	230 / *306*
9. Receipts from the Community	—b / *—b*	—b / *—b*	—100 / *—125*	—b / *—b*	—b / *—b*	—100 / *—133*	—50 / *—66*
10. *Sub-total*: Transfer costs of entry	321 / *401*	504 / *625*	295 / *369*	407 / *509*	416 / *790*	340 / *453*	620 / *827*
11. Total cost	266 / *389*	342 / *657*	345 / *560*	357 / *708*	529 / *1,105*	(665) / *740*	(1,095) / *1,144*

a The figures in roman print are for balance-of-payments costs and those in italics are for welfare costs. The estimates refer to the period after transition. The figures are of costs, so negative signs indicate gains.

b Nil for rows 8 and 9 together.

— indicates nil.

... indicates 'not available, taken as nil'.

Additional notes:

The sources of the estimates are given in the text and footnote references. Figures given for the estimates include elements of attribution based on procedures described in the text. Kaldor's estimates of balance-of-payments effects are drawn from the 1970 White Paper, but not the resource costs; the former include the effects of a wage-spiral and so are given in parentheses. No explicit estimate of import saving in agriculture was given by Kaldor. The Miller-Spencer model assumes a 20 per cent rise in food prices. The Josling-Williamson estimates are derived from Josling's work on agriculture, Chapter 4 above, and Williamson's on manufactures, Chapter 2 above, supplemented by estimates taken from the 1970 White Paper. Josling derived the actual balance of payments figures used in rows 3, 4 and 6 from his own results in Chapter 4. The figure of £81 million in row 6 is given by subtracting the customs duties on mutton and lamb from the £123.5 million appearing in his Table 7 (p.88 above), and then taking 90 per cent of this result. The transfer of customs duties on mutton and lamb is included with other customs duties in row 7. The dynamic effects measured by Williamson in Chapter 2 are not included here. The 1970 White Paper balance-of-payments figures shown in the table are corrected for a wage-price spiral effect (see p. 142). The details of the food cost estimates both for this and for the 1971 White Paper are explained on pp. 133-139.

the method of adjustment is not devaluation, but deflation.

Comparisons of the estimates
Sources of gain and loss

Table 1 associates resource (welfare) costs with the balance-of-payments effects of entry estimated in the various sources. The balance-of-payments effects may be divided into three main categories whose nature can be briefly outlined.

The most easily classified balance-of-payments costs are those incurred in the form of an unrequited or transfer payment. Costs (and gains) of this type are distinguished in the lower half of Table 1. They include the transfer to the Community budget of levies on food (row 6 in the table), of customs duties (row 7) and of some of the revenue from a domestic tax on value-added (VAT) (row 8), although these payments may be in part offset by receipts (row 9).[10]

The second main category of balance-of-payments costs comprises those arising from the need to pay more by way of higher prices for what we import. The principal example here, of course, is food and the extra cost of the higher prices which will have to be paid for the quantities finally imported after entry is what is listed in row 4. In principle there should be a corresponding estimate for manufactures, but only Williamson's study carried such an estimate and this was sufficiently small to be omitted.[11] There is clearly a similarity between making an official transfer of the kind comprised under our first category of costs, and simply paying more for what was previously available at a cheaper price. In fact, this second category of cost can be usefully

---

[10]Under the terms agreed, 90 per cent of the levies and duties on food and other goods will be transferred to the Community (after transition), together with the proceeds of a VAT up to a maximum represented by a VAT at the rate of 1 per cent, the actual amount being determined by the level of Community budget expenditures in relation to receipts of duty and levy revenues. Part of Community budget expenditures, on the other hand, will accrue to the UK.

[11] Pages 28-30 above. The amount involved is approximately £8 million.

thought of as a transfer payment of funds collected by raising a tax on food.[12]

The remaining balance-of-payments effects fall in our third category, and taken together can be treated as the balance-of-payments effects of tariff changes. The effects to be expected from the tariff adjustments are broadly as follows. On the import side the removal of tariffs on manufactured imports by the UK will lead to a rise in imports, while the imposition of the common external tariff (CET) on manufactures from the Commonwealth, and the levying of tariffs and duties on food imports from all non-EEC sources will operate in the other direction. As regards exports, the removal by the EEC countries of their present tariffs against us should lead to a rise in the demand for our exports, but the EEC countries' reduction of tariffs on imports from *other* entrant countries and their reciprocal tariff reduction on imports from the EEC together with, in due course, the end of Commonwealth preference for UK manufactures, will operate in the other direction. The net effect of these changes, on the balance of payments in manufactures and in food,[13] is set down in rows 2 and 3 respectively.

From the point of view of calculating the resource costs or welfare effects associated with the three main categories of balance-of-payments effects described, use may be made of the analogy suggested above between the costs arising from higher food prices and a transfer funded by taxing food. That is, we can amalgamate the balance-of-payments effects associated with official transfers and the costs of higher priced imported foods into a single category from this point of view. This would leave us with just two categories of balance-of-payments effects for the welfare calculations: those associated with official transfers or items of a transfer-like nature, and those associated with the tariff changes.

---

[12] The main reason for treating the two separately in the basic table is that whereas the higher cost of partner imports is an unavoidable cost of joining the union and is so treated in standard customs union theory, the pure tax transfers of the first category are not. Customs union theory normally excludes such transfers by the assumption that consumers in a member country receive back as a lump sum any tariffs paid on imports (and do not transfer them to a partner).

[13] At world prices. For the breakdown of food cost figures into two categories, see below, pages 133-139.

The welfare estimates corresponding to the two categories of balance-of-payments effects relevant for the purpose are arrived at on the following basis.[14] For the tariff-induced changes, the method of calculation was to divide the balance-of-payments deficit figure by the familiar 'sum of the import elasticities minus one'. The basic idea is that the balance-of-payments deficit must involve a relative over-pricing of UK goods; so its rectification must involve raising the relative price of foreign goods, i.e. a worsening in the terms of trade. It is this worsening in the terms of trade which is the resource cost measured in rows 2 and 3. For the transfer or 'transfer-like' effects, the calculation is different. To compute the resource costs here one might, as first approximation, simply take the amount to be transferred and add to it the extra cost of improving the balance of payments by that amount, using the formula mentioned above for the latter calculation. But calculating the extra cost (the so-called 'added burden' of the transfer) in this way neglects the fact that the raising of taxes in the paying country and their reduction in the recipient countries will have income effects which also affect the balance of payments. If, as a result of these income effects, UK residents import less and the EEC countries import more—from the UK among others—this should help improve the balance of payments and so place less burden on the need for price adjustment.[15] The formula used to calculate the resource costs consequently takes approximate account of this feature of transfer payments and the welfare effect associated with transfer payments in rows 4 and 6-10 of the table is the transfer plus the added burden after allowing for income effects.

The division of the balance-of-payments and welfare effects set out in the table and described above is fairly straightforward except perhaps for the division into two parts of the balance-of-payments effects on the food bill in rows 3 and 4. The change in the cost of (net) imports of food is broken into two com-

---

[14] The details of the calculations are given below in the section headed 'The calculation of the welfare estimates', pp. 139-143 below.
[15] Indeed if the allocation of the marginal unit of income by source and type of product in the EEC were identical to that in the UK, there would be no need for price adjustments and hence no added burden.

ponents as follows (where M is the quantity of imports and p their price):

$$\Delta(pM) = (p+\Delta p)(M+\Delta M)-pM$$
$$= pM+p\Delta M+\Delta p(M+\Delta M)-pM$$
$$= p\Delta M+\Delta p(M+\Delta M)$$

= change in quantity at initial prices (row 3) *plus* change in price of terminal quantity (row 4).

The first part of this change is the kind of balance-of-payments effect one might expect from levying a tariff on food, the revenue from which is retained in the country. The second part would be the revenue yielded by such a tariff, which in this case is also a balance-of-payments effect as it is paid over as a higher price for food. Even though the two may cancel in balance-of-payments terms it is very important to realise that they will not cancel in resource terms as the import saving (row 3) requires additional resources or involves a loss of consumers' surplus, while the extra price paid for food buys nothing that was not enjoyed before.

At this stage it is necessary to recognise, however, that static welfare effects may (indeed usually will) also arise in situations of balanced trade, i.e., where there are no balance-of-payments effects. These welfare effects, recognised in tariff theory as gains in the efficiency of production and consumption resulting from the removal of tariff 'distortions', are represented in row 1 of the table. The estimates reported in this row are derived directly from the sources quoted, where they are available.

This general account of the classification used in the table clears the way for discussing the estimates in detail.

Trade creation

Row 1 comprises the estimates of welfare gains associated with increased efficiency, the classical gains in producers' and consumers' surpluses at a balanced level of trade. In fact only two of the sources reviewed yield such estimates and even these are not strictly comparable. The figure attributed to Josling-Williamson relates only to manufacturing, so takes no account of losses arising in agriculture.[16] The figure attributed to Miller-

---

[16]On the other hand the gains due to economies of scale given in Chapter 2 are excluded. Allowing for these gains would add £170 million to this entry.

Spencer is in fact a residual estimate, being the amount remaining after all other resource costs had been accounted for. In principle, however, it should therefore incorporate effects arising in agriculture as well as in manufacturing.

The trade creation figures were incorporated separately in the table to give some idea of the order of magnitude of the *static* gains due to reallocation of consumption and production but not directly associated with the balance of payments. As appears to be common in such cases, the resultant figures are very small.

The balance of trade in manufactures

Balance-of-payments and associated welfare effects arising from the balance of trade in manufactures appear in row 2.

Comparison of the balance-of-payments effects is complicated by the possibility of a wage-price spiral arising on entry. The figures attributed to Kaldor include such an effect; and those given for the 1970 White Paper are based on figures which initially included a spiral but have been re-worked here (on assumptions indicated on pp. 142-3 below) to exclude the estimated amount of the spiral effect. Both the Josling-Williamson and the Miller-Spencer studies exclude the effects of any such spiral from their balance-of-payments estimates (assuming, therefore, either no spiral or one which is offset by a corresponding devaluation). The 1971 White Paper dismisses the prospect of a spiral on the grounds that the fall in prices of manufactured goods will offset the rise in food prices (para. 43).

Aside from the question of the wage-price spiral, it is clear that the balance-of-payments effect in row 2 would be difficult to predict. Nevertheless, the 1970 White Paper talked of an exercise using demand and supply elasticities and tariff changes underlying its estimates (*ibid.*, para. 58), and the Miller-Spencer results are derived from such an exercise in tariff changes in general equilibrium. In the face of such large changes as are in prospect, Williamson and the 1971 White Paper doubt the value of such calculations and prefer to appeal to the historical experience of the other members of the EEC.[17] Whatever they may feel about the short-run reactions of industry to the

---

[17] 1971 White Paper (para. 45).

tariff changes over the transitional period, the Government are confident that the longer-run structural changes will have a "positive and substantial" effect upon the balance of trade (*loc. cit.*). No official forecast was given for the effect on the balance of payments in manufactures by the end of the transition period, so it is taken to be zero in Table 1. It is interesting to note that Williamson, who makes the same appeal to the experience of the present EEC countries, provides an estimate of a £100 million deficit, which is actually more pessimistic than the 1970 White Paper, net of the assumed effects of the wage-price spiral.

It is important to observe that on the basis for calculating the associated resource costs employed in this paper—which is that adjustment takes place through the exchange rate—the wage-price spiral effect is irrelevant.[18] The reason is that the spiral itself may be looked upon as a revaluation which is cancelled by an equal devaluation. The welfare calculation given in row 2 therefore excludes any cost in respect of the wage-price spiral effect, and this is true even for Kaldor's estimates despite the fact that the effects of such a spiral are still present in Kaldor's balance-of-payments figures. On this basis the various welfare figures are fully comparable and it appears that the welfare losses associated with the balance-of-payments deficit in manufactured goods are relatively slight. The highest estimate is that associated with the 'inelastic' variant of the 1970 White Paper and this is a result of the assumption of inelastic demand responses which mean that a larger movement in the terms of trade is required to wipe out a given deficit.

Import saving on food

Row 3 incorporates estimates of the net effect of consumption and production responses on the net balance (exports minus imports) of trade in food valued at *world* prices. The working underlying some of the figures shown is explained in a later section. It is important to realise that not all the rise in market prices of food which is foreseen will stimulate production, as

---

[18] If, however, the assumption of exchange rate flexibility is ruled out, then any inflation is likely to impose an adjustment cost due to the deflation required to correct the resultant deficit. An analysis of this kind of adjustment is given in Appendix II.

some part of such a rise will merely be raising the prices facing consumers towards the level at which prices are now set for producers through the medium of subsidies.

The Kaldor estimates do not include any figure for this part of the effect of entry on the food bill (his figure of £200 million is on account of the higher food prices paid on imports from EEC countries and is treated by him simply as a transfer payment).[19] The balance-of-payments estimate derived from the Miller-Spencer model is unrealistically high because of the very high import elasticity assumed for food. For the White Papers there is some contrast between the higher figures for import saving associated with the larger price gap assumed for the 1970 White Paper and the lower figure associated with the smaller price gap of the 1971 White Paper. Josling's estimate is based on similar price-gap assumptions as the later White Paper, but predicts a higher figure for import saving which suggests that he has higher demand elasticities.

The rise in price of imported food; levies and duties on food

The difference in assumption about the price gap is more evident in the entries in rows 4 and 6. It is convenient to take these two rows together because it is easier to predict the total of food imports than the composition, [20] and so the sum of the two rows is rather more reliable than the distribution between them.[21]

On this basis, there is a contrast between the Kaldor, Miller-Spencer and 1970 White Paper estimates on the one hand, and the Josling-Williamson and 1971 White Paper figures on the other hand. The total balance-of-payments costs arising in the first group of estimates lie in the range of £400-£450 million, whilst the second group of estimates range from £150 million to £270 million. An important reason for the difference lies in the smaller price gap assumed by the latter two estimates. (Further details are given in a later section.) As between the two White Papers

[19] *op. cit.*, p.91.
[20] cf. 1970 White Paper, paras. 35-37.
[21] Special arrangements as regards New Zealand imports after transition, for example, would probably have the effect of lowering the figures in row 4, but raising them in row 6 with little effect on the total.

the difference in cost may be very roughly related to the fall in the predicted rise in retail food prices, as follows. The 1970 White Paper put the total rise in retail food prices at 18-26 per cent (mid-point 22 per cent) whilst the 1971 White Paper suggests an increase of 15 per cent. Lowering the 1970 White Paper figure of around £400 million by the proportionate reduction in the predicted retail price rise gives roughly the figure attributed to the 1971 White Paper in Table 1 for the sum of rows 4 and 6. The Josling estimate also assumes a food price increase of the order of 15 per cent in the UK aggregate food price index as a consequence of joining the EEC.

The commodity-by-commodity study on which Josling's estimates are based assesses the rise in the aggregate retail food price index in the UK as a result of adopting the common agricultural policy to be 15 per cent, and in producer prices to be 10 per cent, but the figure for the extra cost of food imports together with levies, a total of £151 million, is significantly lower than the figure of £270 million attributed to the 1971 White Paper, which has similar price assumptions. The detailed breakdown between rows 4 and 6 is also rather different as between the studies. The calculations underlying Josling's estimates are given in Chapter 2 above, where considerable changes in the pattern of consumption are predicted. Further detail on the food cost estimates attributed to the White Papers is given on pages 133-139 below.

Transfers of customs duties

The figure of £240 million given in the 1970 White Paper (para. 42), for this item has been used for both estimates based on this White Paper, and Kaldor used the same figure for his estimates. The sum of £222 million appearing for the Miller-Spencer study was the result of applying an average tariff rate of 5 per cent to all non-EEC non-food imports. This low average rate of tariff was designed to take approximate account of the near zero rates of CET on raw material imports. The White Paper 1970 figure was incorporated in the Josling-Williamson column and also for the 1971 White Paper, although the former make no estimate of their own and the latter does even say that "it is not possible to make any valid estimate of our levy and duty receipts in the 1980s" (*ibid.*, para. 95). The agreement across this row largely reflects a lack of independent estimates.

Value-added tax transfers; receipts from Community budget

Rows 8 and 9 may be considered together, partly because their absolute values are assumed to be practically equal for some of the estimates but mainly because changes in them are likely to be offsetting. The maximum VAT liability, corresponding to a VAT at the rate of 1 per cent, was put at £230 million in the 1970 White Paper (para. 43), but the amount actually paid will probably be less than that. It depends on the difference between the size of the Community budget and the aggregate receipts of levies and duties from all member countries, and, as the 1971 White Paper (para. 45), asserts, "the gap between these two amounts would have to widen very considerably indeed if member countries were to be required to contribute the full 1 per cent of VAT". The same section continues "This gap is only likely to widen . . . if the enlarged Community were to spend much more on non-agricultural activities, such as industrial and regional developments, in which case the UK could expect to enjoy much larger receipts". This last suggests that errors of measurement in the totals here may offset each other.

Kaldor took maximum VAT and minimum (zero) VAT contributions and combined them with the low and high receipts figures (£50 million and £100 million) contained in the 1970 White Paper, para. 40. The 1971 White Paper does estimate receipts of £100 million for 1977 (*ibid.*, Table 2, page 94). This suggests that the figure of £100 million may be the better estimate to use for the 1970 White Paper. Since, moreover, during the negotiations a figure of £100 million emerged as a reasonable estimate of VAT contribution, this gives the zero sum attributed to the 1970 White Paper, and also to the Josling-Williamson and Miller-Spencer columns.

There is one argument which suggests that the narrowing of the gap between EEC and world food prices may lower the £100 million estimate for VAT just mentioned. The argument is that while the cost of food price support policies, which bulk large in Community expenditure, should fall in line with a narrowing price gap, only the income from tariffs and levies on food imports will fall proportionately, there being no reason for non-food duties to change. Hence the difference between expenditure and income from *all* duties and levies, which is filled by the VAT contributions, should fall with the narrowing price gap. A reduced figure of £75 million was attributed to the 1971 White Paper for the VAT contribution on these grounds.

For reasons implicit in the above discussion it is clear that some suggestive evidence exists to narrow the wide range of Kaldor's estimates to a net figure of near zero.

Overall review by source

We turn now to a comparison of the various estimates of these static costs of entry as a whole. The overall balance-of-payments and welfare costs of row 11 are plotted in Chart 1 to assist the comparison.

While the estimates seem fairly widely dispersed, there are some elements of difference that can easily be explained. Firstly,

Chart 1: Estimates of the (Static) Balance-of-Payments and Welfare Costs of Entry

£ million, 1969 prices

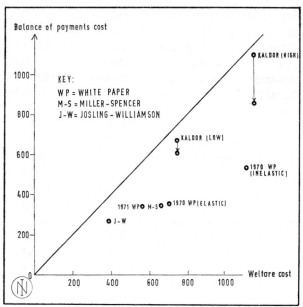

Source: Table 1

the arrows in the chart indicate the effects of 'correcting' the balance-of-payments figures in Kaldor's estimates by the same factors as were used for the White Paper (and Kaldor's figures are those of the 1970 White Paper). This eliminates one source of non-comparability, and narrows the range of the balance-of-payments figures related to our purpose. Secondly, the fact that Kaldor has given a *range* and not a central estimate for the VAT contribution to the budget *less* receipts, whereas the figures attributed to other sources are in the nature of mid-point estimates, also explains why Kaldor's 'high' estimate is so large. The other estimates contain a figure of practically zero for the sum of these two items.

Leaving on one side these reasons for the spread of the estimates we can see that taking the rows in turn, row 1, containing the estimate of the static gains from trade creation, is incomplete for most cases but where estimates are provided they are not very large in any case, and similarly that row 2 does not account for much of the variation between the welfare costs, as large variations in balance-of-payments effects tend to be offset by small resource costs of adjustment for this row. Of the remaining items, row 7, customs duties is, of course, pretty constant for all sources in balance-of-payments terms, although the welfare multipliers put a different interpretation on the resource costs for different assumptions as to trade elasticities. High resource costs of adjustment tend to shift estimates away from the 45 degree line of Chart 1; the best example here is the inelastic version of the 1970 White Paper, which has a welfare cost as large as Kaldor's 'high' estimate on account of the big 'added burden' of 90 per cent.

The added burden of the resource cost of adjustment is of course relevant to the transfer and transfer-like costs in rows 4 and 6, but a key determinant of these costs is also the assumption as to the price gap between EEC and world food prices. For the White Papers, as was discussed above, the balance-of-payments cost falls from around £400 million for the sum of those two items to around £270 million if the gap between EEC and world prices is taken to be such as to raise food prices by only 15 per cent at the retail level. Another important factor appears to be the assumed elasticity of substitution as between different food products, since Josling, who assumes much the same price 'gaps' as the 1971 White Paper, but finds considerable switching in the pattern of consumption, comes out with a significantly lower cost figure of £180 million.

The remaining item, row 3, the import saving on food, is not estimated by Kaldor and in other cases depends on the elasticities assumed. While this last item does account for some of the variation, it is nevertheless true that the bulk of the welfare costs for any source (after correcting for the spiral effects, and ignoring the range of the VAT/receipts net figure) may be explained by the food costs in rows 4 and 6, which depend crucially on the price gap, *plus* a constant figure of around £240 million for customs duties, *plus* the added burden relevant to such transfer or transfer-like costs.

These considerations account for the relative positions of the estimates in Chart 1 as follows. (We have discussed Kaldor's high estimate above, so we leave this aside.) The inelastic version of the 1970 White Paper has a 25 per cent price increase and high resource costs of adjustment and so this gives a high cost estimate. Kaldor (low) and the earlier version of the 1970 White Paper have the same large price gap, but have lower costs of adjustment. The Miller-Spencer study assumes a slightly smaller gap together with a similar low adjustment cost. The 1971 White Paper and Josling-Williamson have a low price gap together with low costs of adjustment.

The food bill in the White Papers

Table 1 distinguishes three elements in the food bill estimates: the net import saving (this was given in row 3) arising from increased domestic production and reduced domestic consumption; the cost represented by the rise in price of the total quantity of food imports consumed (row 4) and the amount of levies and duties raised on food (row 6). The breakdown of the figures given for these items relies on a good deal of 'guesstimation', particularly where the 1970 and 1971 White Paper figures are concerned. This section is devoted to explaining how these figures were derived.

The main source of the figures, or rather of the assumptions behind the figures, is in fact the 1970 White Paper, of which several paragraphs (27-37) were devoted to setting out the results of various possible calculations. The main building blocks of the present estimates are the figuring given there of the expected rise in retail prices, the estimates of possible production responses, the estimates of associated (net) import savings, and the estimates of levies raised.

Chart 2 helps explain how the deductions were made. This shows, for each of the 1970 White Paper estimates, and for the 1971 White Paper, the breakdown of the food 'bill' into the components already described. The value of food imports at 1969 prices is measured along the horizontal axis, and the price of imports along the vertical. Domestic supply (on the left) and demand schedules (on the right) are drawn, their elasticities being indicated to the left of the diagrams.

It is easiest to begin with an account of the 1970 White Paper estimates represented in the top two panels of the chart. The procedure followed may be set out in the following way. We start with an estimate of the value of food imports at 1969 prices before import saving, which is taken to be £2,000 million (this assumption afterwards appears justified by the results). We then inquire what consumer demand response is implied by the adoption of the common agricultural policy: this calls for estimates of the rise in *retail* prices and of the relevant demand elasticity. We next inquire what the producer response will be; this calls for estimates of the rise in *wholesale* prices, allowing for current producer subsidies and making an assumption about the supply elasticity. Finally, we need a figure for levy income, which, when known, allows us to obtain as a residual the value of the higher cost of food imported. At various stages checks are available, from the information given in the 1970 White Paper, on the consistency of the estimates produced.

So far as retail prices are concerned, the White Paper (para. 28) stated that "on the basis of present price differentials at the wholesale stage, and making certain assumptions about distributive and retail margins, the retail index for food might be 18-26 per cent higher than it would otherwise have been". This variation in the predicted retail price rise can be explained on the assumption that the value added at the distributing stage adds about 50 per cent to the wholesale value and that this margin either rises by 26 per cent, in proportion to a rise of the same amount in wholesale prices, or alternatively remains constant, thus reducing the rise in retail prices to between 17 and 18 per

Chart 2: The Construction of the Food Cost Estimates

£ million, 1969 prices

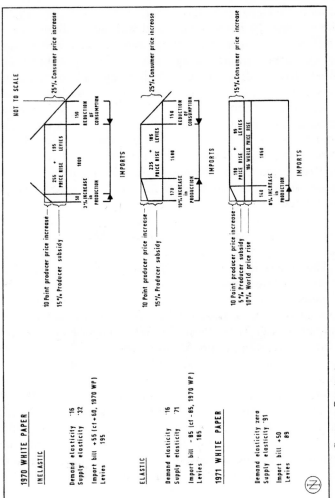

Source: See text

cent.[22] The assumption made here is that both retail and wholesale prices could be assumed to rise by 25 per cent. It is the rise
in the *wholesale* price which is most important for measuring the
rise in the import bill (the retail price movement counts only in
assessing the change in the demand for imports, and the higher
the increase the *lower* the demand will be) so choosing a figure
of 25 per cent for both is not choosing the high end of the scale
for the purpose of measuring the rise in the import bill.[23] The rise
in effective producer prices, which is relevant to measuring the
production response, is, however, less than the rise in wholesale
prices to the extent that part of the rise only makes good the
removal of producer subsidies. These latter were taken as
amounting to 15 per cent, a figure consistent with the White
Paper indication (para. 34) that a narrowing of the price gap
by 10 percentage points would virtually eliminate the production
response, while a widening of the gap by 5 percentage points
would add a half to the production response. In this way then,
the price rises underlying the White Paper calculations were
estimated as 25 per cent for retail and wholesale prices, and 10
per cent for producer prices. These are indicated in the chart.

The underlying estimate of the supply elasticity was deduced
from the White Paper's results given for high and low production
responses. First of all, the value of agricultural production
computed to be consistent with the White Paper's results was
estimated as £1,770 million. The White Paper gives estimates of
a lower and an upper production response of 3 per cent and 10
per cent respectively (para. 33), on the "present price differential", and indicates (*ibid.*, Table 8, rows 1 and 2) that the
associated increases in imports and levies would be £100 million
on the 3 per cent variant and £255 million on the 10 per cent
variant.[24] Thus a cost-saving difference of £155 million is
associated with a difference of 7 per cent in the production
response. Since we are assuming wholesale prices to rise by 25
per cent, an estimate of the value of agricultural production of

[22] See Kaldor, *op. cit.*, p.71.
[23] A recent study of European agriculture, for example, interprets the
same information in the 1970 White Paper as implying a 45 per cent
rise in wholesale prices, see P. Uri *et al.*, *A Future for European
Agriculture*, The Atlantic Institute, Paris, 1970.
[24] This is for the case of the "larger change in consumption".

£1,770 million seemed justified, such a figure producing the correct estimate of cost saving, viz.: $0.07 \times £1,770$ million $\times 1.25 = £155$ million. Given this, the 3 per cent and 10 per cent production responses imply increases of £50 and £170 million (approximately), and these are shown in the left-hand side of the charts; the corresponding supply elasticities—given the 10 per cent estimated rise in producer prices—are of course about 0.3 and 0.7 respectively.

For the demand elasticity, the White Paper statements about the expected elasticity of total expenditure provided the clue, and from the range shown there (para. 30), it appeared that the demand elasticity was of the order of 0.16.[25] In the absence of any other indication this was taken to be the demand elasticity implied in the White Paper figures for what it called "the larger demand response", and both White Paper variants reported here are based on this assumed demand elasticity. The assumptions made above can now be combined to give us the required estimates: considering the top diagram in Chart 2 and recalling that we have assumed for the moment a value of imports before production and demand responses can take place of £2,000 million, we can see that the rise in retail prices of 25 per cent together with a demand elasticity of approximately 0.16 yields a fall in demand of £150 million (shown on the right of the chart). The producer price rise of 10 per cent together with a supply elasticity of 0.32 and a value of production of £1,770 million are consistent with an increase in production of £50 million. The figure of £195 million for levies is taken from the White Paper. For the quantity of imports remaining after production and consumption responses (£2,000 million less £50 mn less £150 mn $= £1,800$ mn), the increase in prices must imply a rise in expenditure of £450 million. If £195 million of this is levy income, the rest is the rise in the cost of purchasing food imports due to higher prices, £255 million, as indicated in the chart.

A comparable analysis applies to the 'elastic' White Paper case, where the only difference is the assumed higher supply

---

[25] The elasticity of demand is given as equal to one minus the elasticity of total revenue or expenditure, in this case as equal to 1-15/18 or 0.16.

elasticity (in line with the White Paper's "higher production response"), which leads by the steps just described to a bigger figure for net import saving and smaller ones for the extra cost of imports and for levy income.

The starting figure of £2,000 million assumed in this exercise for the value of imports before the responses take place seems justified by the outcome. As shown in the chart, the computed figures of cost saving on imports (excluding levies) come out very close to the White Paper figures. Thus if the other assumptions are appropriate, so is the £2,000 million figure.

There is very much less detail in the 1971 White Paper but it is possible to use the same kind of framework as outlined above and incorporate what there is. The 1971 White Paper reckons the rise in retail food prices as $2\frac{1}{2}$ per cent per annum for six years, i.e. approximately 15 per cent overall (para. 88). But the production response is put at 8 per cent (para. 87). If the narrowing of the price gap were the result of a *fall* in EEC food prices then the arguments of the 1970 White Paper would lead to the expectation of a zero production response since the price rise would just absorb the present producer subsidy and no more. But the gap has presumably narrowed from the other direction, world food prices tending to rise towards the level of the present subsidy leaving EEC prices some 10 per cent above it. This is indicated in the bottom diagram of the chart, where the 8 per cent production response applied to a base of £1,770 million gives a figure of £140 million for the production increase. The different implications of these two different ways in which the price gap can narrow may explain some of the problems of reconciling the 1970 and 1971 White Paper results alluded to by Kaldor.[26]

The extra cost of imports, exclusive of levies, is given as £50 million in para. 43. But this cost is the cost of the rise in prices *less* import saving. Assuming there is no consumption response, for reasons indicated below, the implied cost of the rise in prices is therefore £190 million, as shown in the chart. The figure for levies, derived as a residual after subtracting this £190 million from 15 per cent of the reduced quantity food imports, is put at £89 million. Allowing for a consumption response implied by

---

[26] N. Kaldor, The Distortions of the White Paper, *New Statesman*, 16 July 1971.

the demand elasticity of 0.16 would lead to the odd estimate of no levy payments, as levy payments are here calculated as a residual which becomes smaller the higher the import saving. Hence no allowance has been made for import saving by reduced food consumption.

On this basis the total cost of the food bill including levies attributed to the 1971 White Paper is £139 million, with a production increase of £140 million offsetting levies of £89 million and the cost of the rise in prices of imports of £190 million. Exclusive of levies, the food bill rises by the £50 million given in paragraph 43 of the White Paper.

The reason for separating out the levies figure (£89 million) from the cost of the rise in price of food imports (£120 million) is that only 90 per cent of the levies figure is entered as a transfer payment in Table 1, while the whole of the price rise has to be paid. Separating out the import quantity reduction from the import price (and levy) increases is justified by the reasoning that consumers are worse off consuming a smaller quantity at a higher price even though the total cost of imports may remain virtually unchanged, as in the 1971 White Paper.

The calculation of the welfare estimates

In the majority of cases, the welfare effects attributed to the estimates in Table 1 had to be separately calculated on the basis of approximative formulae using various key assumptions, and were not generally available directly in the source documents.[27]

The general basis for the derivation of the welfare effects has already been indicated at the beginning of this chapter and the main purpose of this section is to supply the detailed adjustments. As described earlier, the basis of measurement is the assumption that balance-of-payments deficits are adjusted by devaluation.

The basic formulae[28]

Given this assumption of exchange rate flexibility, the welfare cost of restoring the trade balance is given by the required change in the terms of trade; and this, in turn, depends upon the

---

[27] The Kaldor and Miller-Spencer estimates were exceptions in this respect.
[28] For a full account of the formulae see, for example, I. F. Pearce, *International Trade*, Book I, Macmillan, London, 1970; or R. A. Mundell, *International Economics*, Macmillan, New York, 1968.

value of the elasticities of demand for imports and for exports. As these values differ as between the various estimates reviewed in this paper, the relationship between the balance-of-payments cost and the welfare cost—the welfare 'multiplier'—also varies from estimate to estimate.

The basic formula turns on the well-known 'condition' for a successful devaluation, that the sum of the import and export elasticities is equal to or greater than unity. Using this condition, the welfare cost of correcting a balance-of-payments deficit—being the terms-of-trade loss on imports—can be expressed as follows:[29]

$$dw = -dB/(E_1 + E_2 - 1) \qquad (1)$$

since by definition

$$dw = -Mdp \qquad (2)$$

and, by the condition referred to above

$$dB = Mdp(E_1 + E_2 - 1) \qquad (3)$$

where w is welfare

     p is import prices, with exports as numéraire

     M is imports

     B is the size of the imbalance calling for correction

     $E_{1,2}$ is the elasticity of demand for imports in country 1, 2.

Thus the welfare cost of correcting any balance-of-payments imbalance varies inversely with the value of the sum of the elasticities, which is simply to say that the higher are the elasticities of demand for imports and exports the smaller will need to be the movement in prices (the terms of trade) required to effect any given change in the balance.

Where the balance-of-payments imbalance calling for correction is associated with a transfer payment the analysis calls for an amendment to take account of the fact that the transfer itself directly affects welfare.

But while the transfer itself constitutes a direct loss of welfare, any income effects on the demand for imports or exports associated with it will ease the need for a terms-of-trade adjustment to clear the balance-of-payments deficit. Bearing this in mind, the equation expressing the welfare effect becomes

---

[29] For a two-country, two-commodity world.

$$dw = -dB - Mdp \tag{4}$$

and here

$$dB = Mdp(E_1 + E_2 - 1)/(1 - C_1 - C_2) \tag{5}$$

so that

$$dw = -dB[1 + (1 - C_1 - C_2)/(E_1 + E_2 - 1)] \tag{6}$$

where $C_{1,2}$ refer to the marginal propensity to import, in the UK or the EEC; and where dB is to be set equal to the value of the transfer to be made.

Equation (5) indicates that the balance to be corrected by the terms-of-trade adjustment is less than the initial balance-of-payments change because the change itself effects a transfer of income which raises income (and imports) in the recipient country and reduces income (and imports) in the country making the transfer. The 'added burden' of the transfer (the terms-of-trade cost of righting the balance) is given by

$$a = [1 - (C_1 + C_2)]/(E_1 + E_2 - 1)$$

where a is the added burden. Thus, the added burden is the less, the greater the value of the sum of the marginal propensities to import, and the bigger the sum of the elasticities.

These formulae have been used to provide the welfare multipliers, where these are not indicated by the study in question, and are shown in Table 2. At least for those multipliers not derived from the sources but computed for this table, it is not possible to claim that they will provide anything but broad orders of magnitude for the welfare results, based as they are on crude aggregate elasticities and on analogy with a very simple trade model. We can see the results of varying the key assumptions as follows.

The effect of varying the elasticities is implicit in the different rows of the table (in particular in the comparison between the 'elastic' and 'inelastic' versions of the 1970 White Paper). The effect of varying the (sum of) marginal propensities to import is shown in the second column, where taking the marginal propensity to be double the average lowers the added burden by the amount shown. The burden using an income elasticity of one was used for the White Papers in Table 1, but the effects of the higher income elasticity are shown in Table 3 below, where the detail of Table 1 is compressed to illustrate the application of the two multipliers.

Following the procedure indicated on page 124 we may

Table 2: The Welfare Multipliers: the Terms-of-Trade Costs of Removing a Deficit

Per unit of deficit

	I Cost of curing a deficit	II Added burden of transfer	
		Income elasticities	
		Ey = 1	Ey = 2
Kaldor	n.a.	33%	
Miller-Spencer	36%	24%	—
Josling-Williamson	33%	25%	—
1970 White Paper (inelastic)	120%	90%	60%
1970 White Paper (elastic)	33%	25%	19%
1971 White Paper	33%	25%	19%

Notes: (1) Multiplier I is the percentage cost of improving the balance of trade $=100/(E_1+E_2-1)$, see text. (2) The values of the first multiplier had to be estimated for the White Papers only. This was done by taking the inverse of the sum of the elasticities of demand for imports (manufactures only) given in the 1970 White Paper p. 28, as 0.83 for the inelastic case, and 3 for the 'elastic' case. Adding in non-manufactures, with the appropriate weights, is not likely to alter these estimates substantially (cf. R. N. Cooper, The Balance of Payments, in R. Caves *et al.*, *Britain's Economic Prospects*, Allen and Unwin for Brookings Institution, 1968, p. 189). (3) Multiplier II is the percentage added burden of a transfer $=100$ $(1-(C_1+C_2))/(E_1+E_2-1)$, see text. (4) The sum of the average propensity of the UK to import foreign goods, and the average propensity of the EEC to import UK goods is approximately 0.25 as estimated from data used in the Miller-Spencer study. Hency $C_1+C_2=25$ if the income elasticity (Ey) = 1 and 0.5 if the income elasticity is 2. These values for $C_{1,2}$ were used to compute the second welfare multiplier from the first, except for the case of Kaldor and Miller-Spencer where the value of the second multiplier is given in the study. (5) The multipliers for the 1970 White Paper (elastic) were used for the 1971 White Paper.

aggregate the balance-of-payments effects in rows 2 and 3 and use the first multiplier to get the resource cost and, treating row 4 as analogous to a transfer payment, aggregate rows 4 and 10 and use one *plus* the second welfare multiplier to obtain the resource cost. The resulting welfare costs correspond to those of row 11 less row 1 of Table 1.

The wage-price spiral

The wage-price spiral effect was removed from the 1970 White Paper balance-of-payments figures by use of a similar approach to the one outlined above.

On the fairly modest assumption that the spiral turns the terms of trade in favour of the UK by 1 per cent, we can compute the 'correction' as follows. Rewriting the formula (3) above as

$$dB = pM \times (E_1 + E_2 - 1) \times dp/p$$

and using the figures given in the footnotes to Table 2 for the elasticities, together with a figure of £8,000 million for the value of imports, gives the following results (in £ million):

1970 White Paper: (elastic) 240 = 8,000 × 3 × 0.01
(inelastic) 67 = 8,000 × 0.83 × 0.01

Subtracting these 'correction' factors from the figures for the change in the balance of payments in manufacturing given in the 1970 White Paper, Table 13, page 28, gives the figures quoted in Table 1, viz., £35 million (£275—£240 million) for the 'elastic' case, and £58 million (£125—£67 million) for the 'inelastic' case. The corrected figures are then taken as the base for the application of the welfare cost calculations, yielding welfare cost figures of £12 million and £70 million for the 'elastic' and 'inelastic' cases respectively.

The UK contribution to the Community budget

The gross contribution to the Community budget, given as the sum of rows 6, 7 and 8 in Table 1, is clearly only a part of the cost of entry, and yet much public attention and much of the negotiating has focussed on this element of the cost. This may be related to the fact that such contributions are not the inevitable consequence of joining a customs union on the usual assumption that tariff revenues are redistributed (as a lump sum) to the countries consuming the imports bearing the tariff. The other transfer-like costs of high cost food imports from the EEC are the standard trade diversion costs of a customs union and do not involve such an official transfer.[30] It is, of course, the common agricultural policy with the principle that tariff payments are related to food consumption, while benefits depend on food production, which implies that the UK as a large food importer must make a net transfer.

Some of the main proposals made in the course of the negotiations are shown in Chart 3, and the details are given in

---

[30]It was for this reason that the structure of Table 1 distinguishes between official transfers and all other costs of entry.

Table 3: The Welfare Significance of Balance-of-Payments Effects

£ million, 1969 prices

	Variant	Key: (rows of table 1)	Balance of payments cost	Welfare multiplier	Welfare cost	Welfare multiplier (variant)	Welfare cost (variant)
Kaldor	high	2 + 3	(275)		50		
		4 + 10	820	1.33	1,094		
		11	(1,095)		1,144		
Kaldor	low	2 + 3	(125)		20		
		4 + 10	540	1.33	720		
		11	(665)		740		
Miller-Spencer		2 + 3	−329	0.36	−118		
		4 + 10	671	1.24	831		
		11 − 1	342		713		
Josling-Williamson		2 + 3	−125	0.33	− 41		
		4 + 10	391	1.25	488		
		11 − 1	266		447		
1970 White Paper	inelastic	2 + 3	−142	1.20	−170	1.20	−170
		4 + 10	671	1.90	1,275	1.60	1,074
		11	529		1,105		904
1970 White Paper	elastic	2 + 3	−285	0.33	− 95	0.33	− 95
		4 + 10	642	1.25	803	1.19	764
		11	357		708		669
1971 White Paper		2 + 3	−140	0.33	− 47	0.33	− 47
		4 + 10	485	1.25	607	1.19	577
		11	345		560		530

Notes: (1) The welfare multipliers are drawn from Table 2. (2) the last two columns, not used in Table 1, show the results of doubling the income elasticity of demand for imports in deriving the multipliers, see Table 2.

the notes accompanying the table. The 'agreed contribution' shown there, as described in the 1971 White Paper, is clearly a compromise between EEC(2) and Mr. Rippon's proposals (GRHC). The 'forecast' shown in Chart 3 is the build-up to the figure of approximately £400 million attributed in Table 1 to the 1971 White Paper as the *gross* budgetary contribution.

The figure of £400 million is much lower than the figure of £670 million given as a possible contribution in the 1970 White Paper, and considerably lower than the £540 million which results from reducing the estimated VAT included in the £670 million payment from £230 million to £100 million. The chart suggests, however, that £400 million may well be the sort of gross contribution anticipated, because the forecast line is practically a continuation of the 'agreed contribution' and has every appearance of smoothing the transition from the £300 million (gross) negotiated by Mr. Rippon for 1977, to a per-centage contribution of around 25 per cent, which some of the EEC Commission proposals implied (cf. EEC(1) in the chart). This may be taken as some evidence to substantiate the budgetary estimates attributed to the 1971 White Paper in Table 1.

Conclusions

Much of this chapter has been concerned not with simply comparing published figures, but with trying to guess the assumptions underlying the published figures in order to get the estimates required for such a comparison. This has been particularly true of the official White Papers. It may, of course, be politically necessary to conceal one's hand, but the lack of clarity as to the assumptions used makes an economic assess-ment difficult.

It is perhaps surprising that the second White Paper, addressed as it is to the British public at the end of the negotia-tions, is much less explicit than the first White Paper, published when the negotiations in Brussels were still in progress and it was felt that the Government would probably have to adopt a tough negotiating stand.

It is tempting in conclusion to express the resource cost estimates as a percentage of GNP. But this raises an index number problem. This is because the cost figures in the tables are expressed in 1969 prices, but this means 1969 'manufacturing'

Chart 3: The Scale and Timing of the United Kingdom Contribution to the Community Budget: Proposals and Estimates

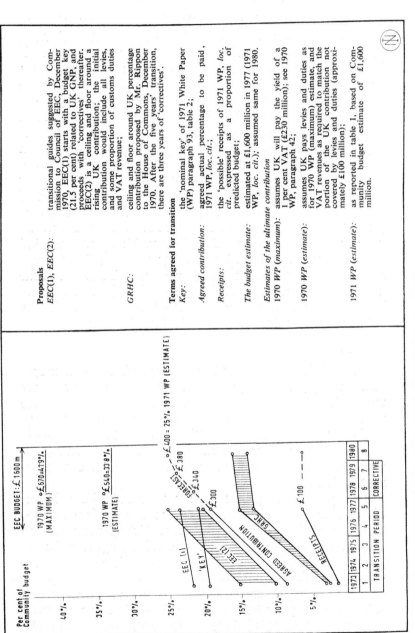

Proposals

EEC(1), EEC(2): transitional guides suggested by Commission to Council of EEC, December 1970. EEC(1) starts with a budget key (21.5 per cent) related to UK GNP, and proceeds with 'correctives' thereafter. EEC(2) is a ceiling and floor around a rising UK contribution; the initial contribution would include all levies, and some proportion of customs duties and VAT revenue;

GRHC: ceiling and floor around UK percentage contribution proposed by Mr. Rippon to the House of Commons, December 1970. After the five years' transition, there are three years of 'correctives'.

Terms agreed for transition

Key: the 'nominal key' of 1971 White Paper (WP) paragraph 93, table 2;

Agreed contribution: agreed actual percentage to be paid, 1971 WP, *loc. cit.*;

Receipts: the 'possible' receipts of 1971 WP, *loc. cit.* expressed as a proportion of predicted budget;

The budget estimate: estimated at £1,600 million in 1977 (1971 WP, *loc. cit.*); assumed same for 1980.

Estimates of the ultimate contribution

1970 WP (maximum): assumes UK will pay the yield of a 1 per cent VAT (£230 million); see 1970 WP, paragraph 42;

1970 WP (estimate): assumes UK pays levies and duties as for 1970 WP (maximum) estimate, and VAT revenues as required to match the portion of the UK contribution not covered by levies and duties (approximately £100 million);

1971 WP (estimate): as reported in table 1, based on Community budget estimate of £1,600 million.

prices for the manufacturing figures, and 1969 agriculture prices for the food costs. The former price index will presumably be much the same as the GNP deflator, but it is not usually clear what the studies assume about the trend of agricultural prices relative to manufactures.

Typically an assumption is made as to the gap between EEC and world food prices. But even on the assumption that the price gap between world and EEC prices is a constant proportion, say 15 or 25 per cent, there is still the question of how food prices will move *vis-a-vis* manufacturing prices. If they rise less fast than the prices of manufactures then the real costs of such a constant proportional price gap will fall, as manufactures bulk large in the GNP of this country.

Relating the agricultural costs of Table 1 to a constant price figure of GNP (say, of £50 billion)[31] together with the assumption of a constant price 'gap' is tantamount to assuming food prices will follow the GNP deflator. Subject to this warning, we can take a figure of £500 million as equivalent to 1 per cent of such a constant price GNP and from Table 1 and Chart 1 see that the estimates range from just below 1 per cent to over 2 per cent of GNP, depending on the factors discussed in the survey section above (pages 122-133) but all on the basis of assuming exchange rate flexibility. The different assumptions incorporate variations in the gap that has been assumed between world and EEC food prices. For any gap a comparison of food prices and the GNP deflator would lead one to expect some reduction of the real costs. An estimate of total resource costs of about $1\frac{1}{4}$ per cent of GNP seems, on this basis, a reasonable compromise. It is a cost of this order of magnitude which the dynamic gains described by Williamson in Chapter 2, above, must offset in order to give a *net* benefit and provide an economic case for entry—unless the Josling-Williamson estimates are accepted, in which case the cost to be covered is only $\frac{3}{4}$ per cent of GNP.

Appendix I: Key features of the Miller-Spencer model

There are four 'countries', the United Kingdom, the EEC, Australia/New Zealand, and the Rest of the World. Each country produces two goods, food and non-food. Food products pro-

---

[31] Cf. the 1971 White Paper, para. 57, which indicates a value of 1 per cent of GNP equivalent to £500 million; see also p.26 above.

duced in different countries are close but not perfect substitutes (the elasticity of substitution postulated is 3), and the same applies to non-food. There are thus eight final products, divided into the two categories of food and non-food. But the elasticity of substitution between food and non-food is lower than between products of any one category, and is taken to be unity. Thus each nation spends a constant proportion of its income on each broad category but the share of this proportion going on the product of any one country rises as its price falls. Formally, the demand for each country is derived from a two-stage constant-elasticity-of-substitution utility function.

The substitution elasticity of unity for food implies a unit elastic demand for food as a whole, which is why UK demand for food falls sharply when the price goes up by 20 per cent. The substitution elasticity of three between *different kinds* of food implies a demand elasticity bounded from above by three and the high demand elasticity for UK food by the EEC gives a rise in exports (a fall in *net* imports) from the UK when the EEC abolishes its tariffs and levies on UK food exports. Levies and tariffs on food in the EEC were represented by a 20 per cent tariff. Both the CET and UK tariffs on manufactures were put at 15 per cent. This high figure for tariffs, together with the elastic demand assumptions, tends to exaggerate the effects of entry on manufactures, although the omission of the effects of the loss of discrimination in our favour by other entrants will bias the deficit towards zero. Tariffs are the only taxes in the model, and they are assumed to be redistributed as a lump sum to consumers, except for the UK when in the EEC where a 90 per cent transfer of such tariffs to the EEC is assumed. The other source of income is from aggregate factor payments.

There are two factors, labour and capital, which are perfectly mobile between the two 'industries' in any country, but immobile between countries. The production functions are Cobb-Douglas with constant returns to scale (which of course precludes finding any benefits from increasing returns). The fact that production is efficient (producers maximise profits) precludes finding dramatic gains from 'X-efficiency'.

Appendix II: The cost of devaluing by deflation

The welfare multipliers used in this article were computed on the basis that the adjustment mechanism was a devaluation. An alternative would be to achieve the adjustment by deflation of domestic demand and prices. The welfare losses involved in this kind of adjustment would be greater, and in the short run considerably greater, if the illustrative calculations suggested below are any guide.

Assuming that there is some 'Phillips' relationship between the price level and the level of unemployment, only a limited amount of unemployment will be required, for the deflation of demand will bring about a reduced rate of domestic price rise, and so eventually effect the required deterioration in the terms of trade. But at the same time, the deflation will bring income effects into play to assist the adjustment of the balance of payments and this will enable prices to adjust more slowly while still keeping payments in balance.

The net welfare effect can therefore be thought of as comprising two components—the loss of income through unemployment, on the one hand, and the gain in temporarily reducing the required adverse swing in the terms of trade on the other. The broad orders of magnitude of these two components may be discovered by considering the key values required in the following algebraic expressions of the component costs.

(i) The loss of income through unemployment

Given that no extra unemployment is to be created in the long run the shift in the terms of trade will be given by the equation (3) used above (page 140), rewritten for convenience here as

$$dB = Mdp/a \qquad (7)$$

This requires that import prices must rise (relatively) by

$$dp = aT/M \qquad (8)$$

where T is the transfer to be effected.

Denoting domestic prices by π, setting p initially equal to unity, and $\pi = 1/p$, we can write the requirement as

$$d\pi = -dp = -aT/M \qquad (9)$$

Assuming that a Phillips relationship exists of the form

$$D\pi = k - fu \qquad (10)$$

where D denotes the time rate of change, and u is the level of unemployment, then we can specify, to an approximation, the change in unemployment needed to accomplish the price level change in the following way:

$$d\pi = \int \delta D\pi dt = -f \int \delta u dt \equiv -fdu \qquad (11)$$

The opportunity cost (L) of this unemployment may, in turn, be measured according to the relationship

$$L = r\,du\ Y = -\frac{d_\pi Yr}{f} = \frac{r\,dp\ Y}{f} = \frac{rY}{f}\cdot\frac{aT}{M} \tag{12}$$

where r is 'Paish's ratio'.[32] Some approximate estimates of the values required exist. For example, M/Y, the average propensity to consume imports, is about 0.2; for f, the slope of the Phillips curve, estimates by Parkin[33] suggest a value of about 3; for r also, Cooper[34] suggests a value of about 3.

Using these values in (12) gives the result $L = 5aT$; i.e. that the once for all loss of effecting the transfer by deflation is five times the added burden payable in any one year.

(*ii*) *The gain on the terms of trade*

Deflating in the manner just indicated does postpone the need for an adverse shift in the terms of trade because the deflation would itself induce income effects reducing the demand for imports. This can be expressed as an equivalent *gain* in the terms of trade, as follows:

In the presence of changes in national income, Y, we may rewrite (7) as

$$dB = Mdpa - md\,Y/1 - Sm \tag{13}$$

where m is the marginal propensity to import. The trade-off between dp and dY holding dB constant is

$$dp = amd\,Y/M(1 - Sm) \tag{14}$$

But if we multiply through by M and replace dY by L, the loss of income measured above, we have an estimate of the terms-of-trade gain, G, purchased by suffering L:

$$G \equiv Mdp = amL/1 - Sm \tag{15}$$

The only new parameter here is the marginal propensity to import. While we have assumed the average propensity to be 0.2 in the numerical illustration, it would be realistic to assume a higher marginal propensity, say 0.3, which is approximately the value emerging from the NIESR's forecasting equations. Thus the offset to L would be 0.5 aL.

---

[32] That is, the ratio of the proportionate shortfall of GDP beneath potential to the excess of the unemployment rate over the unemployables; see F. W. Paish, *Studies in an Inflationary Economy*, Macmillan, London, 1966, Chapter 17.

[33] J. M. Parkin, Incomes Policy: some further results, *Economica*, November 1970.

[34] Cooper, op. cit., p.160.

(iii) The net loss (N)

The calculations above indicated the loss associated with the extra unemployment needed to change the price level by the required amount, and the parallel gains generated by the fall in demand for imports directly induced by the deflation of income. On the assumption that the path of adjustment was such as to maintain balanced trade throughout, the unemployment could gradually be reduced as the cumulated effects on the terms of trade reduce the need to curtail the demand for imports through deflation of income. Thus the net cost can be ascertained by subtracting the gains (*G*) just derived from the losses (*L*).

In this way the net cost of devaluing by deflating as a per-centage of national income emerges as

$$N=L-G=L(1-am)/1-Sm \qquad (16)$$
$$=\frac{rY}{f} \cdot \frac{aT}{M} (1-am)/1-Sm$$

To continue with the numerical illustration

$$N=L(1-am/1-Sm)=5aT(1-0.5a) \qquad (17)$$
$$= 5aT -2.5a^2T$$

Thus for $a=1$, $N=2.5T$

and for $a=0.2$, $N=0.9T$

The interpretation of these results is that there will be, in addition to the added burden of transfer, a, an amount, N, which is related to a but is paid only once as it is the cost of *adjustment* to the new prices (while a is the extra cost of those new prices for imports). The *total* cost of this adjustment *over all time* as shown in the formulae is equal to the value of the transfer *per unit time* when price elasticities are high, and the added burden, a, is low. As the added burden rises, so the adjustment cost increases, by more than three times for the example shown. Obviously, the less price-sensitive are trade flows, the greater the unemployment required to eliminate an excess demand for imports.

While N should be expressed as an infinite stream by multi-plying it by an interest rate to make it comparable with a or T, it is nevertheless true that most of the unemployment costs of adjustment have to be paid early in the adjustment process.

It would not be fanciful to interpret the current unemploy-ment as, at least in part, the cost of such a price adjustment process.

Chapter 7

CAPITAL FLOWS

by Stanislas M. Yassukovich

THE question of liberalised capital flows within an enlarged
European Economic Community and more particularly the
impact of potential outflows (and loss of present inflows) on
Britain's payments position after its accession to the EEC is
not susceptible to scientific analysis. The scale and direction
of capital flows to and from the UK will depend largely on the
attitudes of portfolio and direct investors in Britain and abroad.
One can only speculate on the real and psychological forces
which will shape these attitudes, much as one might do in
attempting to analyse the future trend of the Stock Exchange.
It may be possible to project and adjust certain trends established in the past. However, it is not realistic to attempt to
quantify the precise extent of potential capital flows or their
true significance in terms of the future payments position
without making a great many assumptions about the financial
and economic climate which will characterise an enlarged
European Community.

This chapter will review the known facts about the agreement
reached with the European Economic Community during the
recent negotiations for Britain's entry and examine them in the
light of past and current experience with British direct and
portfolio investment abroad. It will also endeavour to make
some assumptions concerning the motivations which will prompt
both inward and outward flows of capital between Britain and
the rest of the Community, as well as examining the possible
impact of flows between Britain and non-EEC areas which
may have the effect of offsetting or intensifying the negative

aspects of inter-Community movements. In this context it is important to recognise the fact that the present exchange control system which emanates from the Exchange Control Act of 1947 as administered by the Bank of England is not destined to disappear for the foreseeable future. It is certainly unlikely to be altered significantly with respect to capital trans-actions with the non-sterling area outside the EEC. Further-more, exchange control will continue to be the medium through which capital movements between the EEC and Britain are supervised and through which they will be gradually freed in conformity with the arrangements negotiated prior to British accession as well as with respect to the further evolution of the EEC towards greater monetary union and total freedom of capital movements. Much has been made of the stated intention in the Treaty of Rome to move towards the creation of an economic block benefiting from complete freedom of capital movements. This is certainly the accepted objective of those who aspire to a high degree of political and economic unification in Europe. On the other hand, the timing of any moves in this direction is open to very considerable doubt. Very substantial reforms of the national and international monetary systems would be required before it became feasible to contemplate total freedom of capital movement within the EEC. Britain would constitute a particularly powerful element in this crucial debate, able to bring to bear its long experience in international finance and certainly in a position to ensure that progress in the direction of monetary union was fully compatible with its own needs. However, it is important to remember that the question of eventual monetary union goes far beyond the scope of the present arrangements and is not relevant to the present discussion on capital flows within the EEC.

The agreement with the EEC about capital flows
Details of the agreement reached with the Community on the question of capital movements were announced on 16 July 1971 in the House of Commons. Further clarification on certain points was contained in a speech by the Chancellor during a debate on 26 July. The Community places various types of international capital transfers into four basic categories, the so-called Lists A, B, C, and D. Community directives call for

the liberalisation of the first two categories either immediately
or within a reasonable period, while restrictions on transactions
of the type covered in List C may be maintained or, if removed,
may be re-introduced. List D transactions are not due for
liberalisation in the foreseeable future. It is therefore not
accurate to argue that membership of the EEC implies complete
removal of exchange control in keeping with the stated intention
of the Treaty of Rome to create complete freedom of capital
movements within the Community. Although this is indeed
the aim of the Community, it is fully recognised by the Commission that substantial progress must be made in other areas
of economic policy and particularly on the question of eventual
monetary union before the definitive dismantling of national
exchange control procedures can be contemplated. The present
negotiations have been centred around Lists A and B, as these
are the two categories where present directives call for freedom
for transactions to take place at (or near) the official rate of
exchange.

The basic and most important item contained in List A is
that of direct investments. The agreement negotiated with the
Community calls for the eventual removal of the limiting
aspects of present exchange control regulations as they affect
both outward and inward flows of direct investment, meaning
industrial and commercial investment as opposed to investment
in securities. Restrictions which at present limit the extent to
which outward investment can be financed through official
exchange as opposed to external borrowing (which is already
permitted) must be removed immediately upon accession to
the EEC. The requirements that some foreign currency inflow
must take place in connection with inward direct investment
must be lifted by the end of the second year of the five-year
transitional period. This means that at that time, foreign direct
investors in the UK will be able to make use of the British
capital market to finance their investments in this country.

It is worth examining the present position with regard to
this important area before speculating on the consequences of
liberalisation. Present exchange control regulations are administered by the Bank of England on a highly flexible basis. A
potential direct investor is required to estimate carefully the
return on the investment and, in particular, how quickly it may

be expected that the investment will produce a significant inflow of funds in the form of dividends or other exchange benefits. As a very basic rule of thumb, the proportion of the total financial requirement allowed through official exchange is usually greatest where the investment promises a quick and significant return. The balance must usually be provided through the investment currency pool (which produces no exchange loss) or through external borrowing. In fact, it would seem that British direct investment overseas has not been greatly frustrated by these limiting regulations. This is because the pressure to finance abroad, rather than use official exchange or investment currency, has been fully consistent with the commercial and financial advantage of the typical direct investor. The structure of international interest rates and the uncertainties surrounding the stability of the current exchange parities has made foreign borrowing both the cheaper and the more prudent course of financing for a British industrial or commercial enterprise expanding abroad. This is likely to remain the case. To the extent that foreign direct investments are becoming larger in scope, particularly in the basic industries, recourse to foreign or international capital markets will be increasingly necessary because of the natural limitations of any one national market. It is equally likely that continued uncertainty on the international monetary front will continue to promote the wisdom of matching assets and liabilities in the same currency.

The present requirements governing inward flows of direct investment have been designed to encourage the import of capital to offset the fact that foreign investors must be guaranteed complete capital repatriation rights and unlimited dividend distribution rights if they are to invest in the UK. Generally speaking again, strict tests of past capital contributions are necessary before foreign investors are able to tap British capital sources for expanded local investment. Other criteria have often been taken into consideration, such as the contribution made by an overseas-controlled enterprise to regional development priorities or export-oriented activities.

The removal, at the end of the second transitional year, of all restrictions governing local borrowing by overseas controlled companies will in theory have the effect of reducing the potential inflow of capital associated with direct investment in Britain by European companies. A certain amount of direct investment financed externally by the country of origin will still involve capital market operations directed at the international market. This portion would imply an inflow to the extent that the contribution of British investment funds to such operations will be limited on the grounds of competitive choice of investment media. However, to the extent that foreign concerns also consider it more convenient to utilise the resources of the British capital market to finance their British investments some potential inflow is lost.

Most of the balance of List A transactions are concerned with personal capital movements such as investments in real estate, gifts and donations, inheritances and legacies and other transfers by emigrants and immigrants. Also included are various types of commercial transfers deriving from royalties and licensing arrangements. These are by and large already permitted and are, in any case, of a volume that need not concern us in discussing the real effect on the UK balance of payments of the liberalisation of capital flows inherent in British membership of the EEC.

The next item of importance dealt with in the negotiations concerns the List B items, which cover designated securities. Since present exchange control regulations are most stringent in the field of UK resident investment in foreign securities, it is this aspect of capital flows that has caused the greatest concern so far. It is true that since the war, British resident investment in foreign securities has involved substantial and complex control designed to limit the negative effect of this activity on the payments position. What may be less appreciated is the fact that the Bank of England's administration of these controls has been dynamic and constantly adapted to the changing circumstances both in the sense of an evolving investment climate and with regard to fundamental changes in the underlying British payments position. As in the case of the provisions for liberalised direct investment, it is worth while understanding the background and current circumstances surrounding Britain's substantial foreign portfolio investment activity before attempting to evaluate the impact of greater freedom which will come into force only at the end of the five-year transitional period.

The basic concept behind the present regulations on foreign

portfolio investment is inherent in the practical implications of the investment currency pool. Stemming from a considerably more complex system evolved as part of Britain's wartime financial measures, the investment currency pool (or 'premium dollar' pool as it is widely known) ensures that portfolio investment outflow essentially matches inflow since new foreign portfolio investment can be effected only through the purchase of the proceeds of sales of foreign portfolio investments by British residents. The concept is simply that if Mr. Jones can buy only what Mr. Smith has sold in terms of foreign currency value, the basic payments position will be unaffected. From time to time the basic principle behind this system has been obscured by the use of the investment currency pool to process other forms of transfer not specifically concerned with portfolio investments, such as reparations payments, charitable donations, returning emigrant remittances, etc. Depending on the prevailing circumstances the use of the pool for non-portfolio investment transfers has had the effect of expanding or contracting its total size. More recently measures have been introduced which should in theory promote a gradual contraction of the pool. These are the stipulations that a resident investor switching from one foreign security to another must surrender 25 per cent of the sale proceeds at the official rate of exchange rather than at the going rate for investment currency. These measures gave rise to some imaginative financing arrangements by professional investors who, under the sanction and supervision of the Bank of England, are now financing their foreign portfolio investments through medium-term external borrowings, emulating in this respect the direct investor. The portfolio investor engaging in arrangements of this type can circumvent the immediate cost of the investment currency premium and the running cost of the 25 per cent surrender arrangements on switching, without cost to the balance of payments. Experience in the past has demonstrated that the quality of British investment management in foreign securities should assure a reasonable net return on investment after the cost of servicing the foreign debt used to finance such investments. An additional inducement leading to continued use of the foreign borrowing technique for financing overseas portfolio investment has been the possibility of protecting the premium dollar content of an existing portfolio

through a switch-and-surrender process, following the negotiation of a foreign loan by an approved investment institution.
As a result of this continuing reform in the exchange control
regulations governing foreign portfolio investment, together
with the evolution of new techniques, an important part of
Britain's present private foreign investment portfolio is in fact
financed abroad.

Further background necessary to any understanding of the
potential drain (or inflow) which might result from a freeing
of the restrictions vis-à-vis EEC countries in the second transitional year concerns the historic geographical bias of British
overseas portfolio investment. From this analysis one must
initially exclude Commonwealth, or more specifically sterling
area, portfolio investment which is now, and will eventually,
be dealt with separately. There are many reasons why British
investors, both private and institutional, have displayed a
marked and continuing preference for North American securities
over the years. Historically, a considerable portion of the
economic development of the United States and Canada was
financed in the UK. In the nineteenth century London was by
far the largest and most consistent market for American
securities. This activity gave rise to the establishment of a
number of investment trusts and other allied institutions in
England and Scotland which continue to exist today and whose
names and styles indicate their US orientation. The North
American leanings of British investors have been reinforced
in recent years by the dynamic development of the US securities
markets, their considerable choice and diversity and the greater
sophistication of the financial community sponsoring such
investment. Furthermore, the corporate structure, disclosure
standards, accounting practices and other visible aspects of
corporate life of North American companies are entirely
compatible and understandable to British investors, bearing
as they do strong similarities to British Company Law and
practice. None of these features pertain to the Continental
investment scene where the evolution of capitalism in this
tradition has been slow and hesitant and the securities markets
necessarily underdeveloped. Many of the forces which have
made the US capital markets the largest and most liberal in
the world are expected to develop in an increasingly unified

Europe, but the gap in this respect between Europe and the US is still immense and will take decades to close.

Possible future capital flows

After this brief examination of the nature of the agreement reached with the EEC and its relationship to the present situation, let us attempt to speculate on the nature and extent of future movements of capital between Britain and the EEC countries. Direct investment can be said to fall into three general categories. The first is investment prompted by the existence of tariff barriers which cannot be effectively breached and are therefore overcome by the establishment of manufacturing facilities on the other side. Somewhat similar to this is investment to overcome natural barriers resulting, for example, in transport costs. The second basic category derives from the nature of the industrial or commercial activity concerned in that it consists of investment activities within a sphere which is naturally multi-national. This sector is best exemplified by the service industries such as banking, insurance and other financially-oriented businesses, or catering and related commercial enterprises. Yet a third category, perhaps eventually the largest, relates to enterprises which have grown to the maximum size permitted by natural economic factors or by monopoly-control legislation within the national boundaries. Such companies are forced to expand abroad, mainly through acquisitions, because the potential for further growth domestically has been limited by the size of the local market and the impossibility of increasing any particular share, or by regulation designed to prevent the excessive concentration of market share in a single entity.

It should be clear that the fundamental nature of the Common Market should serve to prevent the necessity for the first category of direct investment, in so far as the artificial rather than the natural barriers are concerned. Naturally, while Britain was prevented from participating fully in the expansion of markets which resulted from the Treaty of Rome, a second-best solution for British industry was the penetration of these markets through the establishment of manufacturing facilities within the EEC. Direct investment of this nature by British industry on the Continent has been concentrated in the primary industries and those concerned with the manufacture of goods subject to tariff barriers. In many cases other factors intervene such as the necessity of gaining geographic advantages in relation to points of sale and the seeking of labour cost reductions. These questions will remain relevant in motivating investment within the EEC, although the labour-cost factor may diminish in importance owing to the tendency for these costs to equalise within the Community. On the whole, however, it is reasonable to assume that British accession to the EEC will limit to an important extent the category of direct investment which is concerned with the circumvention of tariff barriers.

As is well known, United States direct investment in Europe increased substantially during the 1950s and 1960s. During that period American corporate executives tried to speculate on the eventual chances of Britain joining the European Economic Community. A very natural preference for investment in the United Kingdom has always existed on the part of American industrialists. The similarity between British and American management and accounting techniques, weights and measures, manufacturing standards, legal systems and a host of other important aspects of corporate life, joining with the obvious advantages of common language, would have made the choice between Britain and the Continent an easy one had it not been for the fundamental problem of Britain's isolation from the dynamic market represented by the EEC. A further element adding to the benefits of investment in the UK was the existence of a highly developed and sophisticated financial community in London. Despite all of these natural advantages, it is certain that the UK lost a considerable amount of direct investment from the United States because of its initial decision not to join the EEC and its subsequent lack of success in remedying this initial fault. Although the rate of US direct investment in Europe has slowed considerably in the last two or three years owing to capital controls in the United States and a certain element of saturation, a major disadvantage from Britain's point of view in attracting this investment is now to be removed. It is logical to suppose that further US investment in Europe will be located to a large extent in the United Kingdom in preference to Continental countries. The corresponding inflow should be significant because it must be remembered that the relaxation of controls with respect to local financing by foreign direct investors will apply only to the member countries of the EEC.

The second category of direct investment referred to above will undoubtedly increase as a result of the expansion of the membership of the EEC. This is the category in which one finds primarily service industries or commercial activities whose market is becoming increasingly multi-national in character. As the level of economic activity within an enlarged Community grows, the demand for services of the type developed so far primarily in North America and Britain, and lacking on the Continent, will give rise to a fairly continuing investment flow from Britain to the other EEC countries in the field of financial services, leisure industries, catering, retailing and other activities of a non-capital intensive nature. In fact, this movement has already been under way for some time without encountering insurmountable problems as a result of present exchange control regulations. These are by nature direct investments requiring low financial outlay and yielding a relatively quick return. An increase in the rate of British overseas investment in these areas is not likely to give rise to serious pressures on the payments position.

More problematical is the third type of direct investment, according to the arbitrary distinctions we have suggested for the purposes of this study. Here we are concerned with that growing body of major multi-national corporations (which are not, as is popularly supposed, confined to the United States) whose very size suggests that their future expansion will involve overseas investment. The problems, and benefits, which emanate from the emergence of multi-national corporations, whose annual sales exceed, in many cases, the gross national product of some quite reasonably-sized countries, has been and continues to be studied in great depth by economists and politicians. For our purposes, however, these entities should be examined in the present context merely as possible sources of embarrassing outflows of capital following the liberalisation of direct invest-ment regulations upon British accession to the EEC. It is clear that companies which fall in this general category will seek outlets for their capital within an enlarged European Economic Community since their domestic potential will be limited by the absence of further domestic possibilities owing to the present monopolies legislation. Once again, however, the real impact of this potential problem is difficult to assess because, as explained earlier in this chapter, the tendency to finance international investment in the international capital market will continue to grow as that market becomes the predominant source of long-term capital for the private sector in Europe. Since it is not reasonable to assume that the size of the domestic capital market will grow any faster than it is at present growing, one can only conclude that any major increase in overall investment, domestic or foreign, will have to be financed partially in the international capital market. That portion of major British direct investment in the EEC which is so financed will not constitute an outflow of capital. At the end of the transitional period, of course, greater British participation in the international capital market will be possible. At that stage, to the extent that British direct foreign investment is financed by the sale of international securities which can also be purchased by British residents, the neutralising aspects of external financing will be proportionally reduced.

On balance it is difficult to visualise anything approaching a serious level of net capital outflow as a result of liberalisation of direct investment immediately upon British accession to the EEC. So far as past experience is concerned, a considerable amount of investment has already occurred with limited negative effect owing to the regulations in force. According to statistics published by the Statistical Office of the European Communities, net direct investment by British companies in EEC countries was as follows: 1965, $193 million; 1966, $178 million; 1967, $155 million; 1968, $133 million; 1969, $159 million. Although the pace of Community development is likely to produce a significant increase in the rate of purely European expansion for the major multi-national companies, this same phenomenon will produce balancing inflows as a result of increased United States interest in a Britain within the European Community. The rate of British direct investment in other member states of the EEC will depend to a large extent on the evolution of the whole economic scene, on the corresponding rate of development of capital markets in which such investments can be financed and on the general level of confidence of British management.

In assessing the potential rate of outflow which might be associated with British portfolio investment in an expanded European Economic Community, one must also deal with the present state of development of Europe's financial markets. Capital outflows from portfolio investment are in any case not a problem until the end of the five-year transitional period negotiated in the case of List B transfers. During the transitional period present regulations on foreign portfolio investment will apply although it is reasonable to suppose that gradual reform will take place just as it has over the past few years with respect to overseas investment in general. We have already alluded to the traditional preference for North American securities which has characterised British overseas portfolio investment since the last war. The important question is whether the European financial markets, apart from London, can make up for lost time and begin to demonstrate the same capacity for attracting foreign capital as is evident in the case of New York. In this context one must separate the bond and share markets in attempting to assess the degree of interest which British investors, both institutional and private, might have in buying the securities of other EEC members after the transitional period.

By and large, investors are attracted to fixed income securities denominated in a currency other than their own only where the choice in their national market is limited or where significant interest-rate differentials exist. These two conditions are often present in certain Continental countries where the bond markets are excessively dominated by public sector issues at controlled and therefore artificial interest rates. The substantial appetite for Eurobond issues which has been apparent in recent years in European markets derives largely from the paucity of competitive issues in the national markets. These factors are not to any similar extent present in the UK market, where a substantial fixed-interest securities market exists and where the rate structure is largely influenced by the forces of supply and demand and therefore likely to be more often competitive with foreign issues. In addition, the more important British investors in fixed-income securities are institutional. Pension funds and insurance companies, for instance, have a less dominant role in the Continental bond markets. Such institutions as a matter of policy, and often as a matter of law, must usually match their currency of investment with their currency of eventual liability to their beneficiaries and are thus precluded from buying fixed-interest investments in a currency other than their own. As long as European capital markets remain independent of each other in terms of currency, it seems unlikely that a substantial outflow of capital from the UK could take place as a result of British investment in the bond markets of the other member countries. Eventual monetary unification, of course, would produce unified capital markets in which British investors would participate on an equal basis and without concern for currency conflicts. However, as suggested earlier in this chapter, this possibility is far enough in the future to be beyond the scope of the present discussion on capital flows. A more likely possibility is the development of a freer market in Europe for fixed-income obligations in the tradition already established by the Eurobond market. Naturally, the safeguards, which will be discussed later, will ensure that international issues floated through the EEC countries for non-EEC account will not be treated as List B securities. However, issues of an international nature in terms of interest-rate structure representing obligations of bona-fide EEC debtors would presumably be eligible and might attract some UK interest despite the currency problem.

Potential British investment in EEC equity markets after the transitional period must be measured according to different criteria. In this case currency differentials and comparative yields are of less import since most investors are concerned primarily with assessing earnings growth potential when evaluating equity investments. Undoubtedly the possibility of buying Continental equities without payment of the investment currency premium will stimulate new British interest in the Continental bourses. This interest will be justified by the individuals and institutions concerned on the grounds of diversification and further stimulated by an increased confidence in a continued rapid rate of European economic growth as a result of British entry. To evaluate the possible impact of this in terms of potential outflow of capital one must be mindful of the scale involved. In comparison with the American or British stock exchanges, no informed person would deny that the present state of development of the Continental exchanges is lamentable. Not only are the purely mechanical elements deficient, that is to say, the volume and method of dealing somewhat archaic, but the availability of information required by investors, although improving, is still well below the standards to which British investors are accustomed. Furthermore, the all-important degree of choice is equally bound to be a greatly limiting factor. Because of the lack of depth of the Continental securities markets, many industrial enterprises which might have qualified to be quoted as public companies have remained as family businesses or under the control of banks and other financial institutions. This means that a potential investor in Continental equities is by and large limited to a restricted number of large and mature enterprises in each given country. This is likely to act as a natural deterrent to large-scale British institutional investment in the equities of the other member countries of the European Community.

One is quickly made aware of the enormous disparity in volume between the principal markets of the European Economic Community and the United States market, that traditional home of British overseas portfolio investment, by studying the statistics of net new issues in domestic capital markets given in the annual report of the Bank for International Settlements. For the year 1970, total net new issues including both the public and private sector were as follows for the principal present members of the EEC:

	($ million)
Belgium	2,147
France	3,477
Germany	5,871
Italy	5,826
Netherlands	659

These figures compare with total net new issues in 1970 for both public and private sector of $57.6 billion in the United States. In other words, by this measurement the US capital market is slightly more than three times the size of the combined capital markets of the present EEC membership. Even more important, in view of the greater attraction which European equity markets are likely to have, are the figures relating purely to net domestic new issues of shares in 1970. These were as follows:

	($ million)
Belgium	391
France	1,575
Germany	1,056
Italy	1,631
Netherlands	49

These amounts compare with total net new issues of shares in the United States for the same year of $9.8 billion, demonstrating a disparity of about 2:1 between United States equity markets and those in the existing EEC.

If one assumes that the net purchases of United States securities by British residents in any given year represented pure capital outflow and therefore a loss to the reserves (i.e. if one assumes that the investment currency system did not exist) experience over the last few years would have produced net outflows as follows:

Net Purchases (+) or Sales (−) of US Securities by British Residents (in £ million)

	Shares	Bonds		Total net outflow
		US Govt.	Other	
1968	− 28	+52	+522	574
1969	−245	+56	+251	307
1970	− 33	+92	+118	210

Even if one were to suppose that outflows to the other member states of the EEC might be at half the rate (since the size of the market is roughly half) the net figure would be well within the range of tolerable outflow. This of course does not give any credit to the reasonable possibility that Continental investors might be drawn to invest in the British market following UK accession to the European Community.

Finally the all-important question of safeguards under the negotiated arrangements is worth commenting on. On 27 July 1971, Mr. Piers Dixon, Conservative member for Truro, asked the Chancellor of the Exchequer what measures were proposed to prevent leakages of capital from the UK to third countries once the restrictions on portfolio investment to the Common Market members are removed. Of course, the Chancellor pointed out that this question would only arise at a future date which he mentioned might be $6\frac{1}{2}$ years away (meaning the period up to accession plus the five-year transitional period). In fact, there are already sufficient powers incorporated within the Treaty of Rome and its subsequent interpretation by the Commission through directives, which allow members discretion to control certain transfers which purport to be inter-Community in nature but are in fact disguised transfers to third countries. Again it must be recalled that the new freedoms foreseen in the negotiated arrangements will continue to be supervised in one way or another by the Bank of England as the traditional administrator of exchange control procedure.

Furthermore, it must also be borne in mind that the Treaty of Rome contains provisions allowing member states to take special action in the event of capital movements on a scale which might endanger a member's balance-of-payments position. In fact, since the inception of the Community, member states have availed themselves of these powers to ward off speculative movements which might be deemed to come within the scale permitted by the stated intention of the adherents to the Treaty to allow freedom of capital movements within the Community. Where these movements clearly threaten the payments position of a member state, the imposition of controls to control or neutralise them is clearly permitted and Britain would obviously benefit from these same safeguards. It is equally worth noting the language of the communique reporting on the general agreement reached with the EEC so far as it affects transactions covered by List B (Operations in Securities). This text refers to arrangements which will be in force at the end of the transitional period and which will permit dealings at (or near) the official rate of exchange with respect to foreign currency securities of the European Economic Community. The important phrase is "or near" the official rate of exchange. This permits the introduction of a two-tier exchange market in special circumstances. For example, Belgium has such a system in force at the present time which, although it is primarily designed to cope with the present tensions in the international exchange markets, also affects dealings by Belgian residents in securities of the other EEC member states. France has also a two-tier exchange market which distinguishes between trade and capital flows and, for capital flows, distinguishes between residents and non-residents as well (for residents there exists a system similar to Britain's own 'premium dollar' market). There can be no question that the present Community arrangements will allow Britain all the necessary scope to deal with movements of a dramatic nature which might adversely affect its payments position, while still remaining within the spirit of the present EEC directives on capital movements.

Chapter 8

INVISIBLE EARNINGS*

by Ronald Cooper and Alan Peacock

IT IS WELL KNOWN that so-called 'invisible accounts'[1] have become an increasingly important element in Britain's balance of payments. The UK is second only to the US in the top 10 invisible earners, earning 12 per cent of the total world invisibles receipts. It is more dependent than any other industrial country on invisible earnings, with over one-third of its total foreign receipts derived from this source. The surplus on invisible earnings has risen dramatically over the last few years, from £116 million in 1966 to £557 million in 1969. Indeed, the surplus in the private sector, when the deficit on government account is excluded, was as much as £1,092 million. It seems more than likely, even if the rate of growth in net invisibles may decline, that invisibles will continue for many years to play a major part in any attempt to preserve a healthy balance-of-payments situation.

It seems curious that during these years of speculation and

---

*The authors are grateful to the Committee on Invisible Exports for permission to reproduce material used in their own draft report to the Committee submitted by the Economists Advisory Group. The report's findings were embodied in *How entry into the Common Market may affect Britain's Invisible Earnings*, published by the Committee on Invisible Exports in July 1971. The Committee are in no way committed to the conclusions reached by the authors in this chapter.

[1] Invisible transactions are most simply defined by enumeration: transport (shipping and civil aviation), travel (including tourist expenditure), other services (including City earnings), interest profits and dividends, private transfers (including migrants' remittances), and government transactions (e.g. military expenditure overseas and grants).

controversy about the economic problems of EEC entry, so little attention has been paid to invisibles. The 1970 White Paper (Cmnd 4289) asserts that "there should be a valuable expansion in our invisible earnings" (para. 91), but without any close analysis of the factors which might affect them. The 1971 White Paper (Cmnd 4715) makes, at most, only oblique reference to invisibles through its very brief discussion of external capital movements. There are two principal reasons for this lack of attention. First and foremost, is the fact that within the EEC itself, invisibles are much less important as a factor in balance-of-payments policies, and, therefore, possibly less in the mind of negotiators in considering what conditions to attach to entry of potential members. Secondly, it is even more difficult than in the case of visible trade to build economic models of a general nature which would help us to quantify the effect on invisible trade of the change brought about by entry. Transactions within the invisible account are extremely heterogeneous and hence dependent upon and related to factors pervading the whole economy. Furthermore, there are only broad estimates of invisible transactions between Britain and the EEC. Our own attempts to assess the economic factors at work are of a tentative nature but it seems fair to suppose that it is better to examine, however tentatively, the range of possibilities than to turn a blind eye.

In the ensuing analysis, we detain the reader for as few lines as possible with some of the main figures which describe the current level of invisible trading with EEC countries. We then consider what EEC measures are likely to be of most consequence in invisible trading if we enter the Common Market and follow this with a look at the possible effects on particular sectors. Our conclusions are tentative but they suggest, to put it at its lowest, that there is no cause for alarm in viewing the prospects for invisibles in an enlarged EEC.

Invisible transactions with the EEC: the present position

The statistical essence of the situation is that (i) invisible transactions are more important for the UK than for EEC countries; (ii) over recent years the UK has shown an increasingly favourable balance while EEC countries as a whole have experienced increasing deficits; and (iii) invisible transactions by Britain with EEC countries are not at present a large part of invisible transactions as a whole.

In 1969, the latest year for which balance-of-payments estimates for both the UK and EEC countries are available,[1] the surplus of £557 million which the UK had on invisible account more than covered the deficit of a much smaller magnitude on visible trade. In the same year, EEC countries as a whole showed a deficit on invisibles account of over £800 million and within this total both Germany and France were in deficit, though not to any significant extent in the case of France. Moreover, between 1964 and 1969, the UK balance had showed a fairly steady improvement from a surplus of £124 million whereas the EEC countries had experienced a deterioration from a deficit of £140 million.

The invisible balance is of course struck as the difference between two large credit and debit sums: for the UK respectively £4,129 million and £3,572 million in 1969. These sums amount to one-third or more of the corresponding total current account transactions. The corresponding proportions for the EEC countries as a whole are about one-quarter. Another way of appreciating the magnitudes of invisible transactions is to look at them in relation to national income. UK 'invisible exports', which enter as credits in the balance of payments, are for example as much as 8 per cent of national income, twice the proportions for Germany and France.

Although on any count total invisible transactions of the UK are large, the amount of trade in invisibles which is carried out with EEC countries is relatively small. Thus in 1969, while 20 per cent of visible exports went to the EEC, only 12 per cent of invisible receipts originated with the EEC. Table 1 sets out the invisible transactions between the UK and EEC for 1969 according to the main heads of the account and compares them with the UK's transactions with all countries.

For UK-EEC transactions, the dominant head is *transport* (including shipping and civil aviation) with UK credits and debits respectively 23 per cent and 21 per cent of total UK credits and debits. It is not unexpected that these proportions are comparable in magnitude with the corresponding figures for

---

[1] The source of the statistics of this section is the Report of the Committee on Invisible Exports, *op. cit.*

The Economics of Europe

Table 1: UK Invisible Transactions with EEC Countries and with all Countries in 1969

	EEC Countries			All Countries			EEC as % of total	
Transport	credit	debit	net	credit £ million	debit	net	credits percentages	debits
Shipping, Civil aviation }	291	242	+ 49	{ 959 287	914 246	+ 45 + 41 }	23	21
Travel	70	83	− 13	359	324	+ 35	19	26
Other services	19	94	− 75	1,010	490	+ 520	2	19
Interest, profits and dividends	95	51	+ 44	1,292	841	+ 451	7	6
Private services (inc. IPD)	475	470	+ 5	3,907	2,815	+1,092	12	19
Government services	4	131	−127	46	329	− 283	8	39
Private transfers	18	14	+ 4	176	253	− 77	10	6
Total*	497	615	−118	4,129	3,397	+ 732	12	18

*Excluding government transfers, which are negligible for EEC countries. These transfers amounted to £175 million in 1969, which accounts for the difference between the total invisibles surplus of £557 million given in the opening paragraph of this chapter and the £732 million given in this table.

visible trade though the transport head includes a wide variety of items dependent upon many factors other than the level of visible trade between this country and the EEC.

The only other significant head within the UK-EEC private sector invisibles account at present is *travel*. Credits and debits in 1969 were respectively £70 million and £83 million, being about one-quarter to one-fifth of UK transactions with all countries. Travel credits from the EEC have increased substantially over the past five years along with travel credits generally. But debits to the EEC have fallen, one important factor having been the expansion of package holidays in Western Europe outside the EEC, particularly in Spain.

The head '*other services*' forms a large and heterogeneous collection: as well as transactions relating to the operations of the City of London's financial institutions, it includes such items as royalties and advertising and commercial services. In recent years, 'other services' have been one of the most important and dynamic components of the UK invisibles account and by 1969 the net surplus with all countries had reached £520 million, not much less than the net surplus on the whole invisibles account. However, transactions with EEC countries remain a small proportion of the whole. Credits from the EEC, at £19 million, accounted for only 2 per cent of credits from all countries. The corresponding proportion for debits (19 per cent) was higher and has been increasing in recent years so that 'other service' transactions with the EEC in 1969 showed a net deficit of £75 million. However, this movement is an apparent one. Higher interest payments from borrowings in the Eurodollar market are largely debits to EEC countries but the corresponding interest credits arising from Eurodollar lending arise mainly from non-EEC countries.

The relatively small magnitude of UK-EEC transactions arising from *interest, profits and dividends* reflects the still low level of capital investment between the two areas. The large debit of £130 million under *government services* arises mainly from the support costs of British forces in Germany. The remaining head in the UK-EEC invisibles account, *private transfers*, is small. But this item includes remittances of workers' earnings which in some EEC countries is very substantial given the labour movements between EEC countries and into the EEC (particularly Germany) from Greece and elsewhere. Thus, in 1968 payments of workers' earnings from Germany were over £125 million and for France £70 million.

The current position may thus be summed up. The UK-EEC invisibles account is dominated by transport and travel transactions and payments for military expenditure in Germany. Receipts from 'other services' (including City earnings) are relatively small.

EEC policies and invisibles

The principal aim of the EEC, in the sphere of economic policy, is to increase the prosperity of its members. We are apt in this country to see this aim as being best fulfilled by appropriate 'macro-economic' policies designed to promote eonomic stability and growth. It is certainly true that this view is also shared in the EEC, and some measures under discussion might even require the eventual acceptance of a supranational armoury of fiscal and monetary controls. It is nevertheless true that in the EEC such macro-economic policies are still basically the responsibility of the member governments, and that policy-making at the Community level has been directed mainly towards creating an environment in which a unified market in goods and services can flourish and in which barriers to competition have been removed. Removing such barriers requires that there is no discrimination within EEC countries against the free movement of goods and services and factors of production originating in member countries. We must now see what 'non-discrimination' means when it is applied to invisible earnings and payments.

Let us look first of all at the main *fiscal measures*. The Common External Tariff (CET) is already in being and it, together with the removal of tariff and quota restrictions between the UK and present ECC members, will have important 'trade-creating' and 'trade-diverting' effects which are considered in other chapters in this book. At first sight, the CET, which is likely to increase the value and volume of trade between the EEC and the UK at a faster rate than with Commonwealth countries which would no longer enjoy preferential treatment, would appear to have no effect on invisible trade. However, it must be remembered that many forms of invisible earnings— shipping and air freight are examples—are closely linked to visible trade.

The second set of fiscal measures now in process of being adopted are designed to harmonise taxation on both goods and services through a value-added tax (VAT) and thus to equalise tax burdens on similar products and services available for sale in any one country, including imports. The UK Government has already announced the replacement of the Selective Employment Tax (SET) and the Purchase Tax by a VAT which will be introduced in 1973. If the doctrine of 'non-discrimination' were to be consistently applied it would require that invisible exports, like manufactured articles, should be exempted from VAT in the country of origin. As many suppliers of invisible services, e.g. banking and insurance concerns, catering industries, etc., are at present subject to SET, the announced changes in the structure of indirect taxes could in principle benefit invisible exporters. However, there are formidable administrative problems in identifying services provided to overseas customers particularly if they enjoy them as visitors to this country. It will be interesting to see whether or not the Government will accept the principle that invisibles exports should be treated similarly to manufactured exports and, even if they do, what form any alleviation in tax might take.

Looking further into the future, the EEC is conscious of the influence which corporation taxes have on the free movement of capital. Non-discrimination would require tax measures which would eliminate double taxation of dividends and interest and the equalisation of rates of withholding taxes on dividends. The recent Green Paper on Corporation Tax favours a 'two-rate' system similar to the German system which would encourage distribution of profits through a lower rate on distributed as distinct from undistributed profits. If such a system were adopted throughout the EEC, the role of the capital market rather than undistributed profits as a source of business finance might increase in importance, and this might bring consequential benefits to the City as a source of expertise in floating new issues. Until recently, the German method seemed the frontrunner for EEC corporate tax structure, but this is no longer certain. Several other proposals for tax harmonisation are under consideration which could affect invisible earnings, but these are unlikely to be of major importance. For example, the Council of the EEC has already approved a scheme for the simplification of taxes on the issue and negotiation of securities.

We consider next those measures *which liberalise the movements of factors of production, capital and labour.* Generally speaking, EEC countries allow free movement in personal capital, such as gifts, legacies, emigrants' remittances and purchases of real estate abroad, and also direct investment by member countries' companies is allowed without major restriction. They are more restrictive in respect of portfolio investment and investment by small savers who are 'protected' by a variety of measures, some of which are clearly designed to help governments channel private savings into the purchase of their own bond issues. On entry into the EEC, we would be committed to remove our relatively strict control of outward capital movements by a phased removal, with relaxation of control on direct investment coming first. As is explained in Chapter 7, the controls on portfolio investment are not likely to be removed at a rate that causes any difficulties for the balance of payments. Nevertheless, as these controls are relaxed, there could be a substantial net outflow on this account. So far as invisibles are concerned, any net outward capital flow movement would be counterbalanced in the long run by a return flow of income from earnings abroad. The size and timing of this flow would depend, of course, on the form which investment abroad would take. Some of this investment would be 'unrequited', in the sense that its fruits are meant to be enjoyed abroad. An example of this would be investment in private property abroad for owner occupation.

The fact that the UK has agreed to liberalise exchange control regulations on personal transfers in the form of migrants' remittances within the first two years of entry is a reminder of the importance attached to *freedom of movement of labour* within the EEC. Already workers within (but not from outside) the EEC are free to take up jobs in the Community without a labour permit and with liberal residence requirements, and it is even possible for foreign workers to be admitted to a member country to seek work not having been specifically guaranteed employment. In time, the same rights will be afforded to self-employed persons, but there have been understandable difficulties in securing agreement on comparability of professional qualifications. It is noteworthy that the Government has resisted pressure to demand transitional safeguards for the British labour market, save in the special case of Northern Ireland.

The next policy factor of importance is *monetary union*. At one time it looked as if our negotiators of entry to EEC could be faced with an agreed EEC view on the nature and timing of monetary union, along the lines found in the Werner Report. All that has happened so far is that there is acceptance in principle of the narrowing of exchange margins and the eventual introduction of a common currency. Member countries, under the monetary crises which have resulted in the floating of a number of European currencies this year, have come to lay increasing stress on the common fiscal and financial policies that would increasingly be needed as monetary union was introduced, and whose implications have not yet been studied in depth. It remains an open question, therefore, that will not be settled without the participation of the new members in an enlarged Community, exactly what a monetary union will mean and by what stages, and when, it will be introduced; and it is thus not possible to identify the effect on the invisibles. It is not certain whether EEC countries will take the City's liberal and flexible banking rules and conventions as the model for common monetary and financial policies, but by the time these policies are again under active discussion, the UK, as a member, is bound to have a large say in what is eventually decided. The spirit of the Treaty of Rome points towards liberalisation of banking and financial arrangements and if it were invoked the City of London as the dominant financial centre in Europe would have a much expanded role as an invisible exporter.

A related issue of much more importance in the short run is the Government's commitment *to reduce the role of sterling as a trading and financing currency.* One must admit that little definite can be said about the effects on invisibles. Sterling balances held in London in the form of British government securities and Treasury Bills, when reduced, would mean outward capital movements coupled with a fall in interest payments (invisible imports) to overseas holders; but it is possible that the UK Government could assume a different form of liability to sterling holders acceptable to EEC partners rather than discharge the liabilities by some phased reduction in sterling balances. The concomitant benefits in the form of banking and financial earnings associated with the use of sterling as an international currency would probably fall, but they are now no longer a significant element in our invisible trading account.

Finally, mention must be made of *legal provisions in EEC countries,* which have a bearing on the future of invisible exports. It will clearly be of advantage for British firms to have the same right of establishment in EEC countries as national competitors. The Treaty of Rome clearly indicates that national company laws should not continue to be formulated in a way which discriminates against other EEC members. Progress has been slow even in devising suitable approaches which conform with the Treaty provisions. British insurance companies are much affected by existing company legislation, which is, at present, much more liberal in Britain than in other EEC countries.

To sum up, the range of EEC provisions which are designed to promote fair trading among members and which could affect invisibles is much wider than official publications on entry suggest. The 1970 White Paper concentrated almost entirely on those measures which affected interest, profits and dividends in its discussion of the effect of entry on invisibles, but as yet these items comprise only a small proportion of invisible trade with the EEC. The striking feature of our survey of EEC policies is how few of them affecting invisibles have been instituted.

The possible effect of entry on individual heads of the invisibles account

The invisibles account is a particularly difficult area on which to offer even tentative views about the likely impact of entry. Not only are there the uncertainties regarding the institutional background referred to above. There is also the point that invisibles transactions form an extremely heterogeneous collection of payments and receipts each influenced by many varied economic and social factors. In this situation, no broad-brush approach can carry any conviction. And finally, the central concern is the effect on the invisible net balance between very large outgoings and incomings. Even small errors in predicting gross flows can, as is well known in relation to forecasts of visible trade, imply substantially wrong forecasts of a balance between the two. Nevertheless, it is possible to make some useful qualitative points about the likely direction of change under certain heads of the account. We consider the heads in the order in which they appear in the table above.

Transport. This head comprises shipping and civil aviation; unfortunately there are no figures of UK-EEC transactions for these two components separately. Transport is important if only because of its size. In 1969, credits and debits with the EEC amounted respectively to nearly £300 million and £240 million, accounting for one-third to one-half of total invisible transactions with the EEC. And UK transactions with all countries, particularly for shipping, are very substantial. As a result, even if entry were to have a relatively small effect on gross transactions, the net effect could be significant.

The future institutional setting within the Common Market is uncertain and the EEC common transport policy has not yet been applied to maritime shipping. Although on entry Britain, with Norway and Denmark, would be operating about two-thirds of Community shipping, and will help to shape the common policy, it is not certain that a common policy will emerge which will be completely in tune with British interests. Clearly there is a big question mark here.

As regards the trade factors, the short-run effects on shipping are likely to be unfavourable though to what degree is impossible to say. UK-EEC trade would increase at the expense of longer-haul UK-Commonwealth trade and this would raise problems of adaptation for the British shipping industry. Effects of tax changes on costs are unlikely to be significant and EEC entry will not change the situation on flag discrimination.

As regards civil aviation, again one can expect a disadvantageous diversion of traffic from long-haul to short-haul routes. Additionally, there might well be erosion of the favourable bilateral agreements relating to BOAC routes with Commonwealth countries.

Taking the transport head as a whole, it seems that, at any rate in the short run, the impact of entry may well be disadvantageous to the balance of payments and to British shipping and airlines. But against this there are two general considerations. First the discussion has left out the dynamic effects on international trade of entry. And second, there is the danger that, if Britain were outside the EEC, a protectionist Community transport policy might emerge that would be seriously inimical to British interests.

Travel. Tourist travel is already more or less free between the UK and the EEC and other countries and there are no institutional factors which in themselves would change this situation on entry. The main impact of entry is likely to come from any change in the competitive position of the British tourist industry resulting from changes in the tariff structure and in taxation on expenditure. (At present, about one-third of tourist expenditure in this country is on 'shopping'.) One important unknown is the form of and the tax rate for VAT. It is unlikely that the position *vis-à-vis* foreign tourist competitors in the EEC and other countries such as Spain will be improved and it could worsen. Any adverse change would of course operate on the whole base of travel receipts and payments, and not merely transactions between the UK and EEC countries.

Other Services. The point has already been made above that, although the great miscellany of items under this have contributed very substantially in recent years to the growth in invisible credits, transactions with EEC countries remain a relatively small part of the whole. Whatever the nature of the impact of entry upon transactions under this head, it is unlikely that there will be any substantial effects in the short run.

In transactions with all countries, over one-half of net earnings from 'other services' arise from 'financial and allied services',—the so-called City earnings—and within the latter, *insurance* is by far the most important element. Net earnings from insurance in 1969 from all countries were as much as £188 million but from EEC countries only about £10 million. If the level of business *vis-à-vis* EEC countries were to expand to the degree it has elsewhere there could be considerable benefit to the invisibles account. This kind of thought was presumably behind the optimism of the 1970 White Paper, which foresaw the increase of City earnings as one of the main benefits to the balance of payments.

However, there are good reasons for tempering, though not countering, this rosy view. One reason for the low level of British insurance business in the EEC countries is their restrictive legislation operating on foreign companies. Thus, there are requirements on the local holding of reserve funds, restrictions which run counter to the freedom of investment which British companies have generally enjoyed. The Community is in the process of formulating a common policy in this field. Where the balance will finally lie between liberal and protectionist or restrictive directives is an open question. But at least it can be said that what finally emerges will be more beneficial to British interests if we are party to the policy formulation. If only for this reason the relative impact of entry can fairly be assessed as a favourable one.

By contrast, other sectors under the 'financial and allied services' could in due course be expected to operate in a more liberal competitive environment. Thus in the field of banking, there will be wider opportunities for British and EEC banking and related institutions in each other's areas. The factors affecting banking credits are many and complex, including the degree of exchange control, the level of interest rates and the movements of capital funds, all of which are impossible to forecast. But there seems no reason to dissent from the view expressed in the Report of the Committee on Invisible Exports (*op. cit.*) that it seems likely that the net effect on the overseas earnings of the banking sector will be a beneficial one, probably (though not necessarily), of only moderate proportions.

There is little which can be said about the many other transactions included under 'other services'. Given that the 'dynamic effects' of EEC entry can be expected in many cases to increase the level of transactions for which there is at present a net surplus, it is not unreasonable to expect some favourable effect on balance.

Interest, profits and dividends. The prospects for interest, profits and dividends transactions hang very much upon the impact of entry upon international capital flows. Likely developments in inward and outward investment are considered in Chapter 7. Despite uncertainties, one point of a general nature can usefully be made. Whatever are the developments in the capital account, the financing of capital flows is likely for many years to dominate the associated changes in interest, profits and dividends. In this sense, it can be said that changes in receipts and payments of interest, profits and dividends will be relatively unimportant except in the longer run.

Remittances of workers' earnings. This is so small an item for the UK at present that these remittances are not identified separately in the accounts, being included under the general head of 'private transfers'. Under the Community's regulations for free movement of labour within the EEC, these transactions will certainly grow, but where the balance will lie between credits and debits is highly doubtful. Germany and France are showing net debits of £50 million and £25 million respectively. However, the German figure reflects the large inflow of workers from Greece and other countries outside the EEC.

Government transactions. The cost of support of British forces in Germany (£108 million in 1969) accounts for most of government transactions with the EEC at present. For many years successive British governments have sought in various ways to reduce this cost though without much success. There is no reason to expect any change if Britain were within the Community.

Finally, it should be noted that some of the payments into and receipts from the Community budgets would be statistically attributed to the invisibles account and could indeed swamp the changes we discussed above. These are discussed elsewhere in this book.

Conclusion

In reaching any conclusion at all, formidable methodological problems have to be faced. One can agree with the 1970 White Paper's procedure of comparing an 'entry' and 'no entry' situation, and we have followed it in our own analysis. However, defining what entry means is much more difficult than the White Paper and its 1971 successor suggest. For one thing, the precise nature of the changes which would be a condition of entry are not yet fully known and were even less clear at the time the 1970 White Paper was written. For another, the timing of adjustment to these changes is also still under negotiation. Furthermore, it is difficult to offer any prediction of the influence we would have, once we had entered the EEC, on the negotiation of a whole range of outstanding matters ranging from European monetary arrangements to the formulation of a European company law. If these matters for conjecture were not enough, the reactions of third countries to our entry have still to be brought into account. On this last point, in regard to invisibles at least, the 1970 White Paper was silent. It is not even clear whether the White Paper, when referring to "the valuable expansion" (para. 91) and "improvement" (para. 94) in invisible earnings, means purely the credit or the net position.

Our conclusions are bound to be of a tentative and qualitative nature, in view both of the difficulties in data collection and analysis and of the problems encountered in identifying the relevant political and economic factors which surround entry and quantifying their effects.

In the short run—say during the first five years of membership —the matter at issue is the change in market conditions, which would arise from redirection of trade and movements in relative prices and costs resulting from acceptance of entry conditions. In the case of the currently important sectors on invisibles account, transport and travel, we have suggested above that the short-run changes in market conditions are likely to be disadvantageous though not substantially so. Then travel is not affected by immediate changes in tariff policy, and although changes in tax structure as a result of the introduction of VAT may if anything be unfavourable, they would not make a substantial difference. In any case, the emerging pattern of tourism suggests that improving the invisibles account within the EEC depends on the ability of our passenger transport services, and possibly our tourist agencies, to cater for and attract growing numbers of EEC tourists who wish to travel abroad. With some liberalisation of capital movements, and if freedom of establishment and greater freedom of investment policy for financial institutions in EEC countries were to be allowed in the short period, the City would be well placed to compete in Europe, for in the fields of banking, merchanting and insurance services, British expertise and competitiveness are fully recognised. We have, however, noted that in the important insurance sector, the Community arrangements might not prove to be as liberal as might be hoped. In any case, as short-run expansion would depend upon increasing our present small share of the European markets in these fields, it is doubtful if there would be an immediate jump in net earnings. Taking an overall view of the invisibles account as a whole, it seems unlikely that in the short term entry would have any sizeable effect one way or the other.

In the longer run, entry is commonly supported on the grounds that our rate of economic growth will be accelerated, and the evidence for this is analysed in detail by Williamson in Chapter 2. So far as the balance of payments is concerned, and invisibles in particular, we must look further than the opportunities for expansion of demand for goods and services within the EEC towards the comparative rates of expansion in the EEC and other international trading partners who import goods and services from the UK.

We can agree with the financial pundits who have emphasised the opportunities available for a much-expanded role for the City of London, were the hoped-for expansion in trade between the EEC and the UK to take place. It does not seem unreasonable to suppose that net earnings of banking, merchanting and insurance services would benefit from any dynamic factors. It is worth noting that any expansion in foreign earnings of City institutions would be a function not only of the hoped-for increase in our export trade with the EEC but also of the greater accessibility of their services to EEC exporters to the UK. Thus the expansion in the *total* volume of trade between EEC countries and not solely the volume of UK exports to the EEC would be a better indicator of the opportunities for expansion of net earnings of the City.

However tentative our conclusions must be regarding the net effect of entry in both the short and the long run on invisible transactions, policy negotiations concerning the economic environment in which invisible trade is carried out will be of the utmost importance *subsequent* to entry. Even though a common currency is not likely to be adopted for a long time ahead, it will be desirable that balance-of-payments problems be met with as little recourse as is possible to either deflation or exchange-rate adjustment. In the light of the recent history of the British balance of payments, which reveals the growing importance of invisibles for strengthening our position, it is more than ever necessary for our representatives at the EEC on our joining to promote harmonisation measures which will help exporters of services. Fortunately, in this area the Treaty of Rome offers ample support for harmonisation in the field of company and financial law, particularly in relation to banking and insurance services, which for once would favour adjustment by other EEC countries towards British legal provisions. This may offer no more than a moral advantage, but it suggests a line of argument which British representatives in the Council of an enlarged Community cannot afford to neglect in seeking the fairest terms for the invisibles sector.

Chapter 9

TAXATION*

by Douglas Dosser

TAXATION is a field which is only loosely dealt with in the Treaty
of Rome, but Community policy has been articulated in
Directives, Proposals and Working Parties. Since it is such an
ongoing field of co-ordination of policy, British entry falls, as it
were, in the middle of the formulation of that policy. Some
decisions (in the form of Directives) are mandatory on her.
Some are in an advanced stage of negotiations, so for those our
influence is likely to be over detail only rather than principle.
But in several tax fields, the future is so vague that Britain will
be a major contributor to Community decisions.

These three categories by the stage decisions have reached
each enclose major taxes. The form of the Community general
sales tax is laid down as the Value-Added Tax, together with the
major provisions of that tax. However, the eventual rate or rates
are still undecided. Excises fall into the second stage: the main
lines now apparent but many details (and again rates of tax)
to be decided. Corporation Tax is, at the time of writing, still
uncertain even as to the basic principles, but the shape of the
Community Corporation Tax is likely to be known, in the form
of a Proposal of the Commission, within months. There is
practically no progress on Social Security harmonisation, and no
intention to harmonise Personal Income Taxes.

The present paper reflects this position: a lot can be said about

*The material upon which this chapter is based arises from a wider
study included in the Public Sector Studies Programme of the Institute
of Social and Economic Studies of the University of York, and financed
by the Social Science Research Council.

the VAT and its effects on Britain, since so much is now known about the agreed harmonised Community tax structure; much less can be said about Excises and Corporation Tax in view of the uncertainties.

However, it is important not to ignore the second two fields. For tax harmonisation is a package of tax changes for Britain and looking at VAT alone is likely to give a distorted picture: what some would consider to be pills under VAT are sweetened elsewhere.   The taxation side must furthermore be seen in the light of the expansion of the Community budget, with its expenditure benefits as well as taxation burdens.

The final fiscal impact on Britain of joining arises from this long-term and complicated budgetary development. Unfortunately, only the earliest elements on each side of the Community budget—VAT and the Agricultural Fund—are currently known about. It must be emphasised that what we are looking at now is a short-term and partial picture, and one with an in-built bias against Britain, for it was formulated to suit the Six in the absence of any British presence in its negotiation.

THE VALUE-ADDED TAX

We can pass over the basic principles of a VAT, which can be found in many text-books,[1] and a short summary seen in the recent Green Paper.[2]

What is less well known about VAT is the position reached in the EEC, the consequences of Britain having to conform to that position, and the options still open for British influence once she is a member.

Adoption of VAT in the EEC

The Treaty of Rome is at its firmest in the fiscal field when dealing with indirect taxes. According to Article 99, "The Commission shall consider in what way the law of the various Member States concerning turnover taxes, excise duties, and

---

[1] For example, A. R. Prest, *Public Finance in Theory and Practice*, Weidenfeld & Nicolson, 1960, and C. S. Shoup, *Public Finance*, Aldine, Chicago, 1969. See also Richard W. Lindholm, The Value Added Tax; a Short Review of the Literature, *Journal of Economic Literature*, Vol. VIII, No. 4, December, 1970.
[2] *Value Added Tax*, Cmnd 4621, HMSO, March 1971.

other forms of indirect taxes . . . can be harmonised in the interest of the Common Market".

The Article was given substance by a committee of outside experts, appointed by the EEC, under the chairmanship of Professor Neumark.[3] This committee recommended the form of taxation as value-added, and several subsidiary principles, of which the most important is the 'restricted origin' principle for internationally traded products, according to which goods traded within the Community carry the taxation of the country of origin or production, but trade with outside countries carries the tax of the country of consumption. Unless one retains the existing 'border taxes', which can prevent 'unfair competition' from countries with the lower tax rates, it follows that a harmonisation of rates of VAT is needed within the Community, for imports from fellow-member states can then compete on sufficiently equal terms with home production (the accepted international code for sales taxes on traded products) only if the rate of the fellow member is close enough to one's own.

So, from an early stage, the Commission envisaged an equal-rate VAT within the Community (more recently thinking has moved, for practical reasons, towards a range of rates, or 'fork'), together with the administratively simpler origin principle (no rebating on exports necessary): all conducive to the emotive catch-phrase: 'abolition of fiscal frontiers'. Products could be driven across the borders of the Community without any check being necessary for fiscal purposes. As we shall see, however, no decision has been taken as to how closely the taxes should be harmonised, at what rates, or at what time.

The first part of the scheme, the structural harmonisation to the VAT form, was given effect by the Directive of 11 April 1967. All member-states were to change to this type of general sales tax by 1 January 1971. (Subsequently, extensions were allowed for Belgium to 1 January 1972, and for Italy to 1 January 1973.)

Why was the VAT chosen, compared with the 'cascade'

---

[3] *Report of Fiscal and Financial Committee* (Neumark Report), EEC, Brussels, 1962.

(then current German) system[4] or a single-stage system, like the British Purchase Tax, or Italian retail taxes?

Some claim can be made for the value-added form on economic grounds, at least in comparison with the 'cascade' system. The latter certainly distorts industrial structure, since tax payments are economised by vertical integration of firms, but not by horizontal integration. Again, rebating the tax paid on exports (still necessary in the Community until the restricted origin principle can come into force, and always to be necessary for trade with third parties) is a difficult and disputatious calculation under the 'cascade' system.

However, there were further reasons for the choice of VAT, albeit unspoken ones. First, it minimised disturbance if one of the major existing systems was used, and the choice fell on the French! More to the point, the VAT compels much more elaborate book-keeping by all producers and traders caught in its net—for otherwise they cannot get their own tax liability reduced by the VAT already paid by others on supplies used. This is the big advantage from the viewpoint of tax administration and enforcement, compared with a single-stage tax. A retail tax, for example, does not have the cascade system's disadvantage, and its burden might well be distributed backwards towards producers, and forwards towards consumers in much the same way as a VAT would be. But the high nominal rate required on all retail transactions would lead to a temptation to sell round the side of the net, and one not easily detected. The British Purchase Tax minimises this problem by levying a single stage tax on wholesalers, a smaller and more controllable number of enterprises, and on a limited range of products only.

This is the rationale for the VAT form in Continental Europe. Obviously many of these arguments do not apply to Britain, or only in lesser degree. There is no distorting 'cascade' system to replace, and rebates are easily calculated under the Purchase Tax. So what justification can be made for this wholesale change in a major British tax? It can hardly be justified under tax efficiency and morality, since this is already reasonably high with the British Purchase Tax.

---

[4] Tax is levied on *gross* value of sales, not *net* value, at every stage of production.

None of the arguments relevant on the Continent has much force here, but a new argument which was not strong, at least in France and Germany, takes over in Britain: expansion of the tax base.

That this is desirable in the indirect tax field has been acknowledged by the Labour Government when in office, and implicitly by the Conservatives' announcement of the impending introduction of VAT. The Conservatives' explicit argument[5] of "simplicity" is hardly valid when the VAT is a much more complex tax than the Purchase Tax, and probably than the Purchase Tax and the SET together. The Conservatives' second claim, that VAT will involve a "reduction in distortion of consumer choice", has more validity, but if this is a new objective of tax policy, Excises are way out in front of the Purchase Tax as candidates for reform. Actually, the argument about distortion really reduces to the tax-base problem: it is the high rates, under Purchase Tax and Excises, on a limited number of products which now look objectionable, but which are necessary to pull in the indirect revenues the present British budget requires. That is, the taxable base is too narrow.

The tax base for indirect taxation in Britain is, of course, consumers' expenditure on products subject to Purchase Tax, and on those which carry Excises. The following table shows how this base has been growing over recent years, compared with consumers' expenditure as a whole.

Table 1: The Tax Base for Indirect Taxation in the UK in relation to Total Consumers' Expenditure

	Group 1	Group 2	(£m, current prices) Total consumers' expenditure
1959	4,164	2,386	16,117
1961	4,551	2,803	17,830
1963	5,024	3,153	20,087
1965	5,687	3,774	22,885
1967	6,061	4,303	25,362
1969	6,631	5,036	28,618

Group 1 contains principal items subject to Purchase Tax: household durables, including cars, clothing, chemists' goods, recreational and miscellaneous goods.

Group 2 comprises main excisable items: alcohol and tobacco, oil and petrol.

[5] In the Green Paper, *op. cit.*

The significant fact is that the main British indirect tax base, for Purchase Tax, has been growing more slowly than total consumption expenditure. Between 1959-69, total consumers' expenditure grew by 78 per cent. The total of Group 1 (Purchase Tax) items increased by only 59 per cent. The 111 per cent increase in the Excise base conceals the fact that alcohol and tobacco expenditure have grown a little less than total consumers' expenditure, whilst petrol expenditure has more than trebled. Thus, to keep indirect tax revenues merely in line with the growth of consumption expenditure requires higher and higher rates of either Purchase Tax or Excises.[6]

The VAT provides a perfect opportunity to broaden the tax base in Britain. Of course, not all consumers' expenditure is brought under its wing, but a much higher proportion is than with our existing indirect-tax structure.[7]

Exactly which items are included, which excluded, is virtually decided by the Directives, though with one important proviso.

The list of exempted commercial activities suggested in Chapter 4 of the Green Paper accords in general with the exempt categories in the Community VAT. Principally, they are the activities of small traders, financial institutions, welfare, education, charitable and religious institutions, housing services.

But there are some 'grey areas' in the correspondence of the Green Paper's suggestions and the Community's code.

The most important concerns food. The present British Government has given assurances that the VAT will not be applied to food. But a reduced rate of VAT is to be applied to food sales in the Community, on which the member countries at present have a half rate.

It is possible for these two positions to be reconciled at least to the end of Britain's transitional period if not beyond.

---

[6] And remember both political parties have a reason for desiring indirect tax revenues to form a *rising* proportion of consumers' expenditure: the Labour Party to provide for a public expenditure growth rate above that of national income; the Conservative Party to allow for some shift away from direct personal taxation.

[7] The type of VAT in question is the 'consumption type'. There is also a 'product type' and an 'income type' of VAT, involving varying treatment of the cost of capital assets, depreciation etc. See M. Krauss and P. O'Brien, Some International Implications of Value-Added Taxation, *National Tax Journal*, Vol. XXIII, No. 4, December 1970.

Article 17 of the Directive of 11 April 1967 allows a member state to zero-rate an item for *social purposes*. This is probably to be interpreted as a method of dealing with social and political repercussions of too abrupt a change-over from an existing to a new system. For example, the Dutch have been allowed to zero-rate newspapers for a limited period. The British would certainly be able to apply this exception during the transitional period, when food prices are anyway being raised to the levels of the common agricultural policy. When, by what stages, and at what rate a VAT on foodstuffs was applied thereafter in Britain would depend on decisions in which Britain itself would participate.

To 'zero-rate' is, however, not the same as to exempt an item. If the former, it must be brought into the VAT net and returns made by traders of that item. It has been argued in Brussels that food would have to be included, though it is zero-rated and hence no tax is paid in the British VAT at a fairly early stage.

This is not to follow an EEC dogma, but comes from a good reason. The base for the VAT in the different member states must be harmonised for purposes of the contributions to the Community budget.

It will be recalled (and dealt with more fully later) that, in 1980, the Community budget will be financed partly by payment by member states of 1 per cent (or a slightly lower percentage) of the *base* of the VAT. Now this is an equitable scheme only if indeed the base *is* the same in each member state. If Britain can exclude food from the base, or Italy exclude retail sales, they substantially reduce their contributions.

So food must in due course be included in the VAT though it can be zero-rated. But though a zero rate for food might be held, using Article 17, at least to the end of the transitional period and perhaps for some time beyond that, it is nevertheless possible in the Community only whilst there is structural harmonisation without rate harmonisation. With the latter, and the consequent abolition of fiscal frontiers, food would be included in the coverage of VAT at a reduced rate within a range to be agreed by the enlarged Community—unless Community thinking had moved by then towards the deliberate use of differences in indirect taxation as an instrument of economic or social policy.

The problem of VAT rates

Whilst the structure of VAT in the Community is a settled issue, and the coverage and exemptions are mostly settled, the eventual rate or rates are not at all settled.

There is first of all a debate as to whether harmonisation necessarily implies that the rates of tax in each country be equalised or brought within a relatively narrow range of rates, or whether the possibility of wider agreed differences, perhaps sometimes only temporarily, is not a valuable tool of economic policy for required stabilisation and growth, which ought not to be sacrificed for a handy administrative or ideological formula. [8] Whilst we will pass over this aspect of the rate debate for the present, we might note in passing that its importance will be enhanced if the policy tool of exchange-rate changes between member states is extinguished by a common currency.

The actual position in the Community on rates is this. At present, there are wide divergences; and the two major members lie at extreme ends of the spectrum of rates, France at the high end with a standard rate of 23 per cent, Germany with a low standard rate of 11 per cent.

The great problem that has exercised policy-makers in Brussels has been how to arrive at an equal rate which, if it is to lie in between these extremes, must involve the French in an enormous reduction in indirect tax revenues and the Germans in big increases in the tax rate. To deal with this, they have developed the idea of a convergence over a time so that there is a permissible harmonised range, rather than a single rate. This fourchette is thought of as 12-18 per cent in the near future, with a narrower band envisaged for the longer run. With a fourchette of only 3-4 points wide, it would be possible to abolish fiscal frontiers; for the differences in the tax rate payable in different member states would not be large enough to occasion serious worries about competitive inequities, or tax avoidance by arranging to buy in the next state. It is a

---

[8] The plea for non-equalisation has been mainly an academic one, and whilst courteously studied by Commission officials, has had little impact on administrative policy so far. The arguments can be seen in the author's Economic Analysis of Tax Harmonisation, in *Fiscal Harmonisation in Common Markets*, edited by C. Shoup, Columbia University Press, New York and London, 1967.

Table 2: The French and German Systems of VAT

(percentages)

Category of Consumers' Expenditure	French Rate	German Rate	Modified¹ French System		Modified¹ German System		Amended² French System	
	(1)	(2)	1968 (3)	1969 (4)	1968 (5)	1969 (6)	1968 (7)	1969 (8)
Food	7.5	5.5	3.1	4.8	4.45	6.85	—	—
Maintenance and Repairs	17.6	0	7.0	10.9			8.1	12.5
Fuel and Light	17.6	11.0	7.0	10.9	8.9	13.7	8.1	12.5
Clothing	23.0	11.0	9.4	14.5	8.9	13.7	10.8	16.7
Motor Cars	33.0	11.0	14.0	21.8	8.9	13.7	16.2	25.1
Furniture	23.0	11.0	9.4	14.5	8.9	13.7	10.8	16.7
Radio and Electricals	33.0	11.0	14.9	21.8	8.9	13.7	16.2	25.1
Household soft furnishings	23.0	11.0	9.4	14.5	8.9	13.7	10.8	16.7
Household goods, soap, etc.	17.6	11.0	7.0	10.9	8.9	13.7	8.1	12.5
Books	7.5	5.5	3.1	4.8	4.45	6.85	—	—
Newspapers and Magazines	0	0	—	—	4.45	6.85	—	—
Chemist's goods	23.0	11.0	9.4	14.5	8.9	13.7	10.8	16.7
Recreational goods	33.0	11.0	14.0	21.8	8.9	13.7	16.2	25.1
Miscellaneous goods	23.0	11.0	9.4	14.5	8.9	13.7	10.8	16.7
Travel	17.6	11.0	7.0	10.9	8.9	13.7	8.1	12.5
Communications	—	—	—	—	—	—	—	—
Entertainment	17.6	11.0	7.0	10.9			8.1	12.5
Domestic service	17.6	11.0	7.0	10.9	8.9	13.7	8.1	12.5
Catering and other services	17.6	11.0	7.0	10.9	8.9	13.7	8.1	12.5
Beer	23.0	11.0	} 9.4	} 14.5	} 8.9	} 13.7		
Wine	17.6	11.0					10.8	16.7
Spirits	23.0	11.0						
Tobacco	23.0	11.0	9.4	14.5	8.9	13.7	10.8	16.7

¹ The modified French and German systems differ substantially between 1968 and 1969, since the combined revenues of the Purchase Tax and SET increased from £1,582 million to £1,916 million between those years.

² The amended French system is another rate exercise: an equal yield four-rate system, with French proportionalities but a zero rate on food.

somewhat untidy solution, dictated by the politics of the existing indirect tax structures of the Six.

Now how is Britain to fit into this fourchette? The figure that has been mentioned for the standard rate for the introduction of the VAT in Britain, namely 10 per cent, is somewhat below its lower prong. But, as Table 2 shows, Purchase Tax plus SET raised revenues in 1969 which were no less than would be raised by VAT at rates well within the fourchette which is at present envisaged, and at the least quite close to any narrower range which might be agreed upon in the more distant future. Thus the VAT can be applied in Britain at rates which accord with current Community thinking about harmonisation, without change in the order of magnitude of revenue that we are accustomed to raise by indirect taxation.

A method of seeing this and other implications for Britain of the VAT, whether levied at low or high rates and by two-tier or four-tier systems, is to use the present German system of rates, then the present French system, as hypothetical sets of rates, item-by-item, for British consumers' expenditure. These are the hypothetical sets of rates used in the following sections, on the effect of VAT in Britain on (a) budget revenues; (b) prices; (c) income distribution; and (d) the balance of payments.

The VAT and budgetary revenues

The French VAT system has four rates: besides a standard rate of 23 per cent, a food rate of 7.5 per cent, an intermediate rate of 17.6 per cent and a luxury rate of 33 per cent. The German system has just 11 per cent standard, and a half-rate on food and a few other things. Table 2 shows these rate systems applied to major categories of consumers' expenditure.

Now the application of the rates in columns 1 and 2 of Table 2 to the value of British consumption expenditure on product categories shown at the side of the table would yield a budgetary revenue of some $2\frac{1}{2}$ times and $1\frac{1}{4}$ times the total revenue of the Purchase Tax and Selective Employment Tax respectively in 1968, with corresponding factors of approximately $1\frac{3}{4}$ and nine-tenths for the 1969 case.

It is interesting to rework the percentages, keeping the same proportions between categories, to yield approximately the same revenues as Purchase Tax and SET in 1968 and 1969.

This has been done in columns 3 to 6 of Table 2. Columns 7 and 8 introduce a French-style four-rate system with food zero-rated. It can be seen that in 1969 Purchase Tax and SET revenues were equivalent to the yield from VAT at rates significantly above the German rates, although in 1968 they had been somewhat lower.

The VAT and consumer prices

In appearance, it is not too difficult to calculate the effect on consumer prices of a substitution of the VAT for Purchase Tax and SET.

There are two methods. Firstly, the retail price index can be scrutinised item-by-item and a percentage rate of Purchase Tax on the price of an item (and, possibly, an imputed rate of SET) replaced by a VAT rate. Using the weights of the index, the overall percentage change in the index is calculated. Secondly, use can be made of a recent breakdown of National Income Blue Book aggregates of taxes on categories of consumers' expenditure.[9] The Purchase Tax and SET are removed and an appropriate VAT levy introduced, and the percentage price change in that category of consumers' expenditure calculated. Since these National Income Blue Book consumer expenditure categories accord fairly closely with the weight system of the official general index[10] of retail prices, the price changes can be weighted and the overall implied change in the official index estimated.

Several difficulties do, however, beset these approaches. Each has its own minor statistical problems, but four difficulties are common to both approaches:

(i) *Consumers' response to price changes*

A rigidity is assumed in consumers' expenditure as tax rates increase or decrease. Of course, this is built into the retail price index in the form of the weights, which assume the base of each category of consumers' expenditure remains constant. Thus the effect on consumers of the tax change is *over-stated* since they will reduce

---

[9] *Economic Trends*, No. 205, HMSO, November 1970.
[10] The weight system and current levels of the official general index of retail prices can be seen in *Department of Employment Gazette*, Vol. LXXIX, No. 7, HMSO, July 1971, Table 132.

expenditures on dearer items in favour of cheaper. This could, of course, be dealt with by adjusting each category of consumers' expenditure according to estimates of elasticity of demand, but this is a long and not too fruitful exercise.

(ii) *Shifting and incidence of the taxes*

The assumption is being made that the removal of Purchase Tax and SET would reduce the price of a product or service by the full amount, VAT increase it; that is, full forward shifting and symmetry of shifting for tax increases and decreases.

Very recent experience with the first stage of the removal of the SET, though it is too early for any careful statistical work to have been done, suggests that in the present inflationary climate, forward shifting on to consumer prices for tax increases may be realistic, but true only to a limited extent for tax decreases.

This is very difficult to deal with, and it is likely to lead to accusations against the new VAT—causing price increases—which are not at all connected with that tax as such.

(iii) *VAT rates to be applied*

In attempting the two calculations of cost-of-living change, some set of rates has to be used. We have used modified rate systems which yield roughly the same revenues as the doomed taxes, Purchase Tax and SET, and which would fall within the fourchette at present envisaged as a basis for Community harmonisation, even if it is possible that a narrower band at a moderately higher level may eventually be agreed upon.

But this leaves the problem of whether to use a non-EEC system, à la Green Paper, with a 10 per cent standard rate and zero on food and other exempted categories listed therein, or whether to use a modified (French) four-rate, or modified (German) two-rate, system. An attempt is made at alternative calculations.

(iv) *Other tax harmonisation measures*

Whilst the introduction of VAT has to stand alone, judgement on its price impact ought to be modified by thinking of the package deal which harmonisation will eventually involve. True, this is not the case whilst only the modified (equal revenue) systems are considered. But the thought of higher-rate systems (even 10 per cent standard rate plus a positive rate on food) may be accompanied by other tax reductions on items appearing in the cost of living, for example Excises on tobacco and alcoholic drinks.

We have calculated the overall effect on the official cost-of-living index by the second method of the two described, i.e. using the National Income Blue Book allocation of Purchase Tax and SET to consumer expenditure categories and weighting the price change in each category as VAT comes in by the weights in the official index, appearing in the Department of Employment Gazette, The results are seen in Table 3.

The application of our usual six rate-systems (see Table 2) produces changes in the official index of the order 1.1 to 2.9 per cent. Given its present level of 154.3 (June 1971) this involves a 2.0 to 4.0 point increase in the index.

This appears relatively small; and it is probably biased upward anyway, for the total yield of Purchase Tax and SET has been used to calculate replacement VAT rates, whereas some 10 per cent of Purchase Tax and 40 per cent of SET are levied on intermediate goods.[11] These portions cannot be allocated to heads of consumers' expenditure, whilst the VAT which replaces it has. In effect, the assumption is made that Purchase Tax and SET on intermediate expenditures are *not* passed forward to consumer prices, whilst that part of VAT which replaces it is passed forward completely. To the extent that either assumption is invalid—tax on intermediate expenditures is partly passed forward, VAT not wholly passed forward— the overall change in the index would be reduced.[12]

There is a small bias downward in the amended system as the zero rate on food has, because of the aggregation problems, been applied to a few items currently bearing Purchase Tax,

---

[11] See *Economic Trends*, *op. cit.*, Table 1.

[12] The Reddaway Report reckoned that about half the SET was passed forward but it did not distinguish in this connection between SET impinging on the production of intermediate goods versus final goods. See W. B. Reddaway, *Effects of the Selective Employment Tax, First Report*, HMSO, 1970.

Table 3a. Unweighted Changes in Price Levels as VAT Replaces Purchase Tax and SET

Category	Weight in General Index of Retail Prices %	Modified French System		Modified German System		Amended French System	
		1968 %	1969 %	1968 %	1969 %	1968 %	1969 %
Food	0.250	1.1	2.4	2.4	4.3	— 1.9	— 2.4
Maintenance Repairs	—	4.5	7.7	2.4	2.9	5.5	9.3
Fuel/Light	0.060	7.0	10.9	8.9	13.7	8.1	12.5
Clothing/Footwear	0.087	1.7	5.2	1.3	4.4	3.0	7.2
Motor Cars	(0.038)²	— 6.1	2.5	—10.3	8.9	4.3	0.2
Furniture	(0.018)³	— 0.6	1.8	1.1	1.1	0.7	3.8
Radio/Electricals	(0.018)³	— 5.3	0.1	9.6	6.7	3.5	2.6
Household Goods (i)	(0.025)³	3.2	6.1	2.7	5.4	4.5	8.2
(ii)		3.7	6.7	5.5	9.4	4.8	8.3
Books	—	1.9	3.6	3.2	5.6	1.2	1.2
Newspapers/Magazines	—	— 0.6	— 1.0	3.8	5.8	— 0.6	— 1.0
Chemist's Goods	(0.020)⁴	—11.3	—10.5	—11.7	11.2	—10.2	8.8
Miscellaneous Goods	(0.016)⁴	—27.1	—15.1	—27.4	15.7	—26.2	13.4
Recreational Goods	(0.029)⁴	3.6	8.4	1.1	1.2	5.5	11.6
Travel	(0.044)²	7.0	10.9	8.9	13.7	8.1	12.5
Entertainment	(0.041)⁵	0.8	0.4	0.6	0.6	1.8	5.9
Domestic Service	(0.013)⁵	7.0	10.9	8.9	13.7	8.1	12.5
Catering/Services	(0.044)⁵	3.6	6.8	5.3	9.5	4.6	8.4
Alcohol	0.065	8.6	13.4	8.1	12.6	10.0	15.5
Tobacco	0.059	7.8	12.6	7.3	11.8	9.2	14.8
Running Costs of Vehicles	(0.054)²	5.3	8.6	7.1	11.4	6.3	10.3
	1.000¹						

Table 3b. Weighted Changes in Price Levels as VAT Replaces Purchase Tax and SET

	%	Modified French System		Modified German System		Amended French System	
		1968 %	1969 %	1968 %	1969 %	1968 %	1969 %
Food	0.250	2.8	5.9	6.0	10.8	−4.9	−5.9
Fuel/Light	0.060	4.2	6.5	5.3	8.2	4.9	7.5
Clothing/Footwear	0.087	1.5	4.5	1.1	3.8	2.6	6.3
Cars, etc.	0.038	—	0.9	3.9	3.4	1.7	0.8
Furniture	0.018	−0.1	0.3	0.2	0.2	0.1	0.7
Radio/Electricals	0.018	−1.0	0.0	−1.7	1.2	−0.6	0.5
Household Goods	0.025	0.9	1.6	1.0	1.8	1.2	2.1
Chemist's Goods	0.020	−2.3	2.1	−2.3	2.2	−2.0	1.8
Miscellaneous Goods	0.016	−4.3	2.4	−4.4	2.5	−4.2	2.2
Recreational Goods	0.029	1.0	2.4	0.3	0.4	1.6	3.3
Travel	0.044	3.1	4.8	3.9	6.0	3.6	5.5
Entertainment	0.041	0.3	0.2	0.3	0.3	0.7	2.4
Domestic Service	0.013	0.9	1.4	1.2	1.8	1.1	1.6
Catering Services	0.044	1.6	3.0	2.3	4.2	2.1	3.7
Alcohol	0.065	5.6	8.7	5.3	8.2	6.5	10.1
Tobacco	0.059	4.6	7.4	4.3	7.0	5.5	8.7
Running Costs of Vehicles	0.054	2.9	4.7	3.9	6.2	3.4	5.5
% Change in General Index of Retail Prices		1.1	2.7	1.2	2.9	1.2	2.9

Present Index June 1971: 154.3.

[1] Housing (weight of 0.119) omitted as outside PT, SET and VAT tax system.

[2] Weight of 0.136 for Transport and Vehicles split between Cars (0.038) and Travel (0.044) and Running Costs of Vehicles (0.054) according to relative 1969 consumers' expenditure.

[3] Weight of 0.061 for Durable Household Goods divided between Furniture (0.018) Radio/Electrical (0.018), and Household Goods (0.025) in accordance with 1969 consumers' expenditure.

[4] Weight of 0.065 for Miscellaneous Goods divided between Chemist's Goods (0.020), Miscellaneous Goods (0.016) and Recreational Goods (0.029) in accordance with 1969 consumers' expenditure.

[5] The weight of 0.044 for Meals Out in the Index has been allocated to Catering in the National Accounts categories. The weight of 0.054 for Services has been split between Entertainment (0.041) and Domestic Services (0.013) in proportion to 1969 consumers' expenditure.

e.g. confectionery; probably these would continue to be in the VAT net even when food is zero-rated.

There is another and larger bias upward in the results in that the VAT has been piled on top of our high Excises on Alcohol, Tobacco and Petrol, and weighted by weights of the retail index, high because they also contain the Excises. If Excise later came down as part of the harmonisation programme, there is a kind of multiplier effect downward on the index.

Particularly because of the first point above—the upward bias in the result from shifting assumptions—the once-for-all change in the cost-of-living index ought to be contained to 1 or 2 percentage points. It is interesting to note that the *monthly* change in the index in certain months of 1971 approached 1 point.

The VAT and the distribution of income

Three studies are available on this subject. They each face the same technical problems just discussed in the preceding section on prices: consumers' re-adjustment to changing taxes, the shifting and incidence of those taxes, and which set of rates and set of tax substitutions to apply. As previously, elasticity of demand considerations are ignored, and the classical full forward shifting of indirect taxes assumed. They each make their own assumptions about tax rates and substitutions.

The first is contained in the NEDO Report on the VAT.[13] It used the Central Statistical Office's Family Expenditure Survey. The VAT was applied in place of the Purchase Tax under two schemes: Scheme A, 10 per cent on everything except food; Scheme B, 25 per cent on products bearing Purchase Tax at rates higher than the lowest, $12\frac{1}{2}$ per cent on everything else except food. The increase in inequality, as measured by a concept called a Gini coefficient,[14] was fairly

---

[13] National Economic Development Office, *Value-Added Tax*, HMSO, 1969.

[14] An income distribution can be mapped on a graph with axes of "proportion of population (or households)" and "proportion of national income" so that any point on the so-called Lorenz curve for a particular country shows the proportion of income received by the first (ranked from the poorest) 10 per cent, 20 per cent, etc., of the population. The Gini coefficient is a simple measure of a shift in the Lorenz curve.

slight. A little more will be said about the meaning of 'fairly slight' later in connection with the other studies.

The second study is by Professor Brown.[15] Its scope is different—the VAT is introduced in Britain as a replacement for Purchase Tax and SET first at 8.9 per cent overall including food, then at 11.8 per cent excluding food, both of which bring in about the same revenue as the replaced taxes. And the effect on income distribution is presented by a different method, namely in a table showing the percentage increases/decreases in tax due from representative households of different types. It is apparent that there is some increase in regressivity, but not a lot.[16]

This method has the advantage of giving a more immediate picture of the change in an income distribution. But, especially if the picture shows a rather haphazard pattern across different household types, it holds the disadvantage that it is not always possible to comprise the result in a simple statement that the income distribution has become more even or less even.

In the third study, the author's,[17] both methods of measurement have been used. The Family Expenditure Survey formed the basic data source, as in the NEDO study. But the VAT rate systems applied were the 1968[18] modified, equal-yield, French and German systems. However, the modified systems are based on purchase tax alone, because it is impossible to distribute the SET over different household types as has been done for the Purchase Tax.

In summary, the exercise involved removing the Purchase Tax from each item of expenditure in the typical consumption pattern of a particular type of household (itself based on a sample of households of that type), and summing the Purchase Tax paid. Such an exercise is not possible for SET. The process is repeated for the application of VAT and the total VAT to be paid by a household type can be calculated. The changes in

[15] C. V. Brown, *Impact of Tax Changes on Income Distribution*, PEP Broadsheet 525, February 1971.

[16] Brown, *op. cit.*, Tables 9 and 10.

[17] D. Dosser *et al.*, *British Taxes and the Common Market*, Allen and Unwin, forthcoming.

[18] 1969 modified rates are, of course, higher (see Table 2) but then so are the PT and SET rates they replace. Thus a 1969 regressivity study is not likely to show greatly different results from 1968.

202 *The Economics of Europe*

tax due, increases or decreases, can then be classified by households over income ranges and over family size.

Looking at the results using the method of Gini coefficient, and confining ourselves to average households over income ranges only (the argument about regressivity is usually about distribution over income groups rather than family size), the changes in the Gini coefficient are as follows (a positive result indicates an increase in inequality):

Modified (equal yield PT) French: +2.6
Modified (equal yield PT) German: +2.5

This compares with a range of 0.2 to 1.0 per cent in the NEDO study. Some idea of the meaning of these numbers can be gained as follows. A specimen change in the British income distribution is made, one which one can evaluate for its 'seriousness' according to one's own political or ethical predilections. The change can then be measured in terms of the Gini coefficient. The change taken is a simple one. From the top 50 per cent of income receivers, 10 per cent of their income is shared out equally among the lower 50 per cent. This reduces the Gini coefficient by $5\frac{1}{2}$ points. Thus the regressivity above is to the advantage of richer sections of the population to roughly half of this extent.

The alternative method of presentation is that used by Brown. The results of our 'equal yield PT' calculations are not dissimilar to his.

A general regressive trend can be seen as the increase in tax to be paid falls away as income increases. If the figures are standardised (to meet the Brown-Dosser statistical problem of note 3 to the Table) to make the average change zero, it can be seen that the increase in tax to be paid by lower-income groups would be raised to 2 or 3 per cent and that they would be reduced towards the other end by 1 or 2 per cent. This accords with the order of magnitude just indicated for a 2 to $2\frac{1}{2}$ Gini-point change.

It is reasonable to conclude therefore that if VAT is introduced for Purchase Tax alone, including a half-rate on food, and whether a French style four-rate or German style two-rate system, the effect is a decrease in lower income groups' after-tax income of roughly 3 per cent and a 2 per cent increase in the upper half of the income distribution. But this result has to

Table 4: Net Change in Tax to be Paid by Households with Varying Income in Introduction of VAT

Income Range[1] / Tax Change[2]	1	2	3	4	5	6	7	8	9	10
Modified French Replacing PT	2.54	1.18	1.03	1.23	1.23	1.90	0.79	1.73	0.77	0.68
Modified German Replacing PT	3.42	1.54	1.38	1.51	1.35	1.14	0.97	0.78	0.83	0.58

	11	12	13	14	15	16	Ave.[3]
Modified French Replacing PT	0.63	n.a.	0.34	−0.10	0.02	0.56	0.55
Modified German Replacing PT	0.56	n.a.	0.16	0.27	−0.18	0.45	0.49

Source:
[1] The income ranges are those used in the Family Expenditure Survey, left to right ranks lowest to highest incomes.
[2] The first two tax changes are the French and German systems modified to an equal yield basis with the Purchase Tax.
[3] The statistical problem common to Brown and Dosser is that households on average appear to be worse off with an equal-yield tax substitution. The reason is the under-representation of high income households in the response to the Family Expenditure Survey. See Brown, *op. cit.*, pp. 3-4.

be modified in the light of these facts: (a) the 'interim' British VAT will have a zero rate on food, (b) the VAT will replace SET as well.

Since (a) works to *reduce* the regressivity of VAT, and the incidence of (b) has never been determined, it is probably safe to assume that not much of a regressive effect is left for the particular way VAT is about to be introduced into Britain.

This is not too surprising when it is remembered that (food apart) the Purchase Tax is nowadays by no means a tax on luxuries but falls on items in a wide range of budgets: cars, television and radio sets, clothing, confectionery. These necessities of today are going to be taxed by VAT instead, often at *lower* rates. Further, that part of SET falling on services—hotels, catering, car maintenance, etc.—will simply be replaced by VAT. And many new items coming into the VAT net, such as books and newspapers, are by no means the preserve of lower-income groups.

The regressive argument against the VAT has thus been greatly exaggerated. If food is included, however, certain special groups, e.g. pensioners and students, whose budgets are greatly dominated by basic food purchases, are substantially affected, and there is a significant shift of tax incidence more generally from higher to lower income groups. The special groups can of course be compensated by increases in social benefits and grants—and it will be recalled that the main advantage of the VAT for Britain is that it is a sufficiently broad-based tax to render the raising of revenue for such purposes relatively easy. A general shift of incidence on lower-income groups can likewise be countered by changes in direct tax and social benefits, and would in any case be offset by a reduction of excise duties resulting from harmonisation (see below).

The VAT and the balance of payments

When the VAT was introduced in some Continental countries for a cascade system of indirect taxes, the effects on the balance of trade were considerable. After all, one of the key reasons for its introduction was the facilitation of more efficient rebating of the domestic tax paid on goods exported. Also the influence on the structure of industry would have had an effect on trade.

When we come to Britain, in so far as the VAT is replacing Purchase Tax, we already have a simple structure. Both taxes are rebatable, and efficiently, on exports, so long as the destination principle remains in force for the VAT (remember the restricted origin principle will come into play only when the long-term Community rate problem has been solved). So, theoretically, there is *no* effect on exports from the British introduction of VAT.

But there is an effect on imports. All taxable imported goods carry Purchase Tax rates at present, and will in future carry VAT rates. Imports remain on the same footing as corresponding domestically-produced goods. There is no substitution price effect between the imported and domestically produced version of any goods. But there is an inter-product substitution effect involving imports as the after-tax prices of some rise, some fall.

The following table presents some estimates of the size of this effect on imports. The usual assumptions are required: there is full forward shifting of the tax, the usual rate systems are applied. But since consumers' demand response is now of the essence, the use of some broad price elasticity of demand figures is required.

The method behind the calculation is to apply the price changes (of Table 3a) (as a forward-shifted VAT rate replaces a forward-shifted PT) and price elasticity of demand estimate to each category of goods in turn. This yields a figure for the total increase or decrease in consumption of that category. Finally, the import content of that increase or decrease is taken to be the same proportion that imports form of the total consumption of items (remember there has been no relative price change between imports and domestic production as both face the same change in tax schedules).

A mixture of decreases and increases in imports is shown, as VAT rates are higher or lower than PT rates respectively. They sum to a decrease in imports, or improvement in the balance of trade, in the case of each rate system used.

This simple exercise on the VAT and the British trade balance is now complicated by two factors.

The first is that the VAT is being introduced in place of the SET as well as Purchase Tax. The SET was introduced specifi-

cally with export promotion in mind. The actual effect on
exports arises from the net subsidy per man employed in manufacturing, at the expense of services, which might enable the delivered
price of exports to be slightly lowered. But this effect is modified
by the SET on services used by manufacturers. Nevertheless,
the slight net gain to the balance of trade arising from SET is
lost when the VAT is introduced. So the favourable effect on
the balance shown as arising from VAT in Table 5 has to be
somewhat reduced—it is not possible to say by how much.[19]

The second complicating factor is that, if VAT is seen as
part of the Community's tax harmonisation programme instead
of an isolated British act, the development of the Community
system involves changes in rates of other member states who
are major, and will be increasing, purchasers of our exports.
Thus a falling French rate and rising German rate would,
ceteris paribus, increase our exports to France, decrease our
exports to Germany. No attempt can be made to incorporate
this at present, in view of future uncertainties about rates, the
restricted origin principle, etc. But the result of Table 5, modified by the removal of SET, must be viewed as strictly an interim
picture.

HARMONISATION OF EXCISES AND CORPORATION TAX

It was mentioned at the beginning of this chapter that VAT
was the first of three candidates for harmonisation. And whilst
current interest naturally centres on the VAT, of longer-run
interest are the effects of the whole package. This section
therefore sketches in some outlines of the other two-thirds;
no detailed work on effects is possible yet because the form of
the Community system in these fields is largely still to be decided.

Excises are a little in advance of Corporation Tax as regards
the Community structure. It is clearly the intention that major
excises are to be harmonised—tobacco, alcoholic drinks, and
petrol—but not for the present the myriad minor ones—coffee,
sugar, salt, matches, etc.—existing in individual member states.
The first step is structural harmonisation. This is a very big

---

[19] A second Reddaway Report on the SET which covers the trade effects
is to be published later.

Table 5. Effects on British Imports of the Introduction of VAT

£ million

Category of Consumer Goods	Modified French System		Modified German System		Amended French System	
	1968	1969	1968	1969	1968	1969
Food	− 13.7	− 30.3	− 29.5	− 55.6	− 23.9	− 30.5
Maintenance/Repairs	− 0.5	− 1.0	− 0.3	− 0.4	− 0.6	− 1.2
Fuel/Light	− 7.2	− 11.9	− 9.1	− 15.0	− 8.3	− 13.7
Clothing/Footwear	− 2.3	− 7.0	− 1.7	− 6.0	− 4.0	− 9.8
Motor Cars, etc.	− 5.3	− 1.9	− 8.9	− 6.8	− 3.8	− 0.2
Furniture	− 0.9	− 2.6	− 1.6	− 1.5	− 1.0	− 5.4
Radio/Electricals	− 4.0	− 0.1	− 7.2	− 5.0	− 2.7	− 2.0
Household Goods (i)	− 5.2	− 10.2	− 4.4	− 8.9	− 7.4	− 13.6
(ii)	− 2.5	− 4.6	− 3.7	− 6.5	− 3.2	− 5.7
Books	− 0.1	− 0.2	− 0.2	− 0.3	− 0.1	− 0.1
Newspapers/Magazines	− 0.1	− 0.2	− 0.8	− 1.1	− 0.1	− 0.2
Chemist's Goods	− 2.4	− 2.3	− 2.5	− 2.4	− 2.2	− 1.9
Miscellaneous Goods	− 6.8	− 6.2	− 6.9	− 6.4	− 6.6	− 5.5
Recreational Goods	− 7.9	− 19.6	− 2.5	− 2.8	− 12.1	− 26.5
Travel	− 10.4	− 17.3	− 13.1	− 21.8	− 12.0	− 19.9
Entertainment	− 0.6	− 3.6	− 4.4	− 5.0	− 1.4	− 4.9
Services/Catering	− 4.1	− 8.2	− 6.1	− 11.5	− 5.3	− 10.1
Alcohol	− 2.8	− 4.5	− 2.6	− 4.2	− 3.2	− 5.2
Tobacco	− 1.7	− 2.9	− 1.6	− 3.7	− 2.0	− 3.4
Running Costs	− 4.8	− 8.3	− 6.5	− 10.9	− 5.8	− 9.8
TOTAL	− 44.3	− 107.3	− 44.8	− 122.8	− 27.0	− 93.1

step, since the form of an excise often differs fundamentally from country to country—specific versus ad valorem, state monopoly versus fiscal charge.

What is clear is that the state monopolies will be dismantled, and an *equal* fiscal charge imposed throughout the Community. But the exact form of this, and above all its level, is not decided.[20]

From the British point of view, since we do not have tobacco or liquor monopolies, nothing of importance has yet been committed. But this does not mean the field is wide open, for it is clear that a Community system is bound to go in a certain direction compared with at least some existing British excises, namely involving a reduction. Excises in Britain on alcoholic spirits, beer and tobacco are far in excess of present levels in the Six.[21] Thus the expectation would be a decrease in these duties, but not in petrol duty. It would seem probable, however, that if there is convincing evidence that for reasons of health the price of cigarettes should not be reduced, the Community would not wish, and would certainly not be able, to compel Britain to reduce the Excise on that item.

Whilst the extent of the consequent effects cannot be judged in the absence of any information about the Community levels of excises, we can briefly modify the preceding VAT effects along the following lines:

   (i) Budgetary revenues from excises will decrease, but this will be compensated by the increase in general sales tax revenues, as British VAT rates move to Community levels.

  (ii) The retail prices of cigarettes, cigars, spirits and beer, all important elements in the cost-of-living index, will fall (except in so far as a reduction of Excise on cigarettes is avoided on health grounds), and thus counterbalance the rise indicated under VAT.

 (iii) The distributional effect is difficult to judge, but in view of the high proportional importance of cigarettes and beer in lower-income budgets, the effect of Excise harmonisation on its own may well be actually pro-

---

[20] A Proposal (which precedes a Directive) by the Commission is, however, expected in a matter of months.

[21] See D. Dosser and S. S. Han, *Taxes in the EEC and Britain: The Problem of Harmonisation*, European Series No. 6, Chatham House/ PEP, January 1968, Table III.

gressive. The net effect of VAT and Excises may then be roughly neutral.

(iv) Excisable goods appear on both sides of the balance of trade. Reduced tobacco and spirit (other than whisky) excises may lead to increased imports. Whisky may be affected by changes in excises in the Community. It is not possible at this stage to forecast the effects on trade.

Most of the undesirable effects of VAT—cost-of-living increases and income distribution regressivity—can be countermanded by Britain following the likely programme of Excise tax harmonisation, providing the traditional attitude of penal taxes on drink and tobacco can be more closely aligned with opinion in other West European democracies.

Corporation Tax harmonisation is a subject of very active discussion within the Community. However, the actual basic structure for a Community tax, let alone rates, is not at all settled as yet.

There is a desire to modify the so-called 'double-taxation' of dividends—taxed first under the Corporation Tax, then under the Personal Income Tax—which exists under what is often called the 'classical' system,[22] and which has existed in Britain since 1965. This is a desire shared by the member states of the Six, and by the present British Government.[23]

The problem arises as to the method of achieving this aim. It can be the present (though about to be changed) German two-rate system (a lower rate on distributed profits), also favoured by the Green Paper. Alternatively, there is the French system of allowing some of the tax paid by the corporation as a credit against personal income tax liability.

The arguments between the three systems—classical, split-rate and credit—are involved and inconclusive;[24] in any case, the current political urge to reduce the total charge on distributed profits and the administratively simplest way of doing so will be decisive.

---

[22] In contrast to the political aim, the classical system was recently recommended as the Community system by an EEC committee. See A. J. van dem Tempel, *Corporation Tax and Individual Income Tax*, EEC, Brussels, 1970.

[23] See *Reform of Corporation Tax*, Cmnd 4630, HMSO, March 1971.

[24] See the author's Memorandum in *Minutes of Evidence* taken before the Select Committee on Corporation Tax, 13 July 1971.

The upshot is that Britain will have a 'reformed' system, either following the Green Paper's two-rate method, or the Community's probable credit method.

The only effect which is at all clear and relevant to our present discussion is that the total revenues from Corporation Tax are likely to be reduced from present levels owing to this structural charge.

THE COMMUNITY BUDGET

The harmonisation of taxes which we have been discussing is, of course, intimately connected with the growing Community budget. One reason for harmonisation, as noted in the case of the VAT, is the achievement of identical tax bases in the member states, so that levies for the Community budget, which are beginning with the payment of up to 1 per cent of the VAT base, are equitable.

The present plan for Community budget receipts—levies on agricultural imports, customs duties, and a percentage of the VAT base—is in part only an interim one. The levy system, connected with price support rather than income support, will die a natural death in far-off post-Mansholt days, if and when European agriculture is brought up to world competitive levels; and its incidence will, as Marsh explains in Chapter 5, be reduced as the need for price support in Europe declines. Customs duties ought to diminish if the Community continues an outward-looking commercial policy with less-developed countries and others.

On the other hand, the expenditure side will grow, and grow away from its present pre-occupation with agricultural expenditure.

The long-run perspective is therefore of a tax-financed Community budget, providing expenditures over a wide field of social and economic activities. The finance will come from small percentages of harmonised taxes, not just VAT but perhaps also Corporation Tax. The expenditures may go towards, for example, a European social security system, industrial projects in lagging regions or new-technology industry.

Against this perspective, the effects of tax harmonisation discussed in this chapter can be seen as relatively minor and short-run and, where undesirable, have to be viewed against an embryonic budget formed essentially for the agricultural problems of others. The developing budget and associated tax harmonisation programme, in contrast, can be geared to British economic needs and aspirations as much as to those of her partners.

Chapter 10

THE PHILOSOPHY OF MAJOR CHANGE

by Maurice Peston

THERE is a sense in which everybody knows what is wrong with Britain and the British economy. They can point to low labour productivity, inferior methods of working, poor organisation, lack of enterprise, faulty appointments and promotion policies, dreadful labour relations, excessive concern with finance rather than production facilities—the list is endless. It is obvious what has to be done, but impossible to see how to do it. There is no mystery about industrial efficiency; British workers and management use the same equipment to less good ends than their foreign counterparts. They themselves know this to be the case, and any observer can see it for himself. The problem of economic failure, therefore, lies at a deeper level. It is psychological and sociological. For all we know, it may even be physiological.

Of course, it may be that there is no failure at all. We reveal what we want by what we do. Since we could be more economically productive and are not, the reason must be that we prefer something else. We are, indeed, just as rich as the foreigners, but we prefer to consume our riches in the form of an easy life in the factory rather than in more leisure in the home coupled with more goods. This is an explanation which I have often been tempted to adopt. The trouble with it is that it is in contradiction with what people say they want and some of the things they do. Thus, wage earners demand higher real wages and go on strike for them. Management too is not exactly silent on the subject of their own real purchasing power. Those of us who are concerned more with public welfare and the public sector also have an

212

extremely long list of projects which require vast quantities of resources for their fulfilment. To argue, therefore, that the present position is optimal leaves one with the difficult task of accounting for why most people say it is not good enough, and behave as if it is not good enough (albeit allowing that behaviour to stop short at the point of doing something about it).

A second view is that, while matters are not as we would like them, this is inevitable. Economic failure is in our nature, it is genetical, there is nothing to be done about it. Or, if it does not lie deep within us as individuals, it is equally deep within our society which is incapable of the kind of change we require. Let me say right away that I know nothing of the genetics of economic performance, and the books I have examined are no help to me on this subject. But the hypothesis does not strike me as *prima facie* nonsensical. Just as some nations appear to be disproportionately able at chess, or squash, or sprinting, or mathematics, so others are especially good at manufacturing. In Britain we may be outstanding poets or pop musicians but dreadful industrial workers.

Now, let me repeat that I believe this hypothesis to be worth investigating further, and it should not be rejected out of hand. It could be that we are inherently doomed to relative economic backwardness. Nonetheless, it did not look like that in the last century so that we may require some concept of genetical exhaustion to account for twentieth century experience. (I note that, depending on what point needs to be established, emigrants are sometimes classified as the best of the population and sometimes as the worst.) Equally, there was a tendency to apply precisely this kind of argument not so long ago to people whose current performance is now very much changed. Consider, for example, the image of the Italians who used to be laughed at but whose performance on equivalent machinery is today superior to our own. One wonders what view the average man takes of the Spaniards, but they too appear to be on the verge of an economic miracle. In other spheres, who 25 years ago would have predicted Brazilian dominance in football or the Chinese ascendancy in table tennis? The genetical view, in its casual form at least, is *ad hoc* and conservative, implying that what is must be.

I suggest, therefore, that our present state of affairs is not inevitable, and that one may be seriously misled by concentrating on it to the exclusion of wider horizons. To put the point differently, although by definition they are impossible, miracles do occur. Although there are always explanations *ex post facto* and they are explained away, they are not predicted beforehand. To the academic they cease to be miracles, although they are in flagrant contradiction to what he predicted beforehand. We can account for the British, United States, German, Japanese, Italian or any other 'miracle', but one wonders what research predicted them before they happened.

Which leads me to the Common Market debate, and especially the economists' contributions to it, before some of the work on which this book is based became available. These have, as must be expected, concentrated on the factual material which was closest to hand, and as a result have placed great emphasis on the costs (notably the money costs, and something called the balance-of-payments costs) of the change. The impression has been created, therefore, that entry will be economically disadvantageous, certainly in the short term and quite likely in the long term, and that we are at the best trading these economic costs for political advantages. What is not realised is that it is almost in the nature of the earlier economic studies that this should be the case. It follows that these studies have been essentially myopic, and have treated the big changes that occur as special cases which they are unable to explain. (To repeat, I do not mean to say that they are not wise after the event. The mark of a first class academic is never to be short of a convincing explanation—or two or three or more. It is merely that they are not so good beforehand.) Thus, if it is allocative and free trade inefficiency that is at issue, we know that quantitative empirical research shows this to be of the general order of 1 or 2 per cent of gross national product. Similarly, massive increases of investment of the order of 25 per cent may add again perhaps 1 per cent to national income. Productivity having grown for a number of years at 2.7 per cent per annum, there seems no evidence that it could grow at 3 per cent let alone at 4 or 5 per cent per annum. The point, however, is precisely that past experience is biased in favour of itself, and, where it has been continuous, makes the odd cases look odd. It should be added that even that gives too much weight to the empirical economic study of economic performance, for even there a great deal of growth is left unexplained and variables such as 'human capital' have to be brought in to deal with the 'residual factor'.

Thus, while it is important to pursue as much detailed research as possible, and to get as precise an estimate of the costs as possible, it should be recognised that the economists did not predict and are still unable to account satisfactorily for earlier economic miracles. It follows that, if Britain were to have an economic miracle, brought about by the Common Market or any other way for that matter, the economists would be the last to predict it (although once it happened they would not, of course, be surprised). What is more, it may not even be strange that it is the leading and most distinguished members of the profession who have the gravest doubts since it is their own work which is most related to the existing state of affairs. (Actually, this is rather too glib. It is really impossible to say why so many outstanding economists are against our entry. Apart from the peculiarity of seeing Harrod, Kaldor, and Harry Johnson together with the *New Statesman* and sundry supporters of the Institute of Economic Affairs all united on this issue, these are the very people whose theoretical writings seemed to provide so much of the case for entry. Incidentally, while I am on this theme, it does not seem to me that the opponents have concentrated on the costs that are most likely to occur. These are not the distortions resulting from the common agricultural policy and the Community budget, but the much greater pains of economic and social change which must be borne if we are to get any benefits at all.)

The case for entry, therefore, is not the percentage one derived from a close scrutiny of the most usual experience. That will point out that while miracles happen, they are rare, and there is no reason to expect one in our case. On past experience we shall fail as we have failed before, and get little or nothing from membership. The case for entry must then be seen as a rejection of past experience, and an attempt to find a new way. It is, therefore, a gamble, and a plunge into uncertainty, at that, rather than a calculated risk. Its logic lies in a rejection of present trends because they are not good enough, and a decision to try something different because more of the same is unacceptable. (If I may try an analogy from the sporting world; one may be playing one's best but clearly be losing. In that case a change to what was thought to be a worse strategy is the only possible way of improving matters.) Of course, the risk is not that great because, as I pointed out in my opening remarks, in some sense we know full well that improved economic performance is possible. The gamble is about shaking everything up in the hope that a new environment will emerge in which an economic miracle actually does take place. That is why those who argue that we do not need the Common Market because we can shake things up in other ways are right, but irrelevant. We could in principle generate vast changes, but in practice we do not. In 1963, for example, when we were rejected, I remember enquiring why we did not simulate membership by embarking on a domestic programme of great economic and social change, but got no satisfactory answer at all. Clearly, internally generated change comes not at all easily, which suggests that we should jump at the opportunity provided externally by the Community.

The correct interpretation of a decision to enter is one of decision-making under uncertainty, and here for once all economists are in agreement because they know that in such circumstances there is no such thing as an objectively right or wrong choice. It is all a matter of attitudes to risk, and two equally reasonable people confronted with the same information may choose differently. Thus, I for one, although I favour entry, see no reason to attack those who oppose it with any degree of vehemence or accuse them of such heinous crimes as bad faith or even changing their minds. It is a pity that the press, and especially what is supposed to be the enlightened press, seem to see nothing that is good in its opponents. But, I suppose, it is exactly when the opposing point of view is not unreasonable, that people most work themselves up into a lather.

Having said that, however, there are two further points to be made. One is that those who oppose entry and favour the continuation of present trends cannot also demand to be accepted as protagonists of great change in our society. Their view is a conservative one, and the basis for its validity must be made in those terms. They have not presented an alternative plan for major change so that the issue is not one of choice between alternative dynamic developments, but rather between existing trends and a great shake up produced by joining the Community. Opponents of entry are quite correct in saying that it is an invalid criticism of their position to suggest that they must present an alternative set of proposals. Equally, however, they must accept the interpretation of their approach as essentially one of maintaining the status quo.

The second is that it is hard to believe that entry could be taking place in worse conditions than those created by the Government in the past year. Although I myself have not shifted my view on the desirability of entry, it is easy to understand those who have or who have become doubtful. The inconsistency of economic policy, both macro- and micro-, and the failure to deal with any major issues in a serious way, apart from the actual damage it has already done, maximise rather than mini-mise the risks of entry. The immediate position is dreadful, the short-term outlook is poor, and on the face of it any eventual return to full capacity working will involve a deficit on the balance of payments on current account. It can hardly be said that these are the best conditions to start a new era, unless it be argued that the new pains will hardly be noticed on top of the existing ones!

Of course, it may not be too late, and the latest shifts in public policy suggest that the Government recognise the fact. The beginnings of an incomes policy are emerging, and no doubt eventually an agreement may be arrived at involving price restraint and wage restraint with a reduction of percentage unemployment to at most 2 per cent. There is less sign of any new micro-policies (especially in connection with the regions) but here too the Government must surely soon become tired of *ad hoc* pronouncements against lame ducks coupled with continuing disbursements to them.

To conclude, the case for entry is what it always has been, a means of getting some dynamism into the British economy. Although it is always valuable to engage in detailed quantitative research into the likely costs and benefits, it was never likely that this could be decisive one way or another, because the essence of the situation is one of decision making under uncertainty. The domestic policies of the present Government have in my view added to the risks, but not to the extent of making entry no longer worth while.

INDEX

Abraham, J.P., 20n
Advanced technology, *see*
    High technology industries
Advertising, 173
Aerospace industry, 6, 7, 59-61, 70
African countries, association
    with EEC, 17
Agnelli, G., 51
Agriculture: and Common Market,
    83-93; Commonwealth exports,
    17; devaluation, 9; EEC policy
    for, 92, 94-5, 110-16; GNP,
    104-5; import elasticity, 9, 90;
    population within, 97, 105;
    prices, 3, 9, 15, 72, 81, 82,
    136 n; production and
    consumption, 83-90, 92, 97,
    100-3; temperate zone
    products, 17, 91
    see also Common agricultural
    policy. Farming. Food
Alcohol, 190, 197, 206-9
American Selling Price, 57
Apollo space exploration, 59
Australia, 49, 82, 90, 147-8

BOAC, 179
Balance of payments, 1, 3, 4, 7,
    8-13, 18, 69, 90, 120, 167, 180,
    184; calculation, 139-43;
    estimates, 122-39; and resource
    costs, 117-22; and VAT, 204-6
    See also Invisible trade
    transactions. Trade
Bank of England, 153-4, 156, 167
Bank of International Settlements,
    165
Banking, 180-1, 184
Barber, A, 20
Beckett, T. N., 50
Beer, 208
Belgium, 51, 68-9, 167
Benelux, 20
Birmingham Chamber of
    Commerce, 68
Blue Book on National Income,
    195, 197
Bombach, G., 32 n
Books and newspapers, 204
Bottrill, A., 22n, 24
Brazil, 213
British Leyland, 49, 52;
    in Europe, 51

British forces in Germany,
    173,   181-2
Brittan, Samuel, 47
Brown, C. V., 201-3
Brown Boveri, 65
Budgetary revenues, 194-5
Butter, 8, 17, 75, 81, 82, 88, 90,
    91; margarine as substitute,
    8, 86
'Buy National' policies, 6, 63

CBI, 68, 83
CII, 62-3
Cable, J. R., 35n
Canada, 31, 49, 82, 90
Capital flows, 4, 7, 11, 152-68,
    181; EEC agreement, 153-9;
    EEC safeguards, 166-8
    See also Investment
Capital goods industry, 7, 55-7
Caribbean countries, association
    with EEC, 17, 90
Cattle, 79
Caves, R., 142
Centre for European Industrial
    Studies (Bath University), 48, 70
Cereals, 74, 75-6, 79, 81, 88, 90, 91
Cheese, 75, 81, 90
Chemical Industry Association, 57
Chemicals industry, 7, 57-8, 70
Chenery, H. B., 32n
China, 213
Civil aviation *see* Transport
City of London, 9, 172, 177, 180,
    183-4
Clothing, 204
Cobb-Douglas production
    functions, 148
Coffee, 206
Committee on Invisible Exports,
    169n, 171n, 181
Common agricultural policy
    (CAP), 3, 8-9, 12, 14, 15, 17, 30,
    44, 69, 72-5, 134, 191; and
    prices, 78-83, 112-13; and
    production, 84-6; and
    structural reform, 107-9
Common external tariff (CET),
    123, 174
Commonwealth, 23, 25, 64;
    implications of Common
    Market for, 17, 174; and motor
    market, 49